Second Edition

# Longman PREPARATION SERIES FOR THE TOEIC® TEST

# MORE PRACTICE TESTS

Lin Lougheed

**Second Edition**
**Longman Preparation Series for the TOEIC Test: More Practice Tests**
Formerly published as *More Practice for the TOEIC® Test*
First printed in 1991. Reprinted in 1991, 1993, 1994.







**Addison Wesley Longman, 10 Bank St., White Plains, N.Y. 10606**

**Editorial Director:** Joanne Dresner
**Acquisitions Editor:** Allen Ascher
**Development Editors:** Suzanne Shetler, Jessica Miller
**Production Editor:** Liza Pleva
**Production Editorial:** Literary Graphics
**Text Design:** Literary Graphics
**Cover Design:** Naomi Ganor

**Library of Congress Cataloging-in-Publication Data**

Lougheed, Lin. 1946–
Longman preparation series for the TOEIC test. More practice tests / Lin Lougheed.—2nd ed.
p. cm. —(English for business success)
Rev. ed. of: More practice for the TOEIC test.
ISBN 0-201-87793-7
1. Test of English for International Communication—Study guides. 2. English language—Business English—Examinations—Study guides. 3. English language—Textbooks for foreign speakers. I. Lougheed, Lin, 1946– More practice for the TOEIC test. II. Title. III. Series.
PE1128.L646 1996b
428'.0076 dc20 96-2489
CIP

1 2 3 4 5 6 7 8 9—CRS—00 99 98 97 96

# PHOTO CREDITS

**Australian Embassy, Washington, D.C.**
page 9 (bottom); page 10 (both); page 41 (bottom); page 45 (bottom); page 46 (both); page 49 (bottom); page 77 (bottom); page 81 (top); page 82 (both); page 85 (both).

**Educational Institute of AH&MA, East Lansing, Michigan**
page 7 (both); page 12 (top); page 43 (top); page 48 (top); page 119 (top)

**Educational Testing Service, Princeton, New Jersey**
pages 3, 39, 75, 111

**Instructional Design International, Inc., Washington, D.C.**
page 4 (both); page 5 (both); page 6 (both); page 8 (bottom); page 9 (top); page 11 (both); page 12 (bottom); page 13 (both); page 40 (both); page 42 (top); page 44 (both); page 45 (top); page 47 (both); page 48 (bottom); page 49 (top); page 76 (both); page 77 (top); page 78 (both); page 79 (both); page 80 (both); page 81 (bottom); page 83 (bottom); page 84 (bottom); page 112 (bottom); page 113 (both); page 114 (top); page 115 (bottom); page 116 (both); page 117 (both); page 118 (top); page 120 (both); page 121 (bottom).

**Japan Airlines, New York, New York**
page 8 (top); page 114 (bottom)

**Japan Information and Cultural Center, Washington, D.C.**
page 83 (top)

**Korean Information Center, Embassy of the Republic of Korea, Washington, D.C.**
page 115 (top)

**NASA, Washington, D.C.**
page 84 (top); page 112 (top); page 118 (bottom); page 119 (bottom)

**Schiffgens, Lisa**
page 42 (bottom); page 43 (bottom); page 121 (top)

**Tourist Office of Spain, New York, New York**
page 41(top)

# TABLE OF CONTENTS

# INTRODUCTION

## GENERAL TEST-TAKING DIRECTIONS

***More Practice Tests*** will give you the practice you need to do well on the TOEIC® test. When you take the tests in this book, you should pretend that you are actually taking the TOEIC test. Make sure you have enough time to complete each section of the test. However, it is not necessary to take the whole test all at once if you do not have enough time. But you should not spend more time than is allowed for each part.

You will need a soft lead pencil and one of the answer sheets from the back of the book. Do not write in your book. All answers for the TOEIC test will be marked on a similar sheet. This will allow you to take the test more than once. When you mark your answer sheet, completely fill the oval. Do not make any marks outside of the oval. If you do not know the answer to a question, **guess.** You may guess correctly!

### *Listening Comprehension*

You will need an audio player for the Listening Comprehension sections and, of course, the cassette tape with the Listening Comprehension questions. If you do not have the cassette, you may have someone read you the questions from the tapescripts. The tapescripts are in the back of this book.

There are four parts to the Listening Comprehension section.

| | | NUMBER OF QUESTIONS |
|---|---|---|
| Part I: | Picture | 20 |
| Part II: | Question-Response | 30 |
| Part III: | Short Conversations | 30 |
| Part IV: | Short Talks | 20 |
| | | TOTAL 100 |

### *Reading*

You will only need the test book, an answer sheet, and a pencil to do the Reading section. There are three parts to the Reading section of the test.

| | | NUMBER OF QUESTIONS |
|---|---|---|
| Part V: | Incomplete Sentences | 40 |
| Part VI: | Error Recognition | 20 |
| Part VII: | Reading Comprehension | 40 |
| | | TOTAL 100 |

The answers for the Practice Tests are in the back of the book. Each answer has a short explanation. These explanations refer you to study materials found in other books in the *Longman Preparation Series for the TOEIC Test*. You can help yourself prepare for the TOEIC test by studying these books, titled ***Introductory Course*** and ***Advanced Course,*** which are available at your bookstore or from your local Addison Wesley Longman representative.

## GENERAL TOEIC DIRECTIONS

General Directions

This is a test of your ability to use the English language. The total time for the test is approximately two hours. It is divided into seven parts. Each part of the test begins with a set of specific directions. Be sure you understand what you are to do before you begin work on a part.

You will find that some of the questions are harder than others, but you should try to answer every one. There is no penalty for guessing. Do not be concerned if you cannot answer all of the questions.

Do not mark your answers in this test book. <u>You must put all of your answers on the separate answer sheet</u> that you have been given. When putting your answer to a question on your answer sheet, be sure to fill in the answer space corresponding to the letter of your choice. Fill in the space so that the letter inside the oval cannot be seen, as shown in the example below.

Mr. Jones ________ to his accountant yesterday.

(A) talk
(B) talking
(C) talked
(D) to talk

Sample Answer

(A) (B) ● (D)

The sentence should read, "Mr. Jones talked to his accountant yesterday." Therefore, you should choose answer (C). Notice how this has been done in the example given.

Mark only <u>one</u> answer for each question. If you change your mind about an answer after you have marked it on your answer sheet, completely erase your old answer and then mark your new answer. You must mark the answer sheet carefully so that the test-scoring machine can accurately record your test score.

# PRACTICE TEST ONE

You will find the Answer Sheet for Practice Test One on page 217. Detach it from the book and use it to record your answers. Play the audiotape for Practice Test One when you are ready to begin.

LISTENING COMPREHENSION

In this section of the test, you will have the chance to show how well you understand spoken English. There are four parts to this section, with special directions for each part.

Part I

Directions: For each question, you will see a picture in your test book and you will hear four short statements. The statements will be spoken just one time. They will not be printed in your test book, so you must listen carefully to understand what the speaker says.

When you hear the four statements, look at the picture in your test book and choose the statement that best describes what you see in the picture. Then on your answer sheet, find the number of the question and mark your answer. Look at the sample below.

Now listen to the four statements.

Sample Answer
(A) ● (C) (D)

Statement (B), "They're having a meeting," best describes what you see in the picture. Therefore, you should choose answer (B).

1. 

2. 

3.

4.

5. 

6. 

7. 

8. 

GO ON TO THE NEXT PAGE

9. 

10. 

11.

12.

GO ON TO THE NEXT PAGE

13.

14.

15. 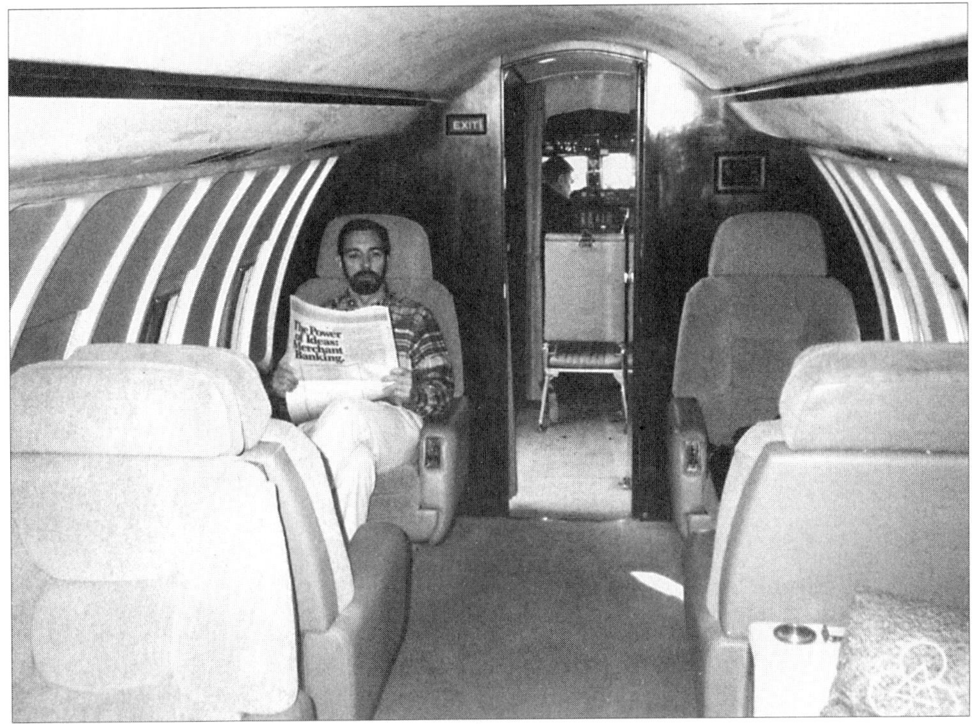
EXIT
The Power
of Ideas:
Merchant
Banking

16. 

GO ON TO THE NEXT PAGE

17.

18.

19.

20.

## Part II

Directions: In this part of the test, you will hear a question spoken in English, followed by three responses, also spoken in English. The question and the responses will be spoken just one time. They will not be printed in your test book, so you must listen carefully to understand what the speakers say. You are to choose the best response to each question.

Now listen to a sample question.

You will hear: Sample Answer

You will also hear: ● (B) (C)

The best response to the question "How are you?" is choice (A), "I am fine, thank you." Therefore, you should choose answer (A).

21. Mark your answer on your answer sheet.

22. Mark your answer on your answer sheet.

23. Mark your answer on your answer sheet.

24. Mark your answer on your answer sheet.

25. Mark your answer on your answer sheet.

26. Mark your answer on your answer sheet.

27. Mark your answer on your answer sheet.

28. Mark your answer on your answer sheet.

29. Mark your answer on your answer sheet.

30. Mark your answer on your answer sheet.

31. Mark your answer on your answer sheet.

32. Mark your answer on your answer sheet.

33. Mark your answer on your answer sheet.

34. Mark your answer on your answer sheet.

35. Mark your answer on your answer sheet.

36. Mark your answer on your answer sheet.

37. Mark your answer on your answer sheet.

38. Mark your answer on your answer sheet.

39. Mark your answer on your answer sheet.

40. Mark your answer on your answer sheet.

41. Mark your answer on your answer sheet.

42. Mark your answer on your answer sheet.

43. Mark your answer on your answer sheet.

44. Mark your answer on your answer sheet.

45. Mark your answer on your answer sheet.

46. Mark your answer on your answer sheet.

47. Mark your answer on your answer sheet.

48. Mark your answer on your answer sheet.

49. Mark your answer on your answer sheet.

50. Mark your answer on your answer sheet.

## Part III

Directions: In this part of the test, you will hear several short conversations between two people. The conversations will not be printed in your test book. You will hear the conversations only once, so you must listen carefully to understand what the speakers say.

In your test book, you will read a question about each conversation. The question will be followed by four answers. You are to choose the best answer to each question and mark it on your answer sheet.

51. What is the woman's job?

    (A) Mail carrier.
    (B) Waitress.
    (C) Typist.
    (D) Grocery clerk.

52. What are the speakers going to do?

    (A) Park a car.
    (B) Run a race.
    (C) Walk in the park.
    (D) Make a wish.

53. When will the phones be installed?

    (A) Monday before noon.
    (B) Monday afternoon.
    (C) Wednesday before noon.
    (D) Wednesday afternoon.

54. How many dozen pens is the woman ordering?

    (A) One.
    (B) Five.
    (C) Six.
    (D) Twelve.

55. What is wrong?

    (A) The man is late for work.
    (B) The man is sick.
    (C) The man is too full.
    (D) The man's house needs repairs.

56. What are the speakers going to do?

    (A) Watch the news.
    (B) Repair a watch.
    (C) Make tea.
    (D) Begin a new book.

57. Where did this conversation take place?

    (A) At the dinner table.
    (B) In the desert.
    (C) In a grocery store.
    (D) At a bakery.

58. What did the man buy?

    (A) A sweater.
    (B) A pair of shoes.
    (C) A tire.
    (D) A car.

59. When does the cleaning staff come?

    (A) Every night.
    (B) Once a week.
    (C) Twice a week.
    (D) Only this evening.

60. What is the woman's concern?

    (A) The numbers are incorrect.
    (B) The accountant is not ready.
    (C) Her sons are in charge.
    (D) There are checks by the figures.

61. Who's giving advice?

    (A) A travel agent.
    (B) A physician.
    (C) A teacher.
    (D) A golfer.

62. When are the speakers going to have lunch?

    (A) Monday.
    (B) Wednesday.
    (C) Thursday.
    (D) Friday.

63. What don't the speakers like?

(A) Spring.
(B) The heat.
(C) The rain.
(D) Standing.

64. Why might the game be canceled?

(A) There aren't enough players.
(B) It's raining.
(C) It's nighttime.
(D) There aren't any lights.

65. Why must the woman hurry?

(A) They will miss the bus.
(B) It's raining.
(C) She lost her raincoat.
(D) Her umbrella won't open.

66. How many pencils does the woman need?

(A) One.
(B) Two.
(C) Six.
(D) Twelve.

67. How many minutes are remaining?

(A) Twenty.
(B) Thirty.
(C) Forty-five.
(D) Fifty.

68. Where does the woman live?

(A) By the school.
(B) By the police station.
(C) By a mountain.
(D) Near work.

69. Why didn't the woman read today's paper?

(A) She didn't have any money to buy one.
(B) She didn't have time to buy one.
(C) It wasn't delivered on time.
(D) She read yesterday's instead.

70. Where are the speakers?

(A) On a sailboat.
(B) In a fruit store.
(C) On a golf course.
(D) In a shoe store.

71. How many hours of sleep does the man usually get?

(A) Four.
(B) Five.
(C) Eight.
(D) Eleven.

72. What are the speakers talking about?

(A) A sports event.
(B) A book.
(C) A newspaper.
(D) A long line.

73. What is the man's profession?

(A) A dentist.
(B) A caretaker.
(C) A waiter.
(D) A brush salesperson.

74. Why can't the woman stay late?

(A) She came to work early.
(B) She's sick.
(C) She's having company.
(D) She's getting an overseas call.

75. What are the speakers talking about?

(A) A shopping trip.
(B) A robbery.
(C) An accident.
(D) An acquaintance.

76. What is the woman's job?

(A) Salesperson.
(B) Tax lawyer.
(C) Cardplayer.
(D) Shipping clerk.

77. When is the plane going to land?

(A) In fifteen minutes.
(B) In thirty minutes.
(C) In one hour.
(D) In three hours.

78. Where is this conversation taking place?

(A) In a coffee shop.
(B) At a diner.
(C) At a restaurant.
(D) On a train.

79. Why can't the man and woman play golf?

(A) They only have one umbrella.
(B) They don't have clubs.
(C) He forgot his shoes.
(D) It's raining.

80. Who are the speakers expecting?

(A) A repairperson.
(B) A photographer.
(C) A secretary.
(D) An office manager.

## Part IV

Directions: In this part of the test, you will hear several short talks. Each will be spoken just one time. They will not be printed in your test book, so you must listen carefully to understand and remember what is said.

In your test book, you will read two or more questions about each short talk. The questions will be followed by four answers. You are to choose the best answer to each question and mark it on your answer sheet.

81. What is being sold?

(A) Office space.
(B) Office supplies.
(C) Down pillows.
(D) Sailboats.

82. How long does this sale last?

(A) One day.
(B) Three days.
(C) One week.
(D) Eight days.

83. When does the sale end?

(A) Thursday.
(B) Friday.
(C) Saturday.
(D) Sunday.

84. What was the weather yesterday?

(A) Rainy.
(B) Foggy.
(C) Sunny.
(D) Clear.

85. When might it snow?

(A) This evening.
(B) Tomorrow morning.
(C) Tomorrow evening.
(D) This weekend.

86. What kind of news item is this?

(A) An analysis.
(B) A review.
(C) A correction.
(D) A warning.

87. When might this announcement be heard?

(A) Spring.
(B) Summer.
(C) Fall.
(D) Winter.

88. What causes power failure?

(A) Excessive use.
(B) Lack of demand.
(C) Increased supply.
(D) Poor quality fans.

89. Who is probably listening to this announcement?

(A) Ticket agents.
(B) Telephone line technicians.
(C) Airline representatives.
(D) Potential travelers.

90. Why is there a delay?

(A) All the agents are busy.
(B) All flights are late.
(C) The fares are going up.
(D) Representatives are on strike.

91. What kind of people are attending the seminar?

(A) Teachers.
(B) Managers.
(C) Waiters.
(D) Gardeners.

92. Which of the following describes Mr. Margalis?

(A) Inexperienced.
(B) Retired.
(C) Speechless.
(D) Young.

93. Where is the announcement being heard?

(A) In a garden.
(B) In a private office.
(C) In a dining hall.
(D) On a train.

94. What is needed to enter?

(A) A special pass.
(B) An authorized signature.
(C) A secure vehicle.
(D) A hunting license.

95. Where can passes be obtained?

(A) Within the secure area.
(B) From authorized personnel.
(C) At the Security Office.
(D) At the License Bureau.

96. What kind of work is advertised?

(A) Full-time.
(B) Part-time.
(C) Overtime.
(D) Volunteer.

97. What qualifications are required?

(A) Law degree.
(B) Medical diploma.
(C) Advertising experience.
(D) Office skills.

98. What time is the report being presented?

(A) At 8:00.
(B) At 10:00.
(C) At 12:00.
(D) At 2:00.

99. What advice is given?

(A) Wear a hat.
(B) Go to bed early.
(C) Have a nice day.
(D) Take your umbrella.

100. What is the weather now?

(A) Rainy.
(B) Clear skies.
(C) Dark clouds.
(D) Windy.

This is the end of the Listening Comprehension portion of the test. Turn to Part V in your test book.

## READING

In this section of the test, you will have the chance to show how well you understand written English. There are three parts to this section, with special directions for each part.

### Part V

Directions: This part of the test has incomplete sentences. Four words or phrases, marked (A), (B), (C), (D), are given beneath each sentence. You are to choose the one word or phrase that best completes the sentence. Then, on your answer sheet, find the number of the question and mark your answer.

Example

Sample Answer

(A) (B) ● (D)

Because the equipment is very delicate, it must be handled with ________.

(A) caring
(B) careful
(C) care
(D) carefully

The sentence should read, "Because the equipment is very delicate, it must be handled with care." Therefore, you should choose answer (C).

Now begin work on the questions.

101. Both companies are ________ the same business.

(A) in
(B) with
(C) from
(D) through

102. ________ there were so many options, everyone was satisfied.

(A) If
(B) Why
(C) Because
(D) When

103. If they ________ more aware of the trends, they could have avoided bankruptcy.

(A) were
(B) are
(C) have been
(D) had been

104. Make checks ________ to the company.

(A) paid
(B) payable
(C) paying
(D) pay

105. Ms. Bolton is both a strong manager ________ a skilled negotiator.

(A) or
(B) with
(C) and
(D) though

106. ________ the stockbrokers said the market was healthy, they refused to invest more money.

(A) Because
(B) Although
(C) In addition
(D) So

107. The seminar will adjourn ________ five o'clock.

(A) in
(B) on
(C) at
(D) the

108. Marketing is important; ________, we're hiring a new public relations firm.

(A) therefore
(B) even though
(C) nevertheless
(D) but

109. The secretary had the messenger ________ the envelope as soon as possible.

(A) delivering
(B) to deliver
(C) deliver
(D) delivered

110. The board meetings usually ________ on time.

(A) have started
(B) start
(C) are starting
(D) have been starting

111. Everyone was disappointed to hear that the company's proposal was ________.

(A) turned up
(B) turned on
(C) turned away
(D) turned down

112. Even though the exchange rate was high, we ________ from them.

(A) buy
(B) must have bought
(C) had to buy
(D) had better buy

113. ________ Dr. Rossi hired the new secretary, the office has become more organized.

(A) When
(B) Before
(C) While
(D) Since

114. Mr. Cutler will ________ as president.

(A) step out
(B) step down
(C) step from
(D) step through

115. Ms. Silva sent the memo ________ it had been approved.

(A) so
(B) but
(C) after
(D) until

116. It's time to take advantage of current ________ rates.

(A) interesting
(B) interest
(C) interested
(D) interests

117. The manager has to ________ the presentation until next week.

(A) put off
(B) put with
(C) put on
(D) put through

118. When the directors ________ a profit, they'll be satisfied.

(A) will see
(B) are seeing
(C) see
(D) have been seeing

119. Do ________ an estimate before getting it in writing.

(A) not ever accept
(B) never accept
(C) accept never
(D) not accept ever

120. Production went down ________ morale was low.

(A) even though
(B) when
(C) but
(D) to

121. The distributors will collaborate ________ a British company.

(A) with
(B) in
(C) from
(D) of

122. If banks ________ the number of credit cards, the economy would improve.

(A) limiting
(B) limited
(C) had limited
(D) are limiting

123. One suggestion was to ________ gasoline taxes.

(A) raise
(B) have raised
(C) be raising
(D) raising

124. The host will want the total amount ________ before paying the bill.

(A) checked
(B) be checked
(C) checking
(D) check

125. The new sales manager cooperates with her colleagues; ________, she is a valued member.

(A) although
(B) however
(C) for example
(D) therefore

126. ________ our office, Mr. James voted against the proposal.

(A) Representation
(B) Representative
(C) Representing
(D) Representative of

127. Paychecks ________.

(A) are twice distributed a month
(B) twice a month are distributed
(C) are distributed twice a month
(D) a month are distributed twice

128. There has been a decline in local ________ national advertising.

(A) therefore
(B) so
(C) but
(D) and

129. ________ Mrs. Lee was calling her husband's office, he was calling hers.

(A) While
(B) Because
(C) So
(D) Then

130. The CEOs will meet ________ Chicago next month.

(A) at
(B) in
(C) to
(D) from

131. The award was contested by one of the ________.

(A) competitors
(B) competition
(C) competing
(D) competitive

GO ON TO THE NEXT PAGE

132. The ________ was considered final.

(A) decisive
(B) decided
(C) decision
(D) deciding

133. Mr. Wong once lived ________ New Orleans.

(A) in
(B) at
(C) from
(D) on

134. The report focused on the ________ of the study.

(A) foundlings
(B) finds
(C) findings
(D) found

135. The staff ________ the office had been burglarized.

(A) suspicion
(B) suspense
(C) suspicious
(D) suspected

136. ________ all the references to verify the information.

(A) Look by
(B) Look out
(C) Look up
(D) Look to

137. Mary is ________ an excellent writer.

(A) considerate
(B) considered
(C) considerable
(D) considers

138. They ________ the launch of their new company only a year ago.

(A) announce
(B) are announcing
(C) have announced
(D) announced

139. After re-evaluating the proposal, the agency ________ the contract to us.

(A) awarding
(B) had awarded
(C) awarded
(D) awards

140. My supervisor had me ________ the morning taking inventory.

(A) spend
(B) to spend
(C) spent
(D) spending

## Part VI

Directions: In this part of the test, each sentence has four words or phrases underlined. The four underlined parts of the sentence are marked (A), (B), (C), (D). You are to identify the one underlined word or phrase that should be corrected or rewritten. Then, on your answer sheet, find the number of the question and mark your answer.

Example

All employee (A) are required to wear (B) their identification (C) badges while (D) at work.

Sample Answer

● (B) (C) (D)

Choice (A), the underlined word "employee," is not correct in this sentence. This sentence should read, "All employees are required to wear their identification badges while at work." Therefore, you should choose answer (A).

Now begin work on the questions.

141. Of all (A) the software the consultants have looked at, (B) the more (C) powerful one (D) is also the most accessible.

142. After much (A) discussion, the negotiators decided not making (B) an offer until they (C) had looked over (D) the contract.

143. The partners agreed that (A) buying a new building (B) will (C) be a solid investment (D).

144. Total amount (A) of the membership dues (B) collected at the annual (C) conference was misplaced (D).

145. Yesterday, (A) Mr. Frank, who was (B) negotiating a new contract, (C) disappoint (D) his supervisor.

146. The home was located (A) in a quiet community; (B) unfortunately, it (C) was much farther than we have (D) originally thought.

147. The result of (A) the studies (B) have had (C) a strong impact on (D) future developments.

148. The director should (A) decide to hire (B) her, we should advise the personnel office to prepare (C) all the necessary paperwork (D).

GO ON TO THE NEXT PAGE

149. We've decided to stop to interview qualified applicants who are not willing to relocate.
A B C D

150. The latest series of articles on trends and innovations have been praised by the readers.
A B C D

151. Your intelligent and energy will help you solve any problem you encounter; use these strengths wisely.
A B C D

152. Employment benefits are given new employees have increased tremendously.
A B C D

153. Paychecks are deposited in the employees' accounts, or an employee can pick it off in Accounting.
A B C D

154. The secretary discovered too late that she transferred the call to the wrong office.
A B C D

155. The concerned customer asked when had the product been sent from the warehouse.
A B C D

156. My colleagues and I did not find the new software program to be easy as the old one.
A B C D

157. The Board of Directors are in the process of dissolving the company.
A B C D

158. If you have just recently purchased a home or are considering to refinance your home, take advantage of our low rates.
A B C D

159. The most popular suggestion with thc office workers is that all smokers could go outside to smoke.
A B C D

160. There is a rumor that the workers are discussing establishing union.
A B C D

## Part VII

Directions: The questions in this part of the test are based on a variety of reading material (for example, announcements, paragraphs, and advertisements). You are to choose the one best answer, (A), (B), (C), or (D), to each question. Then, on your answer sheet, find the number of the question and mark your answer. Answer all questions following a passage on the basis of what is stated or implied in that passage.

Read the following example.

> The Museum of Technology is a "hands-on" museum, designed for people to experience science at work. Visitors are encouraged to use, test, and handle the objects on display. Special demonstrations are scheduled for the first and second Wednesdays of each month at 1:30 p.m. Open Tuesday–Friday 2:30–4:30 p.m., Saturday 11:00 a.m.–4:30 p.m., and Sunday 1:00–4:30 p.m.

When during the month can visitors see special demonstrations?

(A) Every weekend
(B) The first two Wednesdays
(C) One afternoon a week
(D) Every other Wednesday

Sample Answer

(A)  (C) (D)

The passage says that the demonstrations are scheduled for the first and second Wednesdays of the month. Therefore, you should choose answer (B).

Now begin work on the questions.

Questions 161-163 refer to the following job announcement.

**SALES**

We are looking for sales professionals for the Pacific Rim area with a minimum of two years' experience in the clothing industry. Good professional appearance, excellent communication skills, and a college degree are required. We offer an excellent salary and benefits package.

161. Who would most likely apply for this job?

(A) An engineer
(B) A real estate agent
(C) A professor
(D) A clerk in a clothing store

162. Which of the following is NOT mentioned as a requirement?

(A) Good appearance
(B) Previous experience
(C) A master's degree
(D) Good speaking and writing skills

163. Where would this announcement most likely appear?

(A) In a university catalogue
(B) In a telephone directory
(C) In a tourist guidebook
(D) In a newspaper

Questions 164-166 refer to the following article.

The excessive wrapping on compact discs is joining cardboard boxes, plastic jugs, and other packaging in the trash. This trash, then, ends up in the nation's garbage dumps.

Environmentalists believe that this is too much waste. Much of this excessive packaging only makes the products more attractive to consumers; it does not protect the goods from getting damaged.

164. What is this article about?

(A) The excessive packaging of products
(B) The size of compact discs
(C) The use of garbage dumps
(D) A noted environmentalist

165. According to the passage, why are products packaged?

(A) For protection
(B) For attractiveness
(C) For ease of consumption
(D) For environmental safety

166. What happens to most package wrapping?

(A) It's recycled.
(B) It's discarded.
(C) It's stored on shelves.
(D) It's redesigned.

Questions 167-169 refer to the following press release.

Color Crown, Inc., of Hong Kong, a company that makes four-color separations for printing, has announced plans to merge with Graphics IV of Singapore. The company will be known as CrownGraphics.

Color Crown said the merger will enable the company to include desktop publishing support for all types of computers.

167. What does Color Crown specialize in?

(A) Selling computers
(B) Making four-color separations
(C) Producing magazines
(D) Designing furniture

168. What is happening to the two companies?

(A) They are merging.
(B) They are competing.
(C) They are dissolving.
(D) They are separating.

169. What are four-color separations used for?

(A) Computing
(B) Merging
(C) Printing
(D) Dying

GO ON TO THE NEXT PAGE

Questions 170-172 refer to the following table.

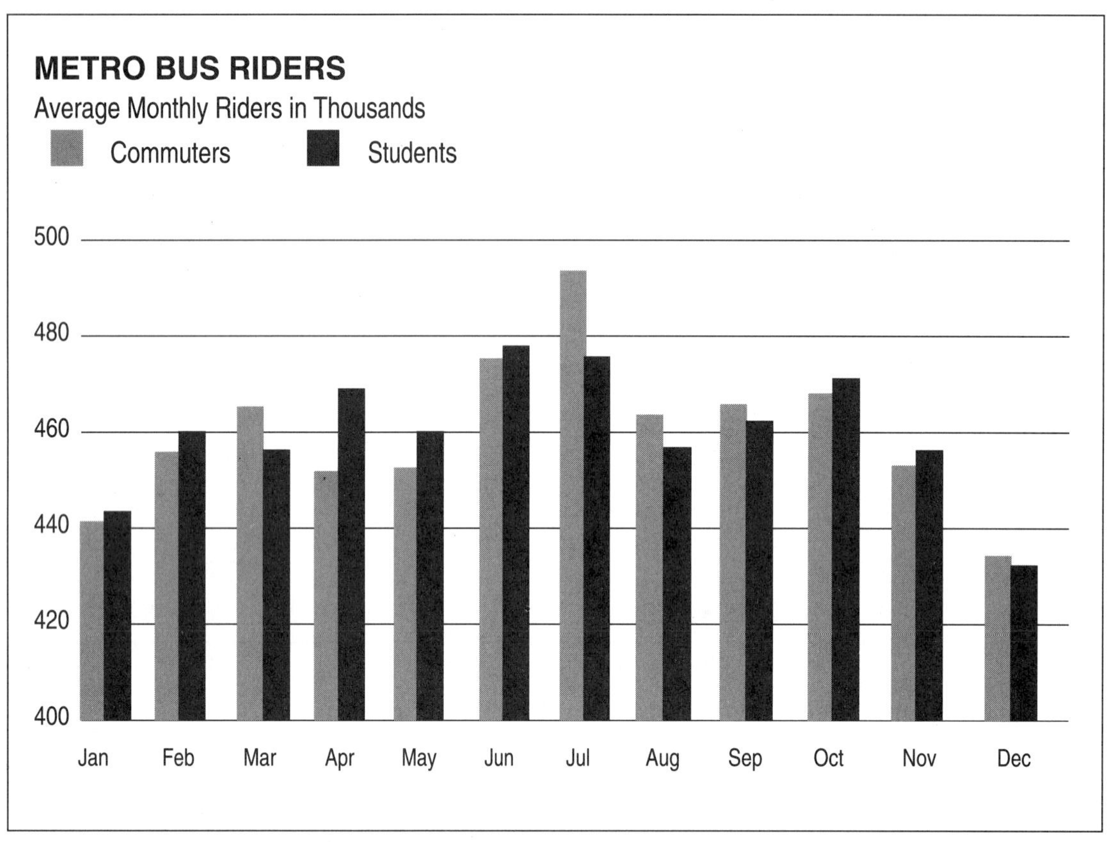


170. What does this table compare?

    (A) Daily schedules
    (B) Means of transportation
    (C) Monthly ridership
    (D) Riders with drivers

171. Which month had the highest number of commuters?

    (A) June
    (B) July
    (C) September
    (D) October

172. In which month were the buses used least?

    (A) February
    (B) May
    (C) August
    (D) December

Questions 173-176 refer to the following report.

> Postal rates are going up again. The price of a first-class stamp will rise from 40 cents to 50 cents. This will hurt many direct-mail companies. These companies include catalogue houses and sellers of mailing lists.
>
> These direct-marketing companies say the proposed postal rate increase will hurt their industry and drive some into bankruptcy. These companies, which mostly use third-class mail, face increases as high as 30 percent.

173. What is the main subject of the report?

    (A) The postal commission
    (B) Mail order catalogues
    (C) Bankruptcy
    (D) Results of a postal increase

174. According to the passage, who will be most affected by this change?

    (A) Direct-mail companies
    (B) Greeting card manufacturers
    (C) Postal employees
    (D) Stamp collectors

175. According to the passage, what rate do most direct-marketing companies use?

    (A) Book rate
    (B) First-class
    (C) Third-class
    (D) Preferred rate

176. What are the catalogue houses in this report?

    (A) Preferred postal clients
    (B) Direct-marketing companies
    (C) Financially stable companies
    (D) First-class mail users

GO ON TO THE NEXT PAGE

Questions 177-181 refer to the following information.

> **1. The One-Call System**
> In most states, petroleum industry–supported laws require contractors and private landowners to call the local One-Call number before beginning any kind of digging. With forty-eight hours' notice, a pipeline operator will locate the pipeline and mark it clearly. Any damage at all to a pipe—even the lightest scratch—could lead to a leak later on. Whether One-Call has become the law in your state or not, you can help keep pipelines safe by calling the number on the right-of-way markers before you dig.
>
> **2. Leak Detection**
> Most pipelines are operated twenty-four hours a day from a control station, using telephone, satellite, or microwave communications systems. Computers are widely used to monitor conditions along the line every ten to sixty seconds, sounding an alarm if they detect any abnormality or sudden change in pressure. In the event of an alarm, valves can be closed and nearby pipeline crews dispatched within minutes.
>
> **3. Emergency Response Preparedness**
> Although leaks occur infrequently and rarely result in a fire, readiness for any emergency is a crucial responsibility for pipeline companies. Federal and state laws supported by the petroleum industry require pipeline companies and local police and fire departments to maintain a coordinated plan of response and to practice for an emergency by staging drills. These drills and personnel training programs emphasize the need for immediate action and for cooperation between the various rescue agencies and the pipeline company.

177. What is the main focus of this passage?

(A) Safety
(B) Personnel training
(C) Computer monitoring
(D) Industry-supported laws

178. What is One-Call?

(A) A telecommunications firm
(B) An excavating company
(C) A contractor
(D) A pipeline detection safety service

179. What do rescue agencies and pipeline companies coordinate?

(A) Leaks
(B) Drilling
(C) Emergency readiness
(D) Microwave communications

180. When does an alarm sound?

(A) If a valve is open
(B) If the pipeline is scratched
(C) If a crew has been dispatched
(D) If pipeline pressure drops suddenly

181. Which of the following would publish this information?

(A) A newspaper
(B) An oil industry marketing firm
(C) A fire safety consultant
(D) An oil company

Questions 182-184 refer to the following table.

| HOTEL | STANDARD RATE | WEEKEND RATE | BENEFITS |
|---|---|---|---|
| Drake | $205 | $145 | Cocktails, refreshments, continental breakfast |
| Park Central | $245 | $125 | Double room in the Towers, dinner |
| Mayfair Regent | $195 | $125 | Parking |
| Nikko | $215 | $99 | Parking |
| Palmer House | $135 | $75 | Continental breakfast |
| Royal Inn | $250 | $215 | Full breakfast, parking |
| Swiss Grand | $350 | $199 | Executive suite, late checkout, parking |

182. Of these hotels, which is the most expensive?

(A) Royal Inn
(B) Park Central
(C) Drake
(D) Nikko

183. Which hotel offers a full breakfast?

(A) Swiss Grand
(B) Royal Inn
(C) Palmer House
(D) Nikko

184. Which is the least expensive hotel?

(A) Palmer House
(B) Nikko
(C) Mayfair Regent
(D) Drake

GO ON TO THE NEXT PAGE

Questions 185-187 refer to the following announcement.

**Yamakura Corporation** announced a plan to double its imports and overseas production over the next four years. The communications electronics firm said it will expand into Southeast Asian markets. The company plans to manufacture its telephone equipment in Singapore.

185. What does Yamakura Corporation specialize in?

(A) Southeast Asia
(B) Overseas travel
(C) Exports
(D) Communications electronics

186. Why is Singapore mentioned?

(A) Yamakura will manufacture telephones there.
(B) The chief market is there.
(C) The weather is very pleasant.
(D) The import duties are low.

187. How much will Yamakura's imports increase in the next four years?

(A) 50 percent
(B) 100 percent
(C) 150 percent
(D) 200 percent

Questions 188-190 refer to the following manual.

## TROUBLESHOOTING

If your TV does not work, check the following points:

| PICTURE | SOUND | POSSIBLE CAUSES | WHAT TO DO |
|---|---|---|---|
| No picture | Noise | Not properly tuned | Adjust tuning |
| Picture visible | No sound | • Volume control dial turned too low<br>• Earphones inserted | • Turn up volume<br>• Disconnect earphones |
| Picture all white | Sound heard | Brightness control not set correctly | Adjust brightness control |
| Picture dark or blurred | Sound heard | Brightness control not set correctly | Adjust brightness control |

188. What is this chart used for?

(A) To determine a problem with a TV
(B) To pick a TV program
(C) To compare prices
(D) To wrap packages

189. What does the manual advise if the picture is all white?

(A) Turn down the volume
(B) Adjust the brightness control
(C) Adjust the tuning
(D) Disconnect the earphones

190. When should the tuning be adjusted?

(A) When the picture is black
(B) When there is a picture but no sound
(C) When the picture is white
(D) When there is noise but no picture

Questions 191-193 refer to the following letter.

April 23, 19—

China Books, Inc.
23405 San Antonio Ave.
San Fernando, CA 94509

Dear Sir / Madam:

I have for the second time received a "Payment Due" notice from your offices.

I am enclosing, for the second time, a photocopy of canceled check #535 in the amount of $23.95 for the book *In a Modern World.*

Note that the date on the check is October 13; it was canceled on the back by your company on October 23.

Please call me at (415) 555-4856 to acknowledge receipt of this letter.

Sincerely,

Margaret Tomkins

Margaret Tomkins

191. Who owes money?

(A) No one
(B) Ms. Tomkins
(C) China Books
(D) The author

192. When was the check written?

(A) April 23
(B) May 30
(C) October 13
(D) October 23

193. According to the letter, which of the following is NOT true?

(A) Ms. Tomkins has paid twice.
(B) This is Ms. Tomkins' second letter.
(C) Ms. Tomkins has received two notices.
(D) The company received the payment.

Questions 194-195 refer to the following report.

When personal computers began showing up on desktops, there was the idea that this business tool would lead to something called the "paperless office."

The "paperless office" theory went like this: people would use magnetic discs and computers in place of file folders and paper. Paper use, therefore, would decrease. This was supposed to help preserve resources and improve the world's solid-waste disposal problem.

194. What is the report about?

(A) Selling computers
(B) Desktop publishing
(C) The "paperless office"
(D) World problems

195. What would the "paperless office" have done?

(A) Preserved resources
(B) Confused secretaries
(C) Cut costs
(D) Improved communication

GO ON TO THE NEXT PAGE

Questions 196-200 refer to the following job announcement.

## Public Health
Pakistan

**Position Available: Division of Public Health and Clinical Nutrition.**
The University of Karachi at Karachi General Hospital (KGH) is recruiting for an assistant clinical professor of medicine for the Division of Public Health and Clinical Nutrition. The candidate will participate in all teaching, clinical, and basic research activities of the division and serve as chief of the public health clinic at KGH. The individual will be expected to develop independently funded clinical research programs dealing with basic public health issues and/or clinical nutrition. Board certification required. Competitive salary in U.S. dollars, airfare, and full board/lodging included. Professional growth and cultural opportunities abound. Send curriculum vitae, summary of clinical research interests, and three letters of reference to Faroque Khan, MD, 572 St. Kilda Road, Sydney 2000, Australia.

196. Where would this information most likely appear?

(A) In a university newsletter
(B) In a medical periodical
(C) In an internal memorandum
(D) In an education periodical

197. Which of the following is part of the job description?

(A) Giving blood tests
(B) Supervising research
(C) Repairing equipment
(D) Diagnosing patients

198. Which of the following is a requirement for employment?

(A) Pakistani medical license
(B) Medical board certification
(C) Clinical nutrition training experience
(D) Abstracts of published articles

199. Which of the following is NOT necessary to apply?

(A) Curriculum vitae
(B) References
(C) Clinical research summary
(D) Abstracts of published articles

200. Who would most likely apply for this job?

(A) A medical school professor
(B) A hospital administrator
(C) A general practitioner
(D) A nutritionist

Stop! This is the end of the test. If you finish before time is called, you may go back to Parts V, VI, and VII and check your work.

# Practice Test Two

You will find the Answer Sheet for Practice Test Two on page 219. Detach it from the book and use it to record your answers. Play the audiotape for Practice Test Two when you are ready to begin.

## LISTENING COMPREHENSION

In this section of the test, you will have the chance to show how well you understand spoken English. There are four parts to this section, with special directions for each part.

### Part I

Directions: For each question, you will see a picture in your test book and you will hear four short statements. The statements will be spoken just one time. They will not be printed in your test book, so you must listen carefully to understand what the speaker says.

When you hear the four statements, look at the picture in your test book and choose the statement that best describes what you see in the picture. Then on your answer sheet, find the number of the question and mark your answer. Look at the sample below.

Sample Answer

Now listen to the four statements. (A)  (C) (D)

Statement (B), "They're having a meeting," best describes what you see in the picture. Therefore, you should choose answer (B).

1.

2.

3. 

4. 

5. 

6. 

7.

8.

9.

10.

11. 

12. 

13.

14.

15. 

16. 

17. 

18. 

19.

DANGER
FLAMMABLE GAS
92271

20.

ICS
Lot No.
DRUM No.
G T N
ERA
RADIOACTIVE LSA

## Part II

<u>Directions:</u> In this part of the test, you will hear a question spoken in English, followed by three responses, also spoken in English. The question and the responses will be spoken just one time. They will not be printed in your test book, so you must listen carefully to understand what the speakers say. You are to choose the best response to each question.

Now listen to a sample question.

You will hear: — Sample Answer

You will also hear: — ● (B) (C)

The best response to the question "How are you?" is choice (A), "I am fine, thank you." Therefore, you should choose answer (A).

21. Mark your answer on your answer sheet.

22. Mark your answer on your answer sheet.

23. Mark your answer on your answer sheet.

24. Mark your answer on your answer sheet.

25. Mark your answer on your answer sheet.

26. Mark your answer on your answer sheet.

27. Mark your answer on your answer sheet.

28. Mark your answer on your answer sheet.

29. Mark your answer on your answer sheet.

30. Mark your answer on your answer sheet.

31. Mark your answer on your answer sheet.

32. Mark your answer on your answer sheet.

33. Mark your answer on your answer sheet.

34. Mark your answer on your answer sheet.

35. Mark your answer on your answer sheet.

36. Mark your answer on your answer sheet.

37. Mark your answer on your answer sheet.

38. Mark your answer on your answer sheet.

39. Mark your answer on your answer sheet.

40. Mark your answer on your answer sheet.

41. Mark your answer on your answer sheet.

42. Mark your answer on your answer sheet.

43. Mark your answer on your answer sheet.

44. Mark your answer on your answer sheet.

45. Mark your answer on your answer sheet.

46. Mark your answer on your answer sheet.

47. Mark your answer on your answer sheet.

48. Mark your answer on your answer sheet.

49. Mark your answer on your answer sheet.

50. Mark your answer on your answer sheet.

## Part III

Directions: In this part of the test, you will hear several short conversations between two people. The conversations will not be printed in your test book. You will hear the conversations only once, so you must listen carefully to understand what the speakers say.

In your test book, you will read a question about each conversation. The question will be followed by four answers. You are to choose the best answer to each question and mark it on your answer sheet.

51. Where does the conversation take place?

    (A) In a light store.
    (B) In a car.
    (C) In a library.
    (D) In the movies.

52. What time will the woman leave?

    (A) At 4:00.
    (B) At 5:00.
    (C) At 5:30.
    (D) At 7:00.

53. What is the man going to buy?

    (A) Toothpaste.
    (B) A TV.
    (C) New glasses.
    (D) Cold medicine.

54. How much money does the man need?

    (A) One dollar.
    (B) Ten dollars.
    (C) Thirty dollars.
    (D) Forty dollars.

55. What time is it now?

    (A) 11:00.
    (B) 1:30.
    (C) 2:00.
    (D) 2:30.

56. What is the woman looking for?

    (A) The closet.
    (B) The office.
    (C) Her coat.
    (D) Her umbrella.

57. What are the speakers doing?

    (A) Buying a watch.
    (B) Watching TV.
    (C) Reading the paper.
    (D) Playing a game.

58. What kind of movies do the speakers prefer?

    (A) Comedies.
    (B) War stories.
    (C) Murder mysteries.
    (D) Westerns.

59. When will the meeting be held?

    (A) On Monday.
    (B) On Tuesday.
    (C) On Thursday.
    (D) On Friday.

60. Why was the woman late today?

    (A) She slept late.
    (B) She walked slowly.
    (C) She took the bus.
    (D) She ran out of gas.

61. How often do the speakers pay their taxes?

    (A) Once a year.
    (B) Every two months.
    (C) Every three months.
    (D) Every four months.

62. Where did the man leave his glasses?

    (A) On his desk.
    (B) In the woman's office.
    (C) In his briefcase.
    (D) In the car.

63. Who are the speakers talking about?

(A) A typist.
(B) A typewriter repairperson.
(C) A runner.
(D) A cleaning person.

64. When will the man start work?

(A) June.
(B) July.
(C) August.
(D) September.

65. Why does the man like the weather?

(A) It's good for business.
(B) He likes it cool.
(C) He wants to go ice skating.
(D) It makes him hungry.

66. What did the man buy?

(A) A shirt.
(B) A tie.
(C) A suit.
(D) A pair of shoes.

67. What is the man's occupation?

(A) Cook.
(B) Construction worker.
(C) Real estate agent.
(D) Painter.

68. When are the reports due?

(A) At noon.
(B) At two o'clock.
(C) At three o'clock.
(D) At five o'clock.

69. Where does this conversation take place?

(A) On a train.
(B) On a plane.
(C) In a clothing store.
(D) In a hospital.

70. Why can't the woman read?

(A) She doesn't know how.
(B) She lost her glasses.
(C) The light is bad.
(D) There's nothing to read.

71. What room are the speakers in?

(A) The bedroom.
(B) The closet.
(C) The dining room.
(D) The kitchen.

72. Who are the speakers?

(A) Office workers.
(B) Building superintendents.
(C) Architects.
(D) Gardeners.

73. How often does the man swim?

(A) Once a week.
(B) Three times a week.
(C) Four times a week.
(D) Every day.

74. What is the woman going to do?

(A) Go hiking.
(B) Read.
(C) Lie in the sun.
(D) Play on the beach.

75. What does the woman want the man to do?

(A) Wash the floor.
(B) Take off his shoes.
(C) Polish his shoes.
(D) Leave the house.

76. When are the speakers leaving?

(A) Today.
(B) Tomorrow.
(C) At the end of the week.
(D) In two weeks.

GO ON TO THE NEXT PAGE

77. What is the woman doing?

(A) Applying for a job.
(B) Telephoning someone.
(C) Filling up the car.
(D) Opening a door.

78. What is the woman's occupation?

(A) Banker.
(B) Barber.
(C) Tree trimmer.
(D) Dressmaker.

79. How often should the buses leave?

(A) Every five minutes.
(B) Every ten minutes.
(C) Every fifteen minutes.
(D) Every thirty minutes.

80. When does the woman like to go to the park?

(A) At dawn.
(B) At noon.
(C) Early in the evening.
(D) At midnight.

## Part IV

Directions: In this part of the test, you will hear several short talks. Each will be spoken just one time. They will not be printed in your test book, so you must listen carefully to understand and remember what is said.

In your test book, you will read two or more questions about each short talk. The questions will be followed by four answers. You are to choose the best answer to each question and mark it on your answer sheet.

81. When will City Hall be open?

(A) From 8 A.M. to noon on Saturday.
(B) Every day this week.
(C) On the weekends only.
(D) From 8 A.M. to 5 P.M., Monday through Friday.

82. What must be filed?

(A) Citizenship papers.
(B) Tax forms.
(C) Time reports.
(D) Housing requests.

83. Why should people come early?

(A) To get a refund.
(B) To become citizens.
(C) To avoid long lines.
(D) To pick up their files.

84. Where would this announcement be heard?

(A) At a subway station.
(B) In a hotel.
(C) On an airplane.
(D) At an airport.

85. Which signs should passengers follow for rental cars?

(A) Blue.
(B) Red.
(C) Green.
(D) Yellow.

86. How can passengers get to their cars?

(A) By city bus.
(B) By shuttle.
(C) By subway.
(D) By walking.

87. When will the speech be heard?

(A) Before lunch.
(B) After lunch.
(C) Next month.
(D) Next Friday.

88. How often are the luncheons held?

(A) Every Friday.
(B) Every month.
(C) Twice a month.
(D) Once a year.

89. What is Dr. Jenny Chang's profession?

(A) Politician.
(B) Criminal.
(C) Saleswoman.
(D) Author.

90. How may visitors enter the building?

(A) With an employee escort.
(B) With permission from security personnel.
(C) With an ID badge.
(D) With proper dress.

91. Who must wear identification badges?

(A) All employees.
(B) Potential employees.
(C) Visitors with escorts.
(D) Visitors alone.

92. What is opening?

(A) The Civic Center.
(B) A new golf course.
(C) A downtown office.
(D) A residential hotel.

93. What is being offered?

(A) Golf lessons.
(B) City apartments.
(C) New watches.
(D) Club memberships.

94. What is the weather perfect for?

(A) Going to the beach.
(B) Bicycling in the mountains.
(C) Playing golf.
(D) Watching the races.

95. How is the sun described?

(A) Rising.
(B) Hazy.
(C) Shining.
(D) Bright.

96. How much was the man's estate worth?

(A) Nothing.
(B) Under two thousand dollars.
(C) A million dollars.
(D) Over two million dollars.

97. Who inherited the money?

(A) His children.
(B) His wife.
(C) His dog.
(D) His best friend.

98. When is the office open?

(A) Every day of the week.
(B) Only on Monday.
(C) Only on Friday.
(D) Monday through Friday.

99. What service is provided only in the afternoon?

(A) Renewal of driver's licenses.
(B) Applications for new driver's licenses.
(C) Driving tests.
(D) Blood tests.

100. When does the office stop taking customers?

(A) At 12:00.
(B) At 4:00.
(C) At 4:30.
(D) At 5:00.

This is the end of the Listening Comprehension portion of the test. Turn to Part V in your test book.

## READING

In this section of the test, you will have the chance to show how well you understand written English. There are three parts to this section, with special directions for each part.

### Part V

Directions: This part of the test has incomplete sentences. Four words or phrases, marked (A), (B), (C), (D), are given beneath each sentence. You are to choose the one word or phrase that best completes the sentence. Then, on your answer sheet, find the number of the question and mark your answer.

Example

Because the equipment is very delicate, it must be handled with ________.

(A) caring
(B) careful
(C) care
(D) carefully

Sample Answer

(A) (B) ● (D)

The sentence should read, "Because the equipment is very delicate, it must be handled with care." Therefore, you should choose answer (C).

Now begin work on the questions.

101. Mr. Doh ________ clients' phone calls.

(A) rarely returns
(B) returns rarely
(C) has returned rarely
(D) rarely had returned

102. Success depends ________ the efforts of the organization.

(A) from
(B) in
(C) on
(D) of

103. There has been strong competition; ________, the new company has made great profits.

(A) instead
(B) nonetheless
(C) then
(D) despite

104. Ms. Shirish will resign her position as chief ________ officer.

(A) operator
(B) operational
(C) operation
(D) operating

105. The weather report predicts it will rain ________ become colder.

(A) neither
(B) nor
(C) and
(D) either

106. The printer ________ paper.

(A) ran into
(B) ran out of
(C) ran without
(D) ran through

107. The electricity went out ________ we were making coffee.

(A) so
(B) because of
(C) while
(D) for

108. ________ all the negotiators, Ms. Neos seems the most reliable.

(A) From
(B) As
(C) Of
(D) But

109. The sales division reported a 64 percent drop ________ the last sales period.

(A) during
(B) with
(C) at
(D) to

110. The company is financially sound; ________, there is no debt.

(A) in spite of
(B) for example
(C) on the other hand
(D) nevertheless

111. Get the invoice ________ upon receipt.

(A) signature
(B) sign
(C) signed
(D) signing

112. ________ time to submit a bid.

(A) Still there is
(B) Is there still
(C) There is still
(D) They're still is

113. Our future will be ________ on what services we can provide.

(A) basic
(B) based
(C) basing
(D) base

114. If there ________ better communication, I would not resign.

(A) were
(B) was
(C) is
(D) will be

115. ________ the critics and answer their questions.

(A) Stand in for
(B) Stand at
(C) Stand with
(D) Stand up to

116. By the end of this century, business ________ greatly.

(A) will be changed
(B) will have changed
(C) changes
(D) changed

117. The ________ market has declined in many parts of the country.

(A) homing
(B) housed
(C) homes
(D) housing

118. ________ saving money, you will purchase a reliable product.

(A) With
(B) So
(C) Besides
(D) Consequently

119. ________ one partner has resigned, others are quitting, too.

(A) Because
(B) Although
(C) If
(D) Before

120. The management makes an assessment ________.

(A) rarely
(B) still
(C) monthly
(D) already

121. The chairman said his ________ would continue his strategies.

(A) successful
(B) successor
(C) success
(D) successive

122. This region ________ as the costliest place to do business.

(A) often is referred
(B) is often referred
(C) is referred often to
(D) is often referred to

123. Since 1970, our customers ________ with our service.

(A) are satisfied
(B) have satisfied
(C) have been satisfying
(D) have been satisfied

124. People either don't have the money ________ they aren't willing to spend it.

(A) and
(B) neither
(C) or
(D) although

125. The group is composed ________ five companies.

(A) in
(B) of
(C) up
(D) from

126. In order to make more money, Mr. Garcia has decided to ________ a second job.

(A) take off
(B) take out
(C) take from
(D) take on

127. A survey of the ________ shows they are satisfied with their jobs.

(A) employment
(B) employs
(C) employees
(D) employing

128. ________ the bad location, the management is confident of success.

(A) Despite
(B) Since
(C) With
(D) As

129. Company officials must disclose their own ________ affairs.

(A) finance
(B) financing
(C) financial
(D) financed

130. The new business has ________ incorporated.

(A) still
(B) once
(C) yet
(D) already

131. The manufacturer listed assets ________ liabilities.

(A) but
(B) nor
(C) and
(D) so

132. The competitor's attempt to ________ the new company was stopped.

(A) take off
(B) take over
(C) take to
(D) take out

133. The new agent has experience ________ not expertise.

(A) but
(B) and
(C) with
(D) however

134. ________ the flight is cancelled, the seminar will have to be postponed.

(A) While
(B) If
(C) Although
(D) Besides

135. The proposal was submitted ________ April 28.

(A) at
(B) the
(C) on
(D) from

136. ________ costs have increased dramatically.

(A) Advertising
(B) Advertisements
(C) Advertised
(D) Advertise

137. Ford Motor Company reported drops ________ quarterly profits.

(A) to
(B) from
(C) in
(D) with

138. The company was ________ by an immigrant.

(A) found
(B) founding
(C) find
(D) founded

139. Mr. Daley is our most skilled speaker; ________, he is unavailable to give the presentation.

(A) besides
(B) nevertheless
(C) for example
(D) while

140. Have Ms. Alva ________ a press release immediately.

(A) writes
(B) to write
(C) writing
(D) write

## Part VI

Directions: In this part of the test, each sentence has four words or phrases underlined. The four underlined parts of the sentence are marked (A), (B), (C), (D). You are to identify the one underlined word or phrase that should be corrected or rewritten. Then, on your answer sheet, find the number of the question and mark your answer.

Example

All employee (A) are required to wear (B) their identification (C) badges while (D) at work.

Sample Answer

● (B) (C) (D)

Choice (A), the underlined word "employee," is not correct in this sentence. This sentence should read, "All employees are required to wear their identification badges while at work." Therefore, you should choose answer (A).

Now begin work on the questions.

141. Mr. Lyons called to find out (A) where (B) was the meeting (C) being held. (D)

142. The opportunity for (A) promotions have increased (B) considerably (C) since the new projects have been funded. (D)

143. The doctor will be giving you (A) a lot of information; if you have (B) questions about them, (C) let us know. (D)

144. Rapidly (A) fallen (B) oil prices caused OPEC ministers to meet (C) and plan (D) a strategy.

145. Book (A) where visitors sign in (B) is (C) kept at (D) the front desk.

146. The director felt more positive (A) steps should be (B) taken before last night's meeting (C) to ensure job security. (D)

147. Ms. Jenkins made the decision (A) that she (B) will promote (C) her administrative assistant before the end of (D) the year.

148. A repair job is costing (A) over $3,000 is automatically (B) discounted (C) $500 from the total (D) cost.

GO ON TO THE NEXT PAGE

149. Although an interior designer had been consulted, the decor was not as impressive we had expected.
A B C D

150. After press conference, the speaker's assistant made a summary of her remarks available.
A B C D

151. The new established advertising agency used innovative demographic studies to attract new clientele.
A B C D

152. The downtown store it is definitely luxurious, with plush carpeting, a sweeping staircase, and
A B C
mirrors everywhere.
D

153. The last job applicant had a background in economics, which are considered critical in
A B C
the new position.
D

154. After the presentation of the developed specially program, the audience reacted positively and
A B C
endorsed it immediately.
D

155. The inspector admitted to offer an estimate for the damage free of charge.
A B C D

156. The size of the new building and their proximity to the center of the business area makes it
A B C
an attractive investment.
D

157. The idea that experience was worth more then education was not unanimously accepted.
A B C D

158. The voters were disappointed since they had expected knowing the outcome of the
A B C
election before now.
D

159. The result of the evaluations and recommendations show that more effort needs to go into research.
A B C D

160. The manager should receive a telephone call from Tokyo this morning, transfer it to his extension.
A B C D

## Part VII

Directions: The questions in this part of the test are based on a variety of reading material (for example, announcements, paragraphs, and advertisements). You are to choose the one best answer, (A), (B), (C), or (D), to each question. Then, on your answer sheet, find the number of the question and mark your answer. Answer all questions following a passage on the basis of what is stated or implied in that passage.

Read the following example.

The Museum of Technology is a "hands-on" museum, designed for people to experience science at work. Visitors are encouraged to use, test, and handle the objects on display. Special demonstrations are scheduled for the first and second Wednesdays of each month at l:30 p.m. Open Tuesday–Friday 2:30–4:30 p.m., Saturday 11:00 a.m.–4:30 p.m., and Sunday 1:00–4:30 p.m.

When during the month can visitors see special demonstrations?

(A) Every weekend
(B) The first two Wednesdays
(C) One afternoon a week
(D) Every other Wednesday

Sample Answer

  (C) (D)

The passage says that the demonstrations are scheduled for the first and second Wednesdays of the month. Therefore, you should choose answer (B).

Now begin work on the questions.

Questions 161-163 refer to the following list.

| LOCAL RESTAURANTS | PRICES | PHONE NUMBER |
|---|---|---|
| Mama Lea's | moderate | 555-1765 |
| Nathan's USA | moderate | 515-0543 |
| Ovid's | high | 555-6821 |
| Papa's Kitchen | low | 555-8116 |
| Peking Palace | moderate | 202-1700 |

161. What is the list of?

(A) Prices
(B) People
(C) Countries
(D) Restaurants

162. What number would you call to make a reservation at Ovid's?

(A) 515-0543.
(B) 555-6821
(C) 555-8116
(D) 202-1700

163. Which is the least expensive restaurant?

(A) Papa's Kitchen
(B) Nathan's USA
(C) Mama Lea's
(D) Ovid's

Questions 164-167 refer to the following fax.

## One Devonshire Gardens

*7 July, 19—*

*Fax to:* *P. Peterman*
*Fax number:* *0101-202-555-1218*

*Dear Mr. Peterman,*

*Thank you for your confirmation fax of today. We take great pleasure in confirming your reservation of one superior double room on the evening of 28 July. The cost of this room will be £ 135.00 inclusive of tax, newspaper, and continental breakfast.*

*We look forward to welcoming you to One Devonshire Gardens.*

*Yours sincerely,*

Debbie Smith

*Debbie Smith*
*Reservations Manager*

164. What is One Devonshire Gardens?

(A) A garden
(B) An office building
(C) A hotel
(D) A newspaper

165. What kind of room was reserved?

(A) A single
(B) A twin
(C) A double
(D) A suite

166. Which of the following is NOT included in the price of the room?

(A) Breakfast
(B) Tax
(C) Newspaper
(D) Dinner

167. How did Mr. Peterman make a reservation?

(A) By fax
(B) Through an agent
(C) By letter
(D) In person

Questions 168-172 refer to the following job announcement.

**Wanted: ACCOUNTANT**

- Large law firm is seeking an Assistant Controller for our Accounting Department.
- Basic responsibilities include supervision of a 7-person department and control of the accounting systems.
- Qualified applicant should have 8 years of accounting experience and have a minimum of 2 or 3 years' supervisory experience.
- Education requirements include an undergraduate degree in accounting.
- The successful candidate must have computer experience and be familiar with automated financial systems.

168. What kind of firm is hiring?

(A) A computer company
(B) An accounting office
(C) An advertising agency
(D) A law firm

169. Which of the following is NOT mentioned as a qualification?

(A) Experience as a supervisor
(B) Familiarity with automated financial systems
(C) A law degree
(D) A degree in accounting

170. What kind of applicant would be most attracted to this job?

(A) A lawyer
(B) An accountant
(C) A computer science major
(D) A personnel director

171. How many people will the Assistant Controller supervise?

(A) 2
(B) 3
(C) 7
(D) 8

172. How many years of supervisory experience are required?

(A) 1
(B) 2
(C) 7
(D) 8

Questions 173-176 refer to the following letter.

◆ ka ◆

October 10, 19—

Dear Customer:

Congratulations! You have just purchased one of the world's most sophisticated microwave ovens. With proper use, the product is designed to give you many years of trouble-free operation. Please follow the instructions in this manual.

Sincerely,

M.S. Fujimoto

M.S. Fujimoto
President
Kitchen Appliances, Inc.

173. Where would this letter most likely be found?

(A) In a microwave manual
(B) In the mail
(C) In an advertisement
(D) In a design store

174. What was purchased?

(A) A globe
(B) A microwave oven
(C) An operation
(D) A manual

175. What is required for trouble-free operation?

(A) Money-back guarantee
(B) A sophisticated customer
(C) A good price
(D) Proper use

176. What must the user do?

(A) Exchange the product
(B) Follow directions
(C) Purchase another model
(D) Redesign the kitchen

Questions 177-179 refer to the following press release.

More than 50,000 electronics retailers and distributors are expected at the McCormick Convention Center in Chicago Saturday when 1,300 manufacturers exhibit the latest high-technology equipment. The new products will generally appear on retailers' shelves next fall. The Summer Consumer Electronics Show will continue through June 5.

177. What is the main topic of the press release?

(A) The McCormick Convention Center
(B) Chicago's convention centers
(C) Electronics retailers
(D) The Summer Consumer Electronics Show

178. How many manufacturers are expected?

(A) 1,300
(B) 5,000
(C) 13,000
(D) 50,000

179. What is on display at the Convention Center?

(A) High-technology products
(B) Distribution of networks
(C) Retail outlets
(D) Shelving samples

Questions 180-181 refer to the following advertisement.

**METROPOLITAN FINANCIAL SERVICES**
**Can Service All Your Mortgage Needs**
Residential • Refinancing • Commercial • Construction • Investor • Home Improvement
Bad Credit • Good Credit • No Problem
**Contact Metropolitan Today (609) 555-7412**

180. Why might people contact Metropolitan?

(A) To apply for a driver's license
(B) To buy stock
(C) To loan money
(D) To receive a loan

181. For which of the following is financing NOT available?

(A) Commercial projects
(B) Home improvement
(C) Hospitalization
(D) Construction

Questions 182-184 refer to the following table.

## Sunday Business TV

| | |
|---|---|
| | **11:30 A.M.** |
| Ch 4 | Business Review<br>A review or this week's business news |
| | **1:00 P.M.** |
| Ch 9, 11 | Company Profiles<br>An in-depth look at significant companies |
| | **1:30 P.M.** |
| Ch 4 | Politics and Economics<br>Discussion of the latest political decisions affecting business and finance |
| | **2:00 P.M.** |
| Ch 7, 13 | Business Today<br>Recent innovations in business |
| | **3:00 P.M.** |
| Ch 4 | World View of Business<br>News on business around the world |
| | **4:00 P.M.** |
| Ch 20 | Making Money<br>Successful personal investing |

182. What do these TV listings feature?

    (A) Concerts
    (B) Business programs
    (C) Travelogues
    (D) Sports events

183. What begins on TV at 2:00 P.M.?

    (A) Business Today
    (B) Company Profile
    (C) Making Money
    (D) Business Review

184. Which station would someone who has money to invest watch?

    (A) Ch 4
    (B) Ch 7
    (C) Ch 11
    (D) Ch 20

Questions 185-187 refer to the following advertisement.

**Upcoming for Tuesday, May 15, SIGMET presents:**

Mr. Sven Anderson, Technical Operations Director, CD-ROM Division, Cirrius Information Systems

Mr. Anderson will give a layperson's introduction to CD-ROM. If you are unsure what CD-ROM is, how it works, what it costs, or what it can do—come and learn from one of the leaders in the industry.

Seating is limited to thirty people, so call (312) 555-3487 for an advance reservation.

185. What will take place on Tuesday?

(A) A price cut
(B) A lecture
(C) A lunch
(D) A sales presentation

186. Who is the session designed for?

(A) Computer specialists
(B) Computer manufacturers
(C) Operators with CD-ROM experience
(D) People who are unfamiliar with CD-ROM

187. How many people can attend?

(A) Thirty
(B) More than thirty
(C) Anyone with an interest
(D) Anyone with a chair

GO ON TO THE NEXT PAGE

Questions 188-189 refer to the following announcement.

As a national leader with over forty years of experience providing TV, radio, and marketing services, **Abington** can offer you outstanding career opportunities.

We are currently seeking applications for Computer Programmers and Analysts.

Please visit our booth at the National Career Center's Job Fair on October 13.

* * * * * * * *

188. What type of announcement is this?

(A) A government proclamation
(B) A job announcement
(C) A television listing
(D) Publicity for the opening of a National Career Center

189. Which of the following people would be most interested in this announcement?

(A) A communications major
(B) A retired radio announcer
(C) A production manager
(D) A computer specialist

Questions 190-193 refer to the following letter.

**International Films, Ltd.**

124 West Houston St., New York, NY 10012

30 July, 19—

E. Denikos, Inc.
Earos 42
Aghia Paraskevi 15342
Athens, Greece

Dear Mr. Denikos,

I am writing to you at the request of Ms. Evangelia Makestos who is applying for a position as secretary in your company.

Ms. Makestos worked for me as a secretary during her summer vacations for the past three years. My colleagues and I found her to be a very competent and reliable employee.

Please feel free to contact me if you need more information.

Sincerely,

Elizabeth Hogan

Elizabeth Hogan, Director
International Films, Ltd.

190. What is Ms. Makestos probably doing?

(A) Job hunting
(B) Quitting her job
(C) Moving to New York
(D) Applying to school

191. Where is Mr. Denikos's company?

(A) In Athens
(B) In New York
(C) In Houston
(D) In London

192. How long did Ms. Makestos work at International Films?

(A) One summer
(B) Three summers
(C) One year
(D) Three years

193. What kind of letter is this?

(A) A letter of complaint
(B) A job inquiry
(C) A letter of recommendation
(D) A request for information

GO ON TO THE NEXT PAGE

Questions 194-197 refer to the following announcement on the Internet.

HOME PAGE

*Current Issue (#148, March 20-26, 19—)*
*SPP Archive of back issues*
*Prospects (SPP Culture & Lifestyle Guide)*

- *How to contact us*
- *More about the* Moscow Daily
- *How to subscribe to the printed newspaper*
- *Staff*



*Return to* Moscow Daily *Web Home Page*

**Subscription Information**

To order an international subscription to the English language edition of the *Moscow Daily*, please e-mail Vladimir Alekseev, subscription service manager.
E-mail: erralls@Mskdaily.com

Please include your name and address to receive a subscription coupon or print out the subscription coupon below.

---

Yes! I want to subscribe to the *Moscow Daily* and have 5 percent of the subscription rate go to the charity of my choice:

Please check one:

- ❑ Protecting our Natural Resources Organization
- ❑ Clean Oceans Today Association
- ❑ Saving Endangered Species Society

Please circle the currency that is most convenient. All subscriptions are honored with a money-back guarantee. The first month's issue is complimentary.

| | ISSUES | USD | DEM | FIM | FRF | SEK | CHF | GBP |
|---|---|---|---|---|---|---|---|---|
| Europe and Scandinavia | 26 issues<br>52 issues | 79<br>135 | 122<br>210 | 373<br>639 | 419<br>716 | 593<br>1012 | 102<br>174 | 50<br>86 |
| All other countries | 26 issues<br>52 issues | 99<br>189 | 153<br>293 | 468<br>894 | 525<br>1003 | 743<br>1417 | 128<br>245 | 62<br>119 |

☐ Please send me your advertising rates.

Name: ______________________________

Job Title: ______________________________

Address: ______________________________

Country: ______________________________

☐ I enclose my check for __________ payable to Moscow Daily, Ltd.

☐ Please charge __________ to my credit card.

Credit card: ______________________

Number: ______________________

Expiration Date: ______________________

Signature: ______________________ Date: ______________________

---

**SEND COUPON TO:**

Moscow Daily
10 Leningradsky Prospect
Moscow, Russia 12504

Tel: 095-368-1654
Fax: 095-368-7214

194. Where would this form most likely be seen?

(A) On a computer monitor
(B) On a movie screen
(C) In a newspaper
(D) In a phone book

195. What would happen if the reader were dissatisfied with the newspaper?

(A) The newspaper would send a complimentary issue.
(B) The subscription would be extended.
(C) The editor would contact the reader.
(D) The subscription price would be refunded.

196. Which type of charities does the newspaper support?

(A) Disadvantaged children
(B) Disease prevention
(C) Environmental concerns
(D) Art and cultural institutions

197. How can a subscriber pay for the newspaper?

(A) In Russian currency only
(B) In monthly installments
(C) By check or credit card
(D) By money order only

Questions 198-200 refer to the following announcement.

**TWO TYPES OF TRAINING**

On-the-job training is the most common form of training. An employee learns from his or her supervisor or coworker how to do the job. On-the-job training is an apprenticeship.

Off-the-job training is the most expensive form of training. An employee is sent to a training program where training is provided.

The purpose of both types is to improve the employee's efficiency.

198. Which of the following best describes on-the-job training?

(A) Expensive
(B) Ineffective
(C) Common
(D) Quick

199. What is on-the-job training similar to?

(A) An apprenticeship
(B) Off-the-job training
(C) A supervisory position
(D) A company benefit

200. What is the purpose of training?

(A) To improve employee efficiency
(B) To spend excess capital
(C) To satisfy government requirements
(D) To please a supervisor

Stop! This is the end of the test. If you finish before time is called, you may go back to Parts V, VI, and VII and check your work.

# PRACTICE TEST THREE

You will find the Answer Sheet for Practice Test Three on page 221. Detach it from the book and use it to record your answers. Play the audiotape for Practice Test Three when you are ready to begin.

## LISTENING COMPREHENSION

In this section of the test, you will have the chance to show how well you understand spoken English. There are four parts to this section, with special directions for each part.

### Part I

Directions: For each question, you will see a picture in your test book and you will hear four short statements. The statements will be spoken just one time. They will not be printed in your test book, so you must listen carefully to understand what the speaker says.

When you hear the four statements, look at the picture in your test book and choose the statement that best describes what you see in the picture. Then on your answer sheet, find the number of the question and mark your answer. Look at the sample below.

Now listen to the four statements.

Sample Answer
(A) ● (C) (D)

Statement (B), "They're having a meeting," best describes what you see in the picture. Therefore, you should choose answer (B).

1.

2.

3.

4.

5.

6.

7. 

8. 

9.

10.

11.

12.

13.

14.

15. 

16. 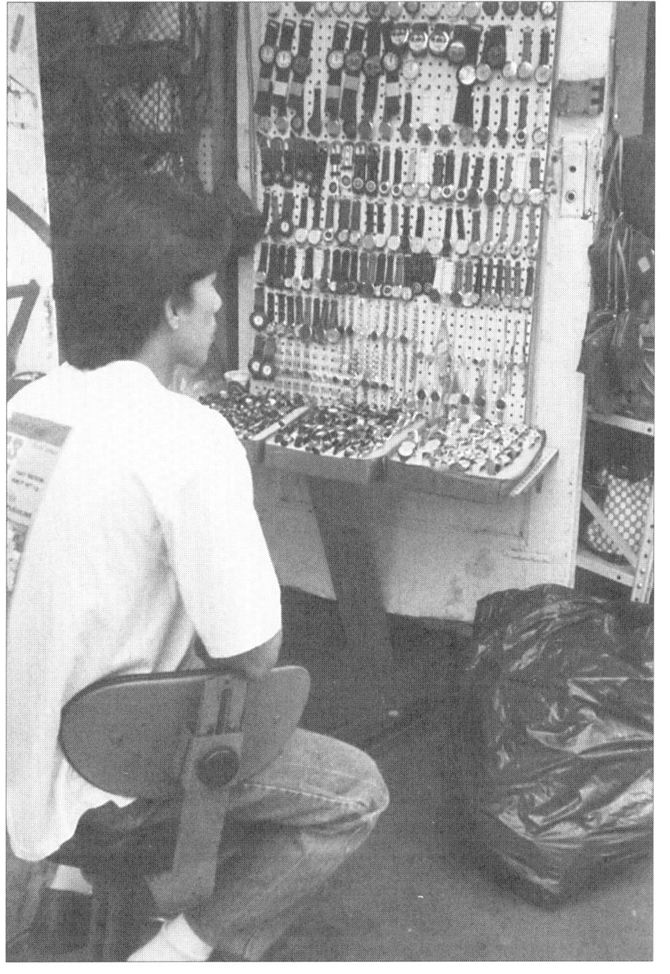

17. 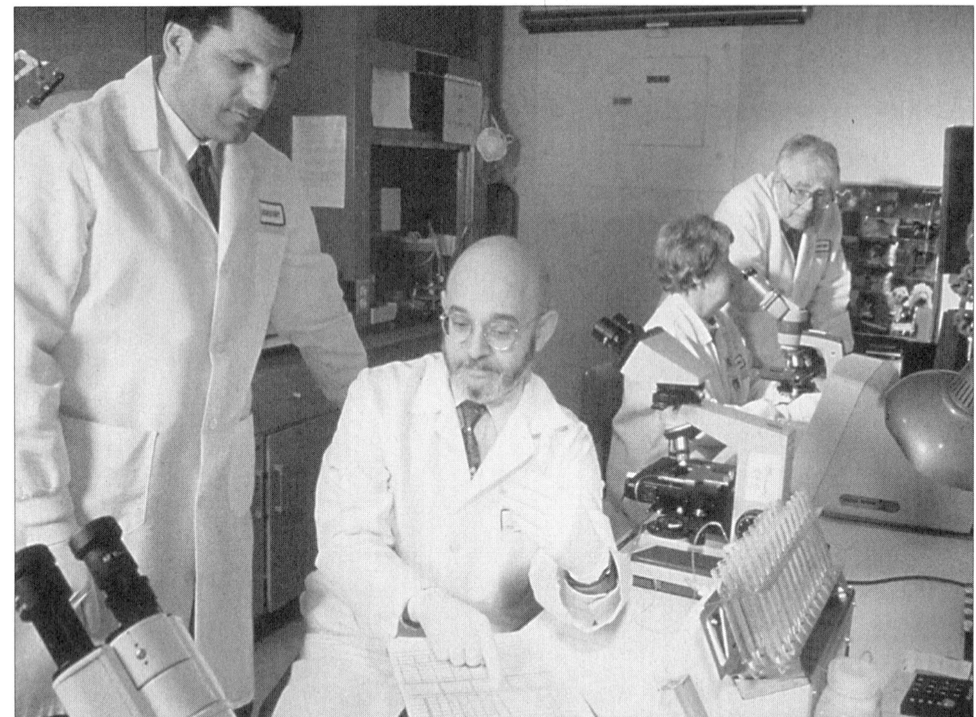

18. 

19.

20.

## Part II

Directions: In this part of the test, you will hear a question spoken in English, followed by three responses, also spoken in English. The question and the responses will be spoken just one time. They will not be printed in your test book, so you must listen carefully to understand what the speakers say. You are to choose the best response to each question.

Now listen to a sample question.

You will hear: Sample Answer

You will also hear: ● (B) (C)

The best response to the question "How are you?" is choice (A), "I am fine, thank you." Therefore, you should choose answer (A).

21. Mark your answer on your answer sheet.

22. Mark your answer on your answer sheet.

23. Mark your answer on your answer sheet.

24. Mark your answer on your answer sheet.

25. Mark your answer on your answer sheet.

26. Mark your answer on your answer sheet.

27. Mark your answer on your answer sheet.

28. Mark your answer on your answer sheet.

29. Mark your answer on your answer sheet.

30. Mark your answer on your answer sheet.

31. Mark your answer on your answer sheet.

32. Mark your answer on your answer sheet.

33. Mark your answer on your answer sheet.

34. Mark your answer on your answer sheet.

35. Mark your answer on your answer sheet.

36. Mark your answer on your answer sheet.

37. Mark your answer on your answer sheet.

38. Mark your answer on your answer sheet.

39. Mark your answer on your answer sheet.

40. Mark your answer on your answer sheet.

41. Mark your answer on your answer sheet.

42. Mark your answer on your answer sheet.

43. Mark your answer on your answer sheet.

44. Mark your answer on your answer sheet.

45. Mark your answer on your answer sheet.

46. Mark your answer on your answer sheet.

47. Mark your answer on your answer sheet.

48. Mark your answer on your answer sheet.

49. Mark your answer on your answer sheet.

50. Mark your answer on your answer sheet.

## Part III

Directions: In this part of the test, you will hear several short conversations between two people. The conversations will not be printed in your test book. You will hear the conversations only once, so you must listen carefully to understand what the speakers say.

In your test book, you will read a question about each conversation. The question will be followed by four answers. You are to choose the best answer to each question and mark it on your answer sheet.

51. Why is the woman upset with the man?

    (A) He has to get gas.
    (B) He didn't plan ahead.
    (C) He got lost.
    (D) He had to wait.

52. How many chairs do the speakers need altogether?

    (A) Six.
    (B) Eight.
    (C) Twelve.
    (D) Eighteen.

53. Where did the woman park the car?

    (A) On the street.
    (B) In the garage.
    (C) In the parking lot.
    (D) Next door.

54. What are the speakers going to do?

    (A) Buy movie tickets.
    (B) Change lines.
    (C) Solve a problem.
    (D) Make change.

55. What does the woman want the taxi driver to do?

    (A) Drive to the store.
    (B) Hire a limousine.
    (C) Open the door.
    (D) Wait for her.

56. What are the speakers going to do?

    (A) Put things away.
    (B) Paint the garage.
    (C) Climb a ladder.
    (D) Clean the brushes.

57. What are the speakers doing?

    (A) Hanging pictures.
    (B) Measuring their children.
    (C) Adding two figures.
    (D) Mountain climbing.

58. What is the man's occupation?

    (A) Runner.
    (B) Pig farmer.
    (C) Carpenter.
    (D) Judge.

59. Where does this conversation take place?

    (A) At the office.
    (B) In a boat.
    (C) In a nursery.
    (D) At a fish store.

60. How much longer will it take the woman to finish the work?

    (A) Two minutes.
    (B) Ten minutes.
    (C) Twenty minutes.
    (D) Thirty minutes.

61. What are the speakers doing?

    (A) Drinking tea.
    (B) Playing golf.
    (C) Going bowling.
    (D) Turning right.

62. Why are the speakers leaving?

    (A) They are bored.
    (B) The play is over.
    (C) They fell asleep.
    (D) They were told to leave.

63. Where does this conversation take place?

(A) In a forest.
(B) In a bank.
(C) By the river.
(D) At a florist shop.

64. When is the van coming?

(A) This morning.
(B) At noon.
(C) Tonight.
(D) Tomorrow.

65. Why shouldn't the woman feed the pigeons?

(A) They are stupid.
(B) They breed diseases.
(C) They can find their own food.
(D) They don't like bread.

66. What is the man doing?

(A) Filing a complaint.
(B) Working in a store.
(C) Shopping.
(D) Interviewing for a job.

67. What is the woman afraid of?

(A) Getting lost.
(B) Being followed.
(C) Driving fast.
(D) Starting the car.

68. Where does this conversation take place?

(A) In a supermarket.
(B) In a garden.
(C) On a farm.
(D) In a theatre.

69. What is the man's occupation?

(A) Gardener.
(B) Banker.
(C) Florist.
(D) Park ranger.

70. How does this year's attendance differ from last year's?

(A) It has doubled this year.
(B) There are half as many people this year.
(C) Last year there were twice as many people.
(D) A thousand people will attend this year.

71. Why didn't the woman call?

(A) She was away last week.
(B) She didn't feel well.
(C) She lost the man's number.
(D) She forgot.

72. How long has the business been in operation?

(A) Sixteen years.
(B) Forty years.
(C) A lifetime.
(D) Four generations.

73. What does the woman want to do?

(A) Go overseas.
(B) Borrow a stamp.
(C) Write a letter.
(D) Buy a postcard.

74. What day does the conversation take place?

(A) Monday.
(B) Wednesday.
(C) Thursday.
(D) Saturday.

75. Who is the woman?

(A) A guest.
(B) A chef.
(C) A hostess.
(D) A dishwasher.

76. Where does this conversation take place?

(A) In a shower.
(B) On a race course.
(C) At a swimming pool.
(D) At a crosswalk.

GO ON TO THE NEXT PAGE

77. When does the plane take off?

(A) 11:30.
(B) 12:00.
(C) 1:30.
(D) 2:00.

78. What does the woman think about the man?

(A) He's a slow reader.
(B) He's interesting.
(C) He's growing taller.
(D) He's a good writer.

79. How many pounds of potatoes will the speakers buy?

(A) One pound.
(B) Five pounds.
(C) Seven pounds.
(D) Ten pounds.

80. Where does this conversation take place?

(A) In an elevator.
(B) At home.
(C) On an escalator.
(D) On the seventh floor.

## Part IV

Directions: In this part of the test, you will hear several short talks. Each will be spoken just one time. They will not be printed in your test book, so you must listen carefully to understand and remember what is said.

In your test book, you will read two or more questions about each short talk. The questions will be followed by four answers. You are to choose the best answer to each question and mark it on your answer sheet.

81. What season is it?

 (A) Spring.
 (B) Summer.
 (C) Fall.
 (D) Winter.

82. What weather is expected this afternoon?

 (A) Rain.
 (B) Stormy winds.
 (C) Cool breezes.
 (D) Dry and windless.

83. What day is Dr. Miller's office closed?

 (A) Monday.
 (B) Wednesday.
 (C) Thursday.
 (D) Friday.

84. Why would someone call 555-3212?

 (A) To report an emergency.
 (B) To make an appointment.
 (C) To reschedule an exam.
 (D) To get lab results.

85. Where is this announcement being heard?

 (A) At a school.
 (B) At home.
 (C) In a theater.
 (D) In a restaurant.

86. Why are the customers requested to leave?

 (A) They refused to pay.
 (B) They lost their belongings.
 (C) There is a fire.
 (D) They were overcharged.

87. Who will participate in the exercises?

 (A) All personnel.
 (B) Only the workers.
 (C) Only the supervisors.
 (D) Only the management.

88. How long will the session last?

 (A) Thirty minutes.
 (B) One hour.
 (C) One hour and a half.
 (D) All morning.

89. Where will the exercises take place?

 (A) In the south gym.
 (B) On the lawn.
 (C) In the parking lot.
 (D) In the lobby.

90. What does this company do?

 (A) Supplies models.
 (B) Rents computers.
 (C) Finds stolen computers.
 (D) Leases cars.

91. What is the minimum rental period?

 (A) Hourly.
 (B) Daily.
 (C) Monthly.
 (D) Yearly.

92. What was this announcement about?

 (A) A riot.
 (B) A tidal wave.
 (C) A volcano.
 (D) An earthquake.

93. How much damage was done to property?

(A) None.
(B) A little.
(C) Extensive.
(D) A great amount.

94. Where is the announcement being heard?

(A) At an airport.
(B) On a plane.
(C) At a consulate.
(D) At a bus station.

95. What is the gate number?

(A) Fifteen.
(B) Sixteen.
(C) Fifty-eight.
(D) Sixty.

96. How many levels are reserved for employee parking?

(A) One.
(B) Two.
(C) Three.
(D) Four.

97. Which vehicles may park in the red spaces?

(A) Maintenance vehicles.
(B) Employees' cars.
(C) Visitors' cars.
(D) Two trucks.

98. What spaces are reserved for management?

(A) Yellow.
(B) Blue.
(C) White.
(D) Any space.

99. Who is listening to this announcement?

(A) Politicians.
(B) Guides.
(C) Diplomats.
(D) Tourists.

100. How is the group traveling?

(A) By van.
(B) By car.
(C) By bus.
(D) By train.

This is the end of the Listening Comprehension portion of the test. Turn to Part V in your test book.

# READING

In this section of the test, you will have the chance to show how well you understand written English. There are three parts to this section, with special directions for each part.

## Part V

Directions: This part of the test has incomplete sentences. Four words or phrases, marked (A), (B), (C), (D), are given beneath each sentence. You are to choose the one word or phrase that best completes the sentence. Then, on your answer sheet, find the number of the question and mark your answer.

Example

Because the equipment is very delicate, it must be handled with ________.

(A) caring
(B) careful
(C) care
(D) carefully

Sample Answer

(A) (B) ● (D)

The sentence should read, "Because the equipment is very delicate, it must be handled with care." Therefore, you should choose answer (C).

Now begin work on the questions.

101. A ________ firm will help us find software.

(A) consultation
(B) consultant
(C) consulting
(D) consult

102. ________ Mr. Jeffries to get the job done.

(A) Count on
(B) Count from
(C) Count in
(D) Count up

103. Ms. Nyguen had submitted her resume before she ________ the position was filled.

(A) will know
(B) knows
(C) has known
(D) knew

104. If Mr. Donna were looking for a permanent job, our recruiter ________ help.

(A) may
(B) will
(C) can
(D) could

105. The purchaser wanted the equipment ________ by Monday morning.

(A) delivered
(B) delivering
(C) will be delivered
(D) must be delivered

106. The company's quarterly earnings were up; ________, the officers felt satisfied.

(A) nevertheless
(B) therefore
(C) however
(D) for this purpose

107. ________ substantial layoffs, costs were reduced.

(A) When
(B) Because of
(C) Although
(D) Since

108. Consumer confidence fell ________ April.

(A) next
(B) on
(C) in
(D) the

109. Price quotes ________.

(A) have daily been announced
(B) have been announced daily
(C) daily have been announced
(D) have been daily announced

110. The administration allows Thailand ________ Indonesia trade benefits.

(A) but
(B) nor
(C) and so
(D) and

111. The talks will take place ________ Brussels.

(A) at
(B) the
(C) in
(D) to

112. Many workers can't use computers; ________, training is required.

(A) on the whole
(B) besides
(C) consequently
(D) for example

113. Management let the employees ________ at two o'clock.

(A) leave
(B) left
(C) was leaving
(D) was left

114. If our candidates ________ elected, we'll have a strong Board.

(A) are
(B) were
(C) have been
(D) will be

115. It's important that the clients ________ interested.

(A) are seeming
(B) will seem
(C) is seeming
(D) seem

116. Find ________ the details and write a report.

(A) up
(B) about
(C) out
(D) around

117. The meeting ________ going on since eight o'clock this morning.

(A) has been
(B) was
(C) is
(D) will be

118. The consultant ________ his business if he had advertised.

(A) doubled
(B) will double
(C) would double
(D) could have doubled

119. Mr. Dalla would like the invoices ________ directly to Milan.

(A) fax
(B) faxing
(C) be faxed
(D) faxed

120. The members would resign if they ________ asked to do so.

(A) was
(B) were
(C) will be
(D) would be

121. Ambition, talent, ________ desire are ingredients for success.

(A) or
(B) never
(C) yet
(D) and

122. Only five years ago, there ________ a shortage of computer specialists.

(A) was
(B) were
(C) has been
(D) have been

123. The Board reported that more funds ________ for training.

(A) was given
(B) could have given
(C) should be given
(D) is given

124. Some employees get their paychecks automatically ________ in their bank accounts.

(A) deposited
(B) depositing
(C) are deposited
(D) deposit

125. Costs should be cut; ________, the number of staff positions will be reduced.

(A) however
(B) therefore
(C) meanwhile
(D) but

126. Office branches are located ________ the metropolitan area.

(A) on
(B) at
(C) about
(D) throughout

127. The company offers a ________ plan for its workers.

(A) retirement
(B) retiring
(C) retire
(D) retired

128. ________ Mr. Hague finished the job interview, he felt relieved.

(A) While
(B) Because of
(C) During
(D) After

129. Ms. Lopez has ________ learned to copy diskettes.

(A) yet
(B) ever
(C) already
(D) certain

130. The paychecks will be delivered ________ they arrive from the accounting department.

(A) before
(B) soon
(C) when
(D) during

131. The report outlines the products for the first quarter ________ the year.

(A) to
(B) at
(C) from
(D) of

132. The benefits package is impressive; ________, the director promotes only from within the company.

(A) for example
(B) when
(C) despite
(D) nevertheless

133. This company attempts to make its employees ________ like family.

(A) feeling
(B) feels
(C) felt
(D) feel

134. If the bills ________ in five days, the company will seek damages.

(A) weren't paid
(B) won't have paid
(C) aren't paid
(D) don't pay

135. The bank ________ another branch in Houston within the next year.

(A) opened
(B) will be opening
(C) have opened
(D) would open

136. Could you have the secretary ________ my office before he leaves today?

(A) stop off
(B) stop for
(C) stop to
(D) stop by

137. The ________ was settled on Saturday.

(A) dispute
(B) disputing
(C) disputable
(D) disputant

138. Make sure to use an ________ dealer.

(A) authority
(B) authorization
(C) authorized
(D) authoritarian

139. The printer apologized for ________ two names on the program.

(A) leaving for
(B) leaving out
(C) leaving to
(D) leaving from

140. Mr. Fox ________ the results tomorrow afternoon.

(A) will be knowing
(B) will know
(C) will have known
(D) is going to be knowing

## Part VI

Directions: In this part of the test, each sentence has four words or phrases underlined. The four underlined parts of the sentence are marked (A), (B), (C), (D). You are to identify the one underlined word or phrase that should be corrected or rewritten. Then, on your answer sheet, find the number of the question and mark your answer.

Example

All employee (A) are required to wear (B) their identification (C) badges while (D) at work.

Sample Answer

● (B) (C) (D)

Choice (A), the underlined word "employee," is not correct in this sentence. This sentence should read, "All employees are required to wear their identification badges while at work." Therefore, you should choose answer (A).

Now begin work on the questions.

141. There is a report in today's (A) newspaper that the (B) bank announces (C) bankruptcy late last (D) week.

142. Many conference (A) attendees were late because the (B) hotel was located far than (C) anyone had anticipated (D).

143. Mr. Spencer advised me talking to (A) my colleague about the problem before filing (B) an official (C) complaint against her (D).

144. The officers (A) of Tiffany & Company decided that they (B) can establish (C) a new branch of their store at Paris (D).

145. It was not (A) a regular luncheon meeting (B); it was held in (C) the more (D) exclusive restaurant downtown.

146. New shopping (A) mall is being planned for the (B) residential area where new (C) homes are being built at a rapid rate (D).

147. Mrs. Pham wanted to know (A) when was the last staff meeting (B) so she could plan (C) the next one (D).

148. The director suggested that you and me (A) report (B) our findings (C) to the team (D) directly.

GO ON TO THE NEXT PAGE

149. Engineers and scientists have had no trouble finding high-level, high-paying positions
A B C

who have experience.
D

150. The opinion holding by most investors is to buy now.
A B C D

151. An annual party for the employees and his families is always held before the holiday season.
A B C D

152. The editors of the weekly newsletter, which contains financial news of local organizations, has agreed
A B C

to accept advertisements.
D

153. The executive's speaking remarks always come across much more powerfully than his
A B C

published reports.
D

154. A new trend is for sales representatives to send the thank-you notes to their customers.
A B C D

155. All the people who is interested in working on the proposal should be invited to tomorrow's meeting.
A B C D

156. The residents of the new housing development need to organize itself and make their complaints
A B C

officially known.
D

157. A group of investors and real estate professionals have discovered an area outside the city that they
A B C

think is perfect for investment.
D

158. Total retail sales they were estimated at more than $4 billion last quarter, nearly double the
A B C

first-quarter figures.
D

159. The client should call and ask for the annual report, you have my permission to send it to him.
A B C D

160. Looking for the perfect location and are assessing the needs of their company, the members of the
A B C

executive committee took a long time before making their decision.
D

## Part VII

Directions: The questions in this part of the test are based on a variety of reading material (for example, announcements, paragraphs, and advertisements). You are to choose the one best answer, (A), (B), (C), or (D), to each question. Then, on your answer sheet, find the number of the question and mark your answer. Answer all questions following a passage on the basis of what is stated or implied in that passage.

Read the following example.

> The Museum of Technology is a "hands-on" museum, designed for people to experience science at work. Visitors are encouraged to use, test, and handle the objects on display. Special demonstrations are scheduled for the first and second Wednesdays of each month at 1:30 p.m. Open Tuesday–Friday 2:30–4:30 p.m., Saturday 11:00 a.m.–4:30 p.m., and Sunday 1:00–4:30 p.m.
>
> When during the month can visitors see special demonstrations?
>
> (A) Every weekend
> (B) The first two Wednesdays
> (C) One afternoon a week
> (D) Every other Wednesday

Sample Answer

The passage says that the demonstrations are scheduled for the first and second Wednesdays of the month. Therefore, you should choose answer (B).

Now begin work on the questions.

Questions 161-163 refer to the following memo.

**Memorandum**

To: All employees
From: Dick Talbot, Director of Personnel
Subject: Vacation leave

All requests for vacation leave must be submitted at least four weeks before your vacation begins. You will be contacted by the Personnel Office when your request is approved. Approval takes two weeks.

161. What is the main topic of the memo?

(A) Termination policy
(B) Amount of vacation time
(C) Requesting vacation time
(D) Contacting employees during vacations

162. When must employees submit their requests?

(A) At the start of the year
(B) Four weeks before vacations
(C) Before two weeks are up
(D) Within two weeks

163. What takes two weeks?

(A) Approval of request
(B) Submission of request
(C) Vacation time
(D) Boat cruises

Questions 164-166 refer to the following chart.

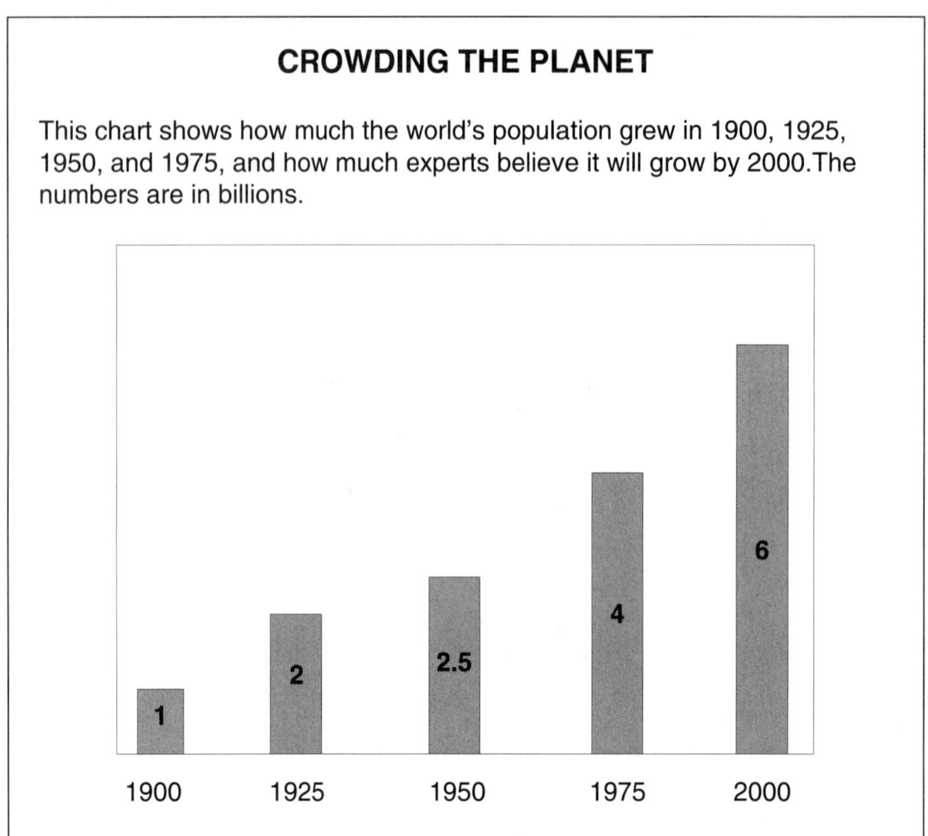


164. What was the world population in 1950?

(A) Half a billion
(B) 2 billion
(C) 2.5 billion
(D) 5 billion

165. In what year did the population reach 4 billion?

(A) 1900
(B) 1925
(C) 1950
(D) 1975

166. When was the population under 2 billion?

(A) In 1900
(B) In 1925
(C) In 1950
(D) In 1975

Questions 167-169 refer to the following article.

Finding new employees who will fit the needs of the company is not always easy. First, the company must think carefully about the tasks involved in each job to be filled and about the skills, abilities, and knowledge a person must have in order to carry out those tasks successfully.

Second, it has to find people who meet these requirements. One of the most common ways to find employees for these positions is to look within the organization. Is anyone currently in the organization who could do the job?

If no one within the firm is qualified, look outside the organization. Some of the most common sources of new employees are high schools, junior colleges, four-year colleges, and universities. Firms also use newspapers to help locate job applicants.

167. What is this article about?

(A) Reading newspapers
(B) Hiring employees
(C) Protecting the organization
(D) Going to high school

168. What is an example of a common outside source?

(A) High schools
(B) Resources within the organization
(C) Spies
(D) Temporary employees

169. What do firms use to help locate applicants?

(A) Yellow pages
(B) Subway ads
(C) Newspaper ads
(D) Word-of-mouth

GO ON TO THE NEXT PAGE

Questions 170-172 refer to the following article.

**Virtual Desktop 2.0,** a new software product, may turn out to be the most important development in the history of compatible personal computers.

Virtual Desktop 2.0 has four main advantages over regular DOS. First, all programs written for Virtual Desktop have a similar look. Second, the program prints on paper what you see on the computer screen. Third, the program makes it easy to transfer data between different programs. Finally, it's possible to load several programs into the computer's memory and switch between them with a single command.

170. Where is Virtual Desktop 2.0 used?

(A) On a desk
(B) On a computer
(C) On paper
(D) On TV

171. What do programs written for Virtual Desktop have in common?

(A) Their appearance
(B) Their cost
(C) Their value
(D) Their printers

172. Why is it advantageous to have several programs in a computer's memory?

(A) It costs less.
(B) It's easier to move from one to the other.
(C) It uses less computer memory.
(D) It's faster when starting a computer.

Questions 173-175 refer to the following announcement.

AERONAUTIC SYSTEMS, INC., the Berlin-based company also known as AeroSys, has made an agreement with three major airlines to provide a satellite system for voice and data communications, a company spokesperson announced last week.

The agreement with Skyways, Air One, and Travelers International will provide communications between aircraft and on-ground systems for operational control and air traffic services.

173. Where is AeroSys based?

(A) In London
(B) In New York
(C) In Berlin
(D) In Tokyo

174. According to the passage, what will be provided by the agreement?

(A) Aircraft
(B) A satellite system
(C) On-ground systems
(D) Air traffic services

175. Which of the following is NOT a part of this agreement?

(A) A satellite system
(B) Communication between aircraft
(C) A system of voice and data communication
(D) Ticketing service

GO ON TO THE NEXT PAGE

Questions 176-178 refer to the following announcement.

## Computer Program at San Juan High

When students at San Juan High Academy fall behind their classmates in reading and mathematics, school officials send a computer to their homes.

For nine weeks, the students get a personal computer with a printer and software. They can work and play with the computer whenever they like and as often as they like. Their families, too, are encouraged to get into the act.

176. Which of the following is NOT part of the program?

   (A) Software programs
   (B) A printer
   (C) A personal computer
   (D) Textbooks

177. When can students use the computers?

   (A) Only during school time
   (B) On weekends only
   (C) At lunch break
   (D) Anytime they wish

178. What are families of the students encouraged to do?

   (A) Become involved
   (B) Be actors
   (C) Drive away
   (D) Supervise the students

Questions 179-182 refer to the following article.

Communication can be in the form of words, pictures, or actions. Words are the most commonly used: we speak or write to communicate ideas. It is, therefore, essential for people to use words effectively.

Pictures are useful, also. Businesses use them successfully in posters, charts, and blueprints. Companies should be careful that the pictures used on posters and charts, as well as in brochures and advertisements, and the words complement, rather than conflict, with each other.

Action is an important comunication medium: actions speak louder than words. This medium is the most important when dealing face-to-face with employees, colleagues, and clients. A frown, a handshake, a wink, and even silence have meaning; people will attach significance to these actions.

179. What is the main topic of the article?

(A) Marketing
(B) Communication
(C) Actions
(D) Businesses

180. According to the article, which of the following is used the most?

(A) Words
(B) Posters
(C) Charts
(D) Telephones

181. Which medium is most important in direct communication?

(A) Charts
(B) Drawings
(C) Posters
(D) Actions

182. Which of the following is NOT given as an example of actions?

(A) Silence
(B) A wink
(C) Television
(D) A handshake

GO ON TO THE NEXT PAGE

Questions 183-184 refer to the following announcement.

Health Network, Inc., of Melbourne and Futura Computing of Perth Amboy agreed to develop handheld, computerized products to help the elderly monitor their health. Items will be made available free or at very low cost to those who could benefit from their use.

183. Who would most likely read this announcement?

(A) Lawyers
(B) Health care professionals
(C) Word processors
(D) Teachers

184. Which of the following could be one of the products?

(A) Dishwashers
(B) Calculators
(C) Blood pressure monitors
(D) All-weather gloves

Questions 185-186 refer to the following announcement.

Less than a year after it started operation, Detroit's giant trash incinerator, the largest in the nation, was stopped last month. Environmental officials said the huge plant, which changes waste into energy, was causing unhealthy levels of mercury. Entire neighborhoods were threatened.

185. According to the passage, why was the plant shut down?

(A) There was too much trash.
(B) It was unhealthy.
(C) It was unable to convert waste into energy.
(D) It could not be regulated.

186. What was the function of the plant?

(A) To collect waste
(B) To monitor air quality
(C) To supply Detroit with mercury
(D) To turn trash into energy

Questions 187-189 refer to the following article.

> The Stummering Corporation has had a problem with absenteeism. Between January and June of this year, the average employee was showing up fifteen minutes late for work three times a week. The management decided that something had to be done.
>
> The personnel department suggested that the management undertake an incentive program. Every worker who was on time during the month of August would be eligible for a cash award. Within five days of the announcement, absenteeism declined to the lowest level it had ever been.

187. What was the problem at the Stummering Corporation?

 (A) The management
 (B) Absenteeism
 (C) Poor pay
 (D) Unprofessional atmosphere

188. How many times was the average employee late?

 (A) Three times a week
 (B) Fifteen times a week
 (C) Three times between January and June
 (D) Fifteen times between January and June

189. What did employees who were on time receive?

 (A) A vacation
 (B) A cash award
 (C) A promotion
 (D) A new watch

GO ON TO THE NEXT PAGE

Questions 190-193 refer to the following letter.

 **WALTERS CORPORATION** 

3255 Trenton Avenue, Columbus, Ohio

---

November 16, 19—

Mr. Allen Porter
2870 Kennewick Dr.
Bloomington, IN 42777

Dear Mr. Porter,

We were pleased to receive your letter of inquiry and resume on November 8. In response to our job announcement, we received twenty applications from qualified accountants. Although we were impressed with your background, we are sorry to inform you that we have hired another applicant.

We wish you the best of luck in your job search.

Thank you for your interest in the Walters Corporation.

Sincerely,

John Simons

John Simons
Personnel Director

190. What is the main purpose of the letter?

(A) To ask for a job
(B) To reject someone who wanted a job
(C) To ask for references
(D) To learn about the Walters Corporation

191. What did Mr. Porter include with his letter?

(A) His resume
(B) A report on the Walters Corporation
(C) A gift for Mr. Simons
(D) A job announcement

192. What is Mr. Porter's profession?

(A) Personnel director
(B) Detective
(C) Accountant
(D) Secretary

193. How many applications were received?

(A) Eight
(B) Eleven
(C) Sixteen
(D) Twenty

Questions 194-196 refer to the following advertisement.

*A Special Invitation*

**Business Monthly**

invites you to sit back and save . . . enjoy free office delivery of each issue at 50% off the $30.00 cover price!

12 issues (1 year) just $15.00

NAME

ADDRESS

CITY STATE ZIP

❑ Payment enclosed ❑ Bill me later

Your first issue will be mailed within 6 weeks.

194. What is this an advertisement for?

(A) A monthly magazine
(B) A daily newspaper
(C) A calendar
(D) Office supplies

195. How much per year would it cost to buy the magazine at a newsstand?

(A) $12
(B) $15
(C) $30
(D) $60

196. When will the first issue arrive?

(A) Next week
(B) This month
(C) Within six weeks
(D) Next year

Questions 197-198 refer to the following notice.

> **WHEN REQUESTING INFORMATION...**
>
> Please feel free to contact our Information Center, toll free, at (800) 555-6843. Call during off-peak times. The busiest day is Monday, and the busiest hours each day are between 12:00 and 2:00. The telephone center is open from 9:00 A.M. TO 5:00 P.M. Monday through Friday.

197. According to the notice, when is the worst time to call?

    (A) Monday through Friday from 9:00 to 5:00
    (B) Any day except Monday
    (C) Tuesday through Friday from 12:00 to 2:00
    (D) Monday from noon to 2:00

198. When is the center open?

    (A) Eight hours a day, Monday through Friday
    (B) Only on Monday
    (C) Only on Monday and Friday
    (D) Only between 12:00 and 2:00

Questions 199-200 refer to the following notice.

> If you can hold a pen, you can use a computer. Forget about keyboards. With our new **Pen-In-Hand** system, all you do is write on paper, and your words appear typewritten on the screen, instantly.
>
> Whether you want to write text or add figures, you simply pick up your pen and write. With our new computer system you can add, delete, and correct with the same stroke.

199. What is being sold?

    (A) An adding machine
    (B) A new computer system
    (C) A ballpoint pen
    (D) A keyboard

200. What is the advantage of this product?

    (A) It is inexpensive.
    (B) You don't need a keyboard.
    (C) You don't have to write.
    (D) You only need an adding machine.

Stop! This is the end of the test. If you finish before time is called, you may go back to Parts V, VI, and VII and check your work.

# PRACTICE TEST FOUR

You will find the Answer Sheet for Practice Test Four on page 223. Detach it from the book and use it to record your answers. Play the audiotape for Practice Test Four when you are ready to begin.

## LISTENING COMPREHENSION

In this section of the test, you will have the chance to show how well you understand spoken English. There are four parts to this section, with special directions for each part.

### Part I

Directions: For each question, you will see a picture in your test book and you will hear four short statements. The statements will be spoken just one time. They will not be printed in your test book, so you must listen carefully to understand what the speaker says.

When you hear the four statements, look at the picture in your test book and choose the statement that best describes what you see in the picture. Then on your answer sheet, find the number of the question and mark your answer. Look at the sample below.

Now listen to the four statements.

Sample Answer

(A)  (C) 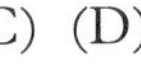 (D)

Statement (B), "They're having a meeting," best describes what you see in the picture. Therefore, you should choose answer (B).

1.

2.

3.

4.

GO ON TO THE NEXT PAGE

5. 

6. 

7.

AMP
ROTTNEST ISLANDER
ROTTNEST ISLANDER

8.

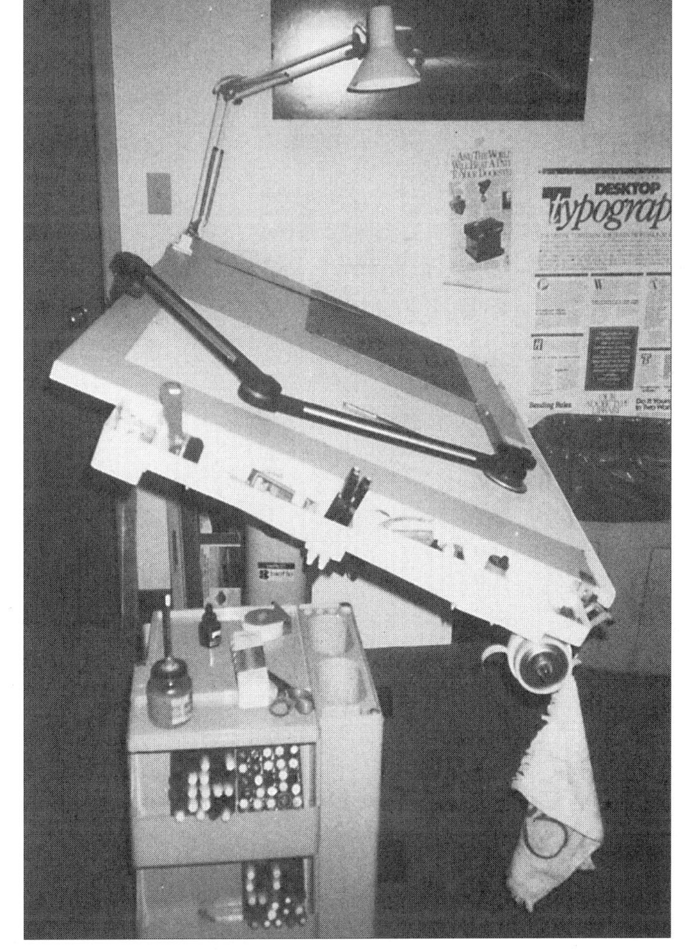
DESKTOP

GO ON TO THE NEXT PAGE

9.

10.

11.

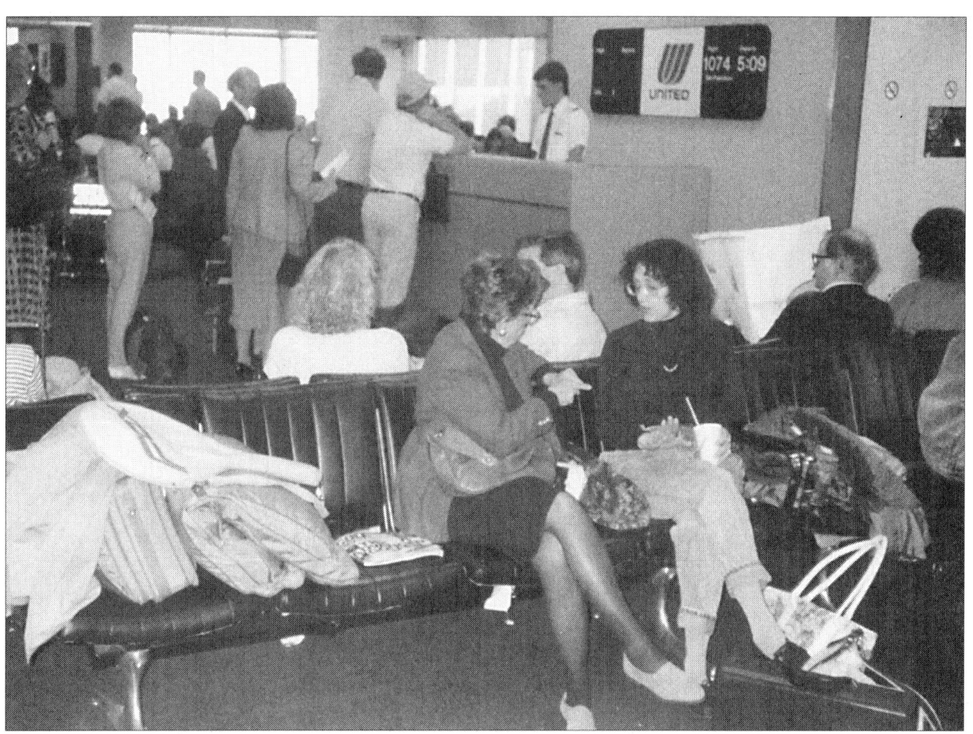


12.

13. 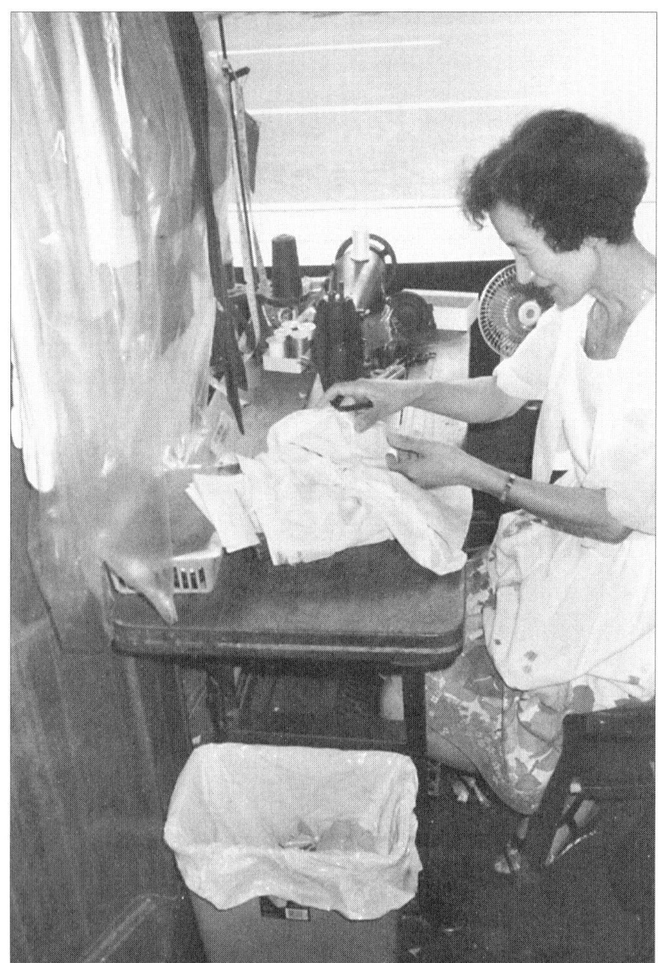

14. 

15.

16.

17.

18.

19.

20.

## Part II

Directions: In this part of the test, you will hear a question spoken in English, followed by three responses, also spoken in English. The question and the responses will be spoken just one time. They will not be printed in your test book, so you must listen carefully to understand what the speakers say. You are to choose the best response to each question.

Now listen to a sample question.

You will hear: | Sample Answer

You will also hear: | ● (B) (C)

The best response to the question "How are you?" is choice (A), "I am fine, thank you." Therefore, you should choose answer (A).

21. Mark your answer on your answer sheet.

22. Mark your answer on your answer sheet.

23. Mark your answer on your answer sheet.

24. Mark your answer on your answer sheet.

25. Mark your answer on your answer sheet.

26. Mark your answer on your answer sheet.

27. Mark your answer on your answer sheet.

28. Mark your answer on your answer sheet.

29. Mark your answer on your answer sheet.

30. Mark your answer on your answer sheet.

31. Mark your answer on your answer sheet.

32. Mark your answer on your answer sheet.

33. Mark your answer on your answer sheet.

34. Mark your answer on your answer sheet.

35. Mark your answer on your answer sheet.

36. Mark your answer on your answer sheet.

37. Mark your answer on your answer sheet.

38. Mark your answer on your answer sheet.

39. Mark your answer on your answer sheet.

40. Mark your answer on your answer sheet.

41. Mark your answer on your answer sheet.

42. Mark your answer on your answer sheet.

43. Mark your answer on your answer sheet.

44. Mark your answer on your answer sheet.

45. Mark your answer on your answer sheet.

46. Mark your answer on your answer sheet.

47. Mark your answer on your answer sheet.

48. Mark your answer on your answer sheet.

49. Mark your answer on your answer sheet.

50. Mark your answer on your answer sheet.

## Part III

<u>Directions:</u> In this part of the test, you will hear several short conversations between two people. The conversations will not be printed in your test book. You will hear the conversations only once, so you must listen carefully to understand what the speakers say.

In your test book, you will read a question about each conversation. The question will be followed by four answers. You are to choose the best answer to each question and mark it on your answer sheet.

51. What are the speakers doing?

    (A) Reading the newspaper.
    (B) Attending a game.
    (C) Playing sports.
    (D) Finishing a puzzle.

52. Who are the speakers talking about?

    (A) A gatekeeper.
    (B) A golfer.
    (C) A chauffeur.
    (D) A car salesperson.

53. What is the man looking for?

    (A) The milk.
    (B) The cabinet.
    (C) The sink.
    (D) The cups.

54. How many children does the man have?

    (A) One.
    (B) Two.
    (C) Three.
    (D) Four.

55. What is the husband's occupation?

    (A) Lawyer.
    (B) Architect.
    (C) City worker.
    (D) Doctor.

56. What's wrong with the batteries?

    (A) They're the wrong size.
    (B) They're too old.
    (C) They're missing.
    (D) They're too expensive.

57. Where are the people allowed to smoke?

    (A) In the lounge.
    (B) In the dining room.
    (C) In their offices.
    (D) Outside.

58. Where does this conversation take place?

    (A) In a hotel.
    (B) On the street.
    (C) In an elevator.
    (D) At the airport.

59. What will the man do tomorrow?

    (A) Take a later bus.
    (B) Come in late.
    (C) Take an earlier bus.
    (D) Stay late.

60. What did the woman borrow?

    (A) Money for lunch.
    (B) A screwdriver.
    (C) A paperback.
    (D) A toolbox.

61. What's the weather like?

    (A) Nice.
    (B) Cold.
    (C) Tropical.
    (D) Windy.

62. By what time does the man have to be home?

    (A) 6:30.
    (B) 7:00.
    (C) 8:00.
    (D) 9:00.

63. Where is the suitcase?

(A) In the dining room.
(B) In the hall.
(C) In the taxi.
(D) Upstairs.

64. What does the woman want to do?

(A) Buy a boat.
(B) Sail around the world.
(C) Learn to fly.
(D) Stop worrying.

65. What is difficult to read?

(A) The signature.
(B) The letter.
(C) The prescription.
(D) The book.

66. What does the man want to do?

(A) Meet some people.
(B) Leave the room.
(C) Remove a chair.
(D) Sit down.

67. How often did the woman call?

(A) Two times.
(B) Three times.
(C) Six times.
(D) Fifteen times.

68. Where are the brochures?

(A) In Singapore.
(B) In the supply room.
(C) In the mail.
(D) At the printer.

69. What will the woman put on the form?

(A) Friday's date.
(B) Her job title.
(C) The company name.
(D) Her phone number.

70. What is the man doing?

(A) Eating breakfast.
(B) Driving a car.
(C) Going to school.
(D) Going to work.

71. Why can't the man drink his coffee?

(A) The water is too hot.
(B) It's too weak.
(C) It's not strong enough.
(D) It's bitter.

72. In which direction does the woman want to go?

(A) Left.
(B) Right.
(C) Forward.
(D) Backward.

73. Where are the speakers?

(A) In an airplane.
(B) In a furniture store.
(C) In a restaurant.
(D) In a living room.

74. What are the speakers talking about?

(A) Air-conditioning.
(B) The refrigerator.
(C) The music system.
(D) The wind.

75. What is the speakers' profession?

(A) Physicians.
(B) Musicians.
(C) Athletes.
(D) Gardeners.

76. What is the problem?

(A) Spring came late this year.
(B) The driver took the wrong road.
(C) The road is full of holes.
(D) The man forgot his watch.

GO ON TO THE NEXT PAGE

77. What is the man doing?

(A) Getting measured for a shirt.
(B) Painting a house.
(C) Taking a long vacation.
(D) Buying a shirt.

78. What are the speakers getting ready for?

(A) A party.
(B) An election.
(C) A parade.
(D) A moving van.

79. How long did the man wait today?

(A) Thirty minutes.
(B) Forty-five minutes.
(C) Sixty minutes.
(D) One hundred and twenty minutes.

80. How long is the woman's vacation?

(A) One week.
(B) Two weeks.
(C) Three weeks.
(D) Four weeks.

## Part IV

Directions: In this part of the test, you will hear several short talks. Each will be spoken just one time. They will not be printed in your test book, so you must listen carefully to understand and remember what is said.

In your test book, you will read two or more questions about each short talk. The questions will be followed by four answers. You are to choose the best answer to each question and mark it on your answer sheet.

81. Why is the airport closed?

    (A) Because of heavy traffic.
    (B) Because of heavy fog.
    (C) Because of strong winds.
    (D) Because of falling snow.

82. When will the airport reopen?

    (A) By this morning.
    (B) By noon.
    (C) By early evening.
    (D) By late evening.

83. What time does the train arrive in New York?

    (A) 9:30.
    (B) 2:40.
    (C) 6:00.
    (D) 6:15.

84. How many stops does the train make?

    (A) None.
    (B) One.
    (C) Two.
    (D) Six.

85. What does this message state?

    (A) That there is a convention in town.
    (B) That city hotel rooms are booked.
    (C) That hotels have closed.
    (D) That there are long lines for tourist attractions.

86. What time frame is mentioned?

    (A) All of August.
    (B) The first week of August.
    (C) The middle of August.
    (D) The last two weeks of August.

87. Why would someone leave his or her name?

    (A) To get on a mailing list.
    (B) To cancel a room reservation.
    (C) To apply for any available job.
    (D) To be put on a waiting list.

88. Where is this announcement being heard?

    (A) In a restaurant.
    (B) In a school room.
    (C) In a meeting room.
    (D) At a train station.

89. What time will the session resume?

    (A) 10:15.
    (B) 10:30.
    (C) 10:45.
    (D) 11:00.

90. What did the participants just finish?

    (A) The question-answer period.
    (B) A coffee break.
    (C) Their resume.
    (D) Ms. Johnson's report.

91. What is the problem?

    (A) High waters.
    (B) Lack of food.
    (C) More homes than families.
    (D) Expensive property.

92. How many people have died?

    (A) None.
    (B) Twenty.
    (C) Thousands.
    (D) Millions.

GO ON TO THE NEXT PAGE

93. What does Carlos do?

(A) Builds new homes.
(B) Paints houses.
(C) Designs interiors.
(D) Supplies servants.

94. Who will provide a reference?

(A) The painters.
(B) The neighbors.
(C) The decorators.
(D) The real estate agents.

95. Who is listening to this announcement?

(A) A football team.
(B) Hospital patients.
(C) Airplane passengers.
(D) A theater audience.

96. How many minutes is the delay?

(A) Five.
(B) Fifteen.
(C) Twenty-five.
(D) Fifty.

97. What kind of organization is this?

(A) Sports.
(B) Music.
(C) Youth.
(D) Scholastic.

98. When is ticket information available?

(A) Between 4:00 and 6:00.
(B) Between 4:00 and 8:00.
(C) At 6:00.
(D) At 7:30.

99. What is this news item about?

(A) Shipping accidents.
(B) Gas tanks.
(C) Civil authority.
(D) Weekend activities.

100. How many accidents were there this month?

(A) One.
(B) Two.
(C) Three.
(D) Four.

This is the end of the Listening Comprehension portion of the test. Turn to Part V in your test book.

## READING

In this section of the test, you will have the chance to show how well you understand written English. There are three parts to this section, with special directions for each part.

### Part V

Directions: This part of the test has incomplete sentences. Four words or phrases, marked (A), (B), (C), (D), are given beneath each sentence. You are to choose the one word or phrase that best completes the sentence. Then, on your answer sheet, find the number of the question and mark your answer.

Example

Because the equipment is very delicate, it must be handled with ________.

(A) caring
(B) careful
(C) care
(D) carefully

Sample Answer

(A) (B) ● (D)

The sentence should read, "Because the equipment is very delicate, it must be handled with care." Therefore, you should choose answer (C).

Now begin work on the questions.

101. Salary increases will not be higher than the cost of ________.

(A) life
(B) live
(C) living
(D) lived

102. Feel free to ________ the engineer for more assistance.

(A) call on
(B) call to
(C) call forward
(D) call at

103. Mr. Goa ________ the proposal before he looked at the guidelines.

(A) writes
(B) had written
(C) has written
(D) will write

104. If the project is a success, the office ________ more help.

(A) would hire
(B) hired
(C) can hire
(D) could have hired

105. The office manager wants the computers ________ by tomorrow.

(A) will be installed
(B) installing
(C) install
(D) installed

106. Suggestions were requested; ________, none were offered.

(A) in spite of
(B) therefore
(C) however
(D) for this purpose

107. ________ the workers put in a lot of effort, profits were not high.

(A) Whatever
(B) Why
(C) Even though
(D) However

108. Ms. Kwak has already conducted market research ________ two new products.

(A) around
(B) from
(C) on
(D) near

109. Transactions ________.

(A) have weekly been documented
(B) have been documented weekly
(C) weekly have been documented
(D) have been weekly documented

110. Clients are invited to write ________ call for additional information.

(A) but
(B) or
(C) not
(D) either

111. An answering machine takes messages ________ weekends.

(A) from
(B) at
(C) in
(D) on

112. The solution cannot be determined ________ the problem is identified.

(A) if
(B) when
(C) until
(D) which

113. The director had her assistant ________ the memo.

(A) signing
(B) signed
(C) will sign
(D) sign

114. If you ________ a touch tone phone, you won't need an operator.

(A) had
(B) are having
(C) have
(D) will have

115. Our company ________ Metro Messenger Service since 1988.

(A) use
(B) used
(C) had used
(D) has been using

116. The new employees will ________ during training sessions.

(A) catch out
(B) catch on
(C) catch in
(D) catch down

117. The ________ result will be announced next week.

(A) finalized
(B) finally
(C) finalist
(D) final

118. The financing deal is expected to ________ in a matter of weeks.

(A) go ahead
(B) go out
(C) go through
(D) go beyond

119. The supervisor wants the inventory ________ by next Thursday.

(A) will be finished
(B) finish
(C) finished
(D) finishing

120. I would ask for a special meeting if I ________ her.

(A) was
(B) were
(C) am
(D) would be

121. The company appreciates not only the president's ambition ________ his ideas.

(A) or
(B) but also
(C) with
(D) and if

122. A new collection of programs ________ in the conference room.

(A) are presenting
(B) are presented
(C) present
(D) is being presented

123. The supplier said the department ________ a surplus in the future.

(A) has been ordered
(B) order
(C) should order
(D) ordered

124. Some managers wouldn't let the secretaries ________ early yesterday.

(A) leave
(B) leaves
(C) leaving
(D) left

125. Sales performance has been poor; ________, the store will close soon.

(A) nevertheless
(B) therefore
(C) on the whole
(D) but

126. Ms. Jacobs is one ________ our best agents.

(A) from
(B) by
(C) of
(D) than

127. Please refer to your personal ________ number.

(A) identify
(B) identifies
(C) identification
(D) identified

128. ________ you transfer your account, sign on the dotted line.

(A) While
(B) Because
(C) During
(D) Before

129. No one has turned on the air conditioner ________.

(A) yet
(B) never
(C) already
(D) soon

130. Akinori remained calm ________ his anticipation.

(A) while
(B) in spite of
(C) with
(D) as

131. All bank branches are open ________ 8:30 A.M. to 4:00 P.M.

(A) in
(B) at
(C) from
(D) by

132. We need more details; ________, who, when, what, and where.

(A) for example
(B) moreover
(C) however
(D) accordingly

GO ON TO THE NEXT PAGE

133. My boss gets her messages ________ by a computer.

(A) take
(B) takes
(C) taken
(D) taking

134. If the company ________ in debt, the accountant would be the first to know.

(A) were
(B) are
(C) would be
(D) will be

135. Who ________ how many offices we have contacted for the survey?

(A) knows
(B) know
(C) is knowing
(D) are knowing

136. There is a rumor that the London office is trying to ________ the Edinburgh office.

(A) take out
(B) take away
(C) take over
(D) take off

137. Before the meeting, a ________ was held to verify information.

(A) brief
(B) briefing
(C) briefly
(D) briefed

138. It is not ________ to argue about small details.

(A) advise
(B) advice
(C) advisable
(D) advised

139. ________ these data before publishing them.

(A) Verification
(B) Verify
(C) Verified
(D) Verifying

140. Either the product ________ the advertisement should be changed.

(A) or
(B) and
(C) but
(D) nor

## Part VI

Directions: In this part of the test, each sentence has four words or phrases underlined. The four underlined parts of the sentence are marked (A), (B), (C), (D). You are to identify the one underlined word or phrase that should be corrected or rewritten. Then, on your answer sheet, find the number of the question and mark your answer.

Example

All employee are required to wear their
A B

identification badges while at work.
C D

Sample Answer

● (B) (C) (D)

Choice (A), the underlined word "employee," is not correct in this sentence. This sentence should read, "All employees are required to wear their identification badges while at work." Therefore, you should choose answer (A).

Now begin work on the questions.

141. The annual picnic for the company and their employees is always planned for the beginning of summer.
A B C D

142. The management team has met and is considering to set up a staff meeting to hear complaints
A B C

directly from those who are not content.
D

143. Because so many unexpected people showed up for the seminar, last-minute arrangements were
A B C

made to find seats for him.
D

144. The company had finally decided that it can start looking into the research and development
A B C D

of new programs.

145. There is article in this morning's newspaper that outlines the reasons for the success of the program.
A B C D

146. Rather the little attention has been given to meeting the need for autonomy among subordinate
A B C

managers of small companies.
D

147. The city commission, is believing in the new transportation system, decided to bring in an advertising
A B C

agency to acquaint the public with the system.
D

GO ON TO THE NEXT PAGE

148. Management consultants are often used to helping solve business problems.
A B C D

149. Local car dealer has been making an estimate of the number of cars his agency will sell next year.
A B C D

150. We request that all employees report to Ms. Huang and I regarding their vacation plans
A B C
for the upcoming holiday.
D

151. This group of recruits is most motivated of all the recruits we have ever trained in this office.
A B C D

152. We are analyzing information which have been collected since the project began more than
A B C D
three years ago.

153. Noted the nervousness of the speaker, the director broke the ice by telling a joke
A B
before introducing her.
C D

154. Mr. Khiet wanted to know where was the personnel office so he could complete his forms
A B C
before going home.
D

155. The vice president itself summarizes and analyzes the ideas presented at the staff meetings.
A B C D

156. The committee have finalized the advertising and marketing strategies for the next fiscal year.
A B C D

157. The person to answer the phone was polite to the caller.
A B C D

158. Mr. Hughes, having consult with his lawyer, decided to manufacture a new product.
A B C D

159. The report should arrive and I'm not here, please get in touch with me as soon as possible.
A B C D

160. When are communicating with the support staff, the office managers must take care to write memos
A B
in clear and precise language.
C D

## Part VII

Directions: The questions in this part of the test are based on a variety of reading material (for example, announcements, paragraphs, and advertisements). You are to choose the one best answer, (A), (B), (C), or (D), to each question. Then, on your answer sheet, find the number of the question and mark your answer. Answer all questions following a passage on the basis of what is stated or implied in that passage.

Read the following example.

> The Museum of Technology is a "hands-on" museum, designed for people to experience science at work. Visitors are encouraged to use, test, and handle the objects on display. Special demonstrations are scheduled for the first and second Wednesdays of each month at l:30 p.m. Open Tuesday–Friday 2:30–4:30 p.m., Saturday 11:00 a.m.–4:30 p.m., and Sunday 1:00–4:30 p.m.
>
> When during the month can visitors see special demonstrations?
>
> (A) Every weekend
> (B) The first two Wednesdays
> (C) One afternoon a week
> (D) Every other Wednesday
>
> Sample Answer
>
> (A) (B) ● (D)

The passage says that the demonstrations are scheduled for the first and second Wednesdays of the month. Therefore, you should choose answer (B).

Now begin work on the questions.

GO ON TO THE NEXT PAGE

Questions 161-164 refer to the following table.

| InterCity Europe | Rail time | Air time |
|---|---|---|
| Paris to Amsterdam | 5 hr | 1 hr |
| Paris to Madrid | 13 hr | 1 hr, 50 min |
| Paris to Nice | 7 hr | 1 hr, 20 min |
| Frankfurt to Rome | 12 hr | 1 hr, 45 min |
| Frankfurt to Brussels | 5 hr, 30 min | 1 hr |
| Frankfurt to Vienna | 9 hr | 1 hr, 20 min |
| London to Edinburgh | 4 hr, 30 min | 1 hr, 15 min |
| London to Paris | 5 hr, 30 min | 1 hr, 5 min |

161. Which city is closest to Paris by air?

(A) London
(B) Nice
(C) Amsterdam
(D) Madrid

162. Which two cities are farthest apart by rail?

(A) Paris and Madrid
(B) Paris and Nice
(C) Frankfurt and Rome
(D) Frankfurt and Vienna

163. How long does it take to get from Frankfurt to Brussels?

(A) 1 hour by rail
(B) 1 hour by air
(C) 5 hours by rail
(D) 5 hours by air

164. What is the longest flight?

(A) Paris to Madrid
(B) Frankfurt to Rome
(C) Paris to Nice
(D) London to Edinburgh

Questions 165-167 refer to the following job announcement.

**BUSINESS INSTRUCTOR**

Major Paris vocational rehabilitation agency seeks instructor for clerical training program. Job duties: teach typing, data entry, office practices to motivated, disabled adults.

*Send resume to:*

PO Box 34256
75008 Paris

165. Who would be most qualified for this position?

    (A) A practical nurse
    (B) A clerical instructor
    (C) An office cleaner
    (D) A typist

166. Who is being taught?

    (A) Disabled adults
    (B) Clerical instructors
    (C) Office managers
    (D) Professional typists

167. What should applicants do?

    (A) Contact the nearest agency
    (B) Submit references
    (C) Mail their resumes
    (D) Call as soon as possible

GO ON TO THE NEXT PAGE

Questions 168-170 refer to the following memo.

## *Memorandum*

To: Juan Gomez
Date: 17 Jan. 19—
From: Maria Johnson, Building Engineer
Subject: Thermostat located in your office

We have noted that the thermostat in your office is frequently being turned off. The thermostat controls the temperature on the entire second floor. Please do not touch it. The other tenants are complaining about the heat in their offices.

168. What is the problem?

(A) Someone keeps turning off the thermostat.
(B) There is no thermostat on the second floor.
(C) The other tenants want a thermostat.
(D) The second floor is without heat.

169. When should the thermostat be turned off?

(A) In the evenings
(B) When it gets cold out
(C) Never
(D) When it gets hot

170. What should Mr. Gomez do?

(A) Change offices
(B) Leave the thermostat alone
(C) Complain to the other tenants
(D) Install a heater in his office

Questions 171-173 refer to the following advertisement.

## *White Shoe Kleen-Kit*

White shoes are handsome, but they've been difficult to keep clean... until now. A two-step, two-minute kit that will keep YOUR white shoes sparkling white, developed by the same company that supplies Wright and Perry Shoes with its finishes.

If you own a pair of white shoes, or plan to enjoy the extra pleasure that they can give, this kit is a must. It solves the problem you've always had . . . of keeping white shoes WHITE!

$7.00 each
**$5.00 with a shoe order**

171. What is this advertisement promoting?

(A) White shoes
(B) Shoe cleaner
(C) Shoe repair
(D) Company supplies

172. How long does it take to use the kit?

(A) Two minutes
(B) Five minutes
(C) Seven minutes
(D) Ten minutes

173. What problem does the product solve?

(A) Improving Wright shoe sales
(B) Finishing first
(C) Staying handsome
(D) Keeping white shoes white

GO ON TO THE NEXT PAGE

Questions 174-175 refer to the following announcement.

**REINHOLD COMPANY,** which had reported three straight periods of declining earnings, said yesterday that its earnings rose 15 percent in the first quarter of its fiscal year.

174. Which of the following statements about the Reinhold Company is true?

(A) Its most recent report shows declining earnings.
(B) It reported four straight periods of declining earnings.
(C) Its first-quarter earnings are up.
(D) Its profits in the current year are fifteen million dollars.

175. What percentage increase were the first-quarter earnings?

(A) 1 percent
(B) 3 percent
(C) 15 percent
(D) 16 percent

Questions 176-178 refer to the following memo.

## Interoffice Memo

To: Mr. Rollings
From: Ms. J. Gibbons
Date: July 17, 19—
Subject: Work schedules

The vice president has asked me to remind you that The Smithson Company observes a 35-hour workweek, from 9:00 A.M. to 5:00 P.M. Monday through Friday, with a 1-hour lunch period.

Individual employees may establish different schedules with their supervisor's approval.

176. What is the topic of the memo?

(A) Schedules
(B) Hiring
(C) Observations
(D) Approval

177. How many hours a week do the employees work?

(A) 17 hours
(B) 25 hours
(C) 35 hours
(D) 40 hours

178. Who must approve any change?

(A) The employee
(B) The employee's supervisor
(C) The personnel director
(D) The vice president

Questions 179-182 refer to the following memo.

## MEMORANDUM

To: ALL EMPLOYEES
From: Security
Date: 30 May
Subject: Visitors

Employees are reminded that a number of our contracts with clients are of a confidential nature. Therefore, visitors are not allowed within the office area unless they are accompanied by a member of the staff.

Your visitors are asked to sign in at the reception desk. The receptionist will call your office to admit them. You must come to the reception area and escort your visitors to your office.

179. Who will read this memo?

(A) Clients
(B) Company employees
(C) Visitors
(D) Security staff

180. Why must visitors be escorted?

(A) They may get lost.
(B) They have appointments with staff members.
(C) Company projects are confidential.
(D) They are special guests.

181. What must visitors do when they arrive?

(A) Call their office
(B) Admit themselves
(C) Leave before closing
(D) Sign in

182. How will employees know when their visitors have arrived?

(A) The visitors will call ahead.
(B) The receptionist will call the employee's office.
(C) The employee must wait in the reception area.
(D) The visitor will be sent to the employee's office.

Questions 183-186 refer to the following article.

Businesspeople find that some jobs take them away from home for longer than a few days. Those who find themselves at a new job site for weeks or months are often choosing to stay at apartment-hotels. These residences offer small and full-sized apartments that can be rented short-term. Apartments are fully furnished with everything from sofas to TV sets to dishes. Best of all, they are run like hotels, with cleaning and linen services, gyms and restaurants, and a desk clerk to take messages and help tenants with questions about the city. Apartment-hotels are often more cost-effective than standard hotels and more comfortable than hastily furnished apartments.

183. Why are these residences called "apartment-hotels"?

(A) They have characteristics of apartments and hotels.
(B) They contain full-sized apartments.
(C) They look like hotels.
(D) They have only short-term tenants.

184. Who would be likely to use an apartment-hotel?

(A) A businessperson on an overnight trip
(B) A family of tourists
(C) An engineer on a ten-week project away from home
(D) A consultant in town for a convention

185. What is NOT mentioned as an advantage of apartment-hotels?

(A) They are furnished.
(B) They have cleaning service.
(C) They are centrally located.
(D) They have a desk clerk on duty.

186. How do apartment-hotels compare with standard hotels?

(A) The rooms are larger.
(B) They are not as comfortable.
(C) There are fewer services offered.
(D) They are less expensive for a long stay.

Questions 187-189 refer to the following article.

When David Bikowski was laid off from his production job at the factory, he immediately found work at another place nearby. This new job pays $100 less a week. Yet, when he was called back to the factory last month, Bikowski chose to stay at his new job because he finds that his new firm is much less stressful than the old one.

187. Why did David Bikowski leave his job?

(A) He wanted a promotion.
(B) He was fired.
(C) He wanted more money.
(D) He was laid off.

188. How does Mr. Bikowski's present salary compare to his salary at his previous job?

(A) It is $100 less a week.
(B) It is $100 less a month.
(C) It is $100 more a week.
(D) It is $100 more a month.

189. According to the article, why did Mr. Bikowski stay at his new job?

(A) The salary is better.
(B) The new job is less stressful.
(C) He has become a supervisor.
(D) He prefers working close to home.

GO ON TO THE NEXT PAGE

Questions 190-193 refer to the following letter.

**GUESS CONSULTING**

121 Market St., New York, NY 10012

January 4, 19—

J.P. Thompson, Esq.
14, rue du Mont Blanc
1201 Geneva, Switzerland

Mr. Thompson,

I have enclosed a copy of the evaluation that I was hired to prepare for the project "Improving Employee Performance."

Please contact me if you have any questions or desire any additional information.

I have enjoyed working with your law firm on this project and look forward to working with you again in the future.

Sincerely,

Amanda Guess

Amanda Guess
Consultant

190. What is the main purpose of the letter?

(A) To submit a report
(B) To inquire about future job possibilities
(C) To request future projects
(D) To ensure prompt payment

191. Which of the following would Mr. Thompson like to improve?

(A) Ms. Guess's writing
(B) Employee performance
(C) The salary
(D) The evaluation

192. According to the letter, which of the following is NOT true?

(A) Ms. Guess would like more projects.
(B) Ms. Guess will discuss her evaluation.
(C) Ms. Guess is a consultant.
(D) Ms. Guess didn't complete the project.

193. What is Mr. Thompson's profession?

(A) Lawyer
(B) Personnel director
(C) Consultant
(D) Landlord

Questions 194-197 refer to the following guide.

| Customer Guide | Page |
|---|---|
| Area Codes | 29 |
| Billing | 10 |
| Choosing a Telephone Service | 7 |
| Consumer Information | 12 |
| Directory Assistance | 4 |
| Special Services | 22 |
| Telephone Repair | 3 |

194. Where would you likely find this guide?

(A) In a telephone booth
(B) On a public telephone
(C) With a telephone bill
(D) In a telephone directory

195. How is the list organized?

(A) In chronological order
(B) By order of importance
(C) In alphabetical order
(D) In order of popularity

196. What page would you turn to for telephone repair?

(A) Page 3
(B) Page 7
(C) Page 12
(D) Page 22

197. Which page has advice about choosing a telephone service?

(A) Page 4
(B) Page 7
(C) Page 12
(D) Page 29

GO ON TO THE NEXT PAGE

Questions 198-200 refer to the following advertisement.

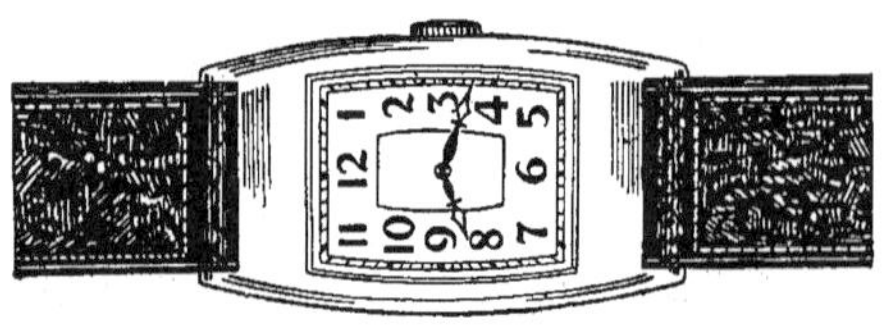

**TRAVELLER**

*A multifunction watch displaying local time sumultaneously in all twenty-four world time zones.*

*Self-winding, water-resistant in a combination of stainless steel and 18 kt. gold. Five-year international limited warranty. Intelligently priced. Also available in all 18 kt. gold or all stainless steel.*

A tradition of excellence in watches, fine jewelry, and unique gift ideas since 1928.

**Paris Jewelers**

*137 Saint Paul Street, Newport, ME*

198. What is being sold?

(A) A suitcase
(B) A watch
(C) A steel band
(D) A gold ring

199. How many time zones can be displayed?

(A) Five
(B) Twelve
(C) Eighteen
(D) Twenty-four

200. How long is the warranty?

(A) Eighteen months
(B) Five years
(C) Eighteen years
(D) Lifetime

Stop! This is the end of the test. If you finish before time is called, you may go back to Parts V, VI, and VII and check your work.

# TAPESCRIPT

# TAPESCRIPT
# PRACTICE TEST ONE

## PART I

Example:

(A) They're looking out the window.
(B) They're having a meeting.
(C) They're eating in a restaurant.
(D) They're moving the furniture.

1. (A) The plane is being fueled.
(B) The plane is flying low.
(C) The plan is to add more guests.
(D) The playing field is wet.

2. (A) He's driving his car.
(B) He's reading his mail.
(C) He's monitoring the systems.
(D) He's mowing his lawn.

3. (A) The hotel is on the corner.
(B) The clerk is looking down.
(C) The pictures are on the counter.
(D) The manager is helping customers.

4. (A) He's going fishing.
(B) He's looking at the locks.
(C) He's bending over the box.
(D) He's watching a movie.

5. (A) They're walking down the sidewalk.
(B) They're looking at one another.
(C) They're dancing in the street.
(D) They're watching a movie.

6. (A) The audience is leaving.
(B) The speaker is in front of the room.
(C) Four chairs are on the lawn.
(D) The plants are in the lobby.

7. (A) They're rubbing their fingers.
(B) They're arm wrestling.
(C) They're leading a band.
(D) They're shaking hands.

8. (A) The conductor is on the train.
(B) The entertainer is on television.
(C) The teacher is behind the desk.
(D) The trainer is in front of the chart.

9. (A) The closets are full of clothes.
(B) The drawers contain supplies.
(C) The storage bins are open.
(D) The boxes are empty.

10. (A) He's preparing food.
(B) He's sawing a board.
(C) He's changing his shirt.
(D) He's cutting his hair.

11. (A) They're riding on a tram.
(B) They're staring at the fight.
(C) They're running across the floor.
(D) They're going down one level.

12. (A) The fireplace is tall and narrow.
(B) Smoke is coming from the chimney.
(C) The skyscraper is on fire.
(D) The construction worker was fired.

13. (A) The assembly is meeting today.
(B) The marchers are walking in line.
(C) The workers are at their stations.
(D) The plant is large and green.

14. (A) They're sitting side by side.
(B) They're purchasing a record.
(C) They're building a studio.
(D) They're signing a contract.

15. (A) The man is reading a newspaper.
(B) All the chairs are occupied.
(C) The pilot light is lit.
(D) The passengers are sitting down.

16. (A) She's going to faint.
(B) She's brushing her hair.
(C) She's painting a picture.
(D) She's discussing art.

17. (A) They're making coffee.
(B) They're having a discussion.
(C) They're painting a picture.
(D) They're using a calculator.

18. (A) The man is pushing a hand truck.
(B) The boxes are on the shelf.
(C) The produce is on display.
(D) The horse is behind the cart.

19. (A) He's buying an umbrella.
(B) He's clearing the table.
(C) He's serving the diners.
(D) He's waiting by the restroom.

20. (A) The roof is new.
(B) The newspapers are on the stand.
(C) The car tracks are narrow.
(D) The man is on the platform.

## PART II

Example:

Good morning, John. How are you?
(A) I am fine, thank you.
(B) I am in the living room.
(C) My name is John.

21. Where shall we sit?
(A) Let's sit in the front row.
(B) Tall people sit in the back.
(C) It's on the table.

22. Which train goes to New York?
(A) New York is my favorite city.
(B) All trains on Track 1 go there.
(C) He goes by train.

23. How much does this suit cost?
(A) It costs thirty dollars.
(B) The suit fits very well.
(C) There are two suits in the closet.

24. Who took the telephone message?
(A) I will phone you tomorrow.
(B) I looked for the telephone.
(C) My secretary took the message.

25. What time are you eating dinner?
(A) I'll have dinner about 6 P.M.
(B) We dined early yesterday.
(C) I always eat a big dinner.

26. Has the mail arrived yet?
(A) Yes, we came by jet.
(B) No, it has failed.
(C) Yes, it came an hour ago.

27. Why is the window open?
(A) Yes, because it's closed.
(B) It's too hot in here.
(C) The windmill turns in the wind.

28. Who are you expecting?
(A) I'll accept your proposal.
(B) I'm expecting my aunt.
(C) I suspected it would happen.

29. Where is the accountant's office?
(A) It's at the end of the hall.
(B) There are five accountants.
(C) The accountant is on the phone.

30. How many students are in the class?
(A) The class meets every day.
(B) There are about fifteen.
(C) My students have to learn English.

31. Which magazines does she read?
(A) The magazine is on the table.
(B) She read it last week.
(C) She only reads business magazines.

32. When are you leaving for Hawaii?
(A) I'm going tomorrow.
(B) You're leaving soon.
(C) Hawaii is in the Pacific.

33. Will the report be finished on time?
(A) It's five o'clock.
(B) No, it won't be finished on time.
(C) Yes, the reporter will be late.

34. Why do you get up so early?
(A) Because I have to be at work at 6 A.M.
(B) I always get what I want.
(C) You had to leave early, didn't you?

35. Would you like soup with your dinner?
(A) I'm not getting thinner.
(B) I ate dinner at 7 P.M.
(C) No, I'd prefer a salad.

36. When did you learn how to swim?
(A) I learned when I was young.
(B) I swim in the evening.
(C) I wondered how you learned.

37. How much did you pay for this car?
(A) Because it was used.
(B) I paid about three thousand dollars.
(C) The car needs repairs.

38. Why did you change your shirt?
(A) The shirt cost forty-five dollars.
(B) I don't have any change.
(C) Because I spilled coffee on it.

39. What was the movie about?
(A) It's about 6 P.M.
(B) He moved here last August.
(C) It was a western film.

40. Where are the office supplies?
(A) That company supplies us with water.
(B) The supplies are in the hall closet.
(C) Our offices are on the fifth floor.

41. When did the doctor leave?
(A) She left at noon.
(B) The boat docked at 8 P.M.
(C) There was no one left.

42. Why hasn't this letter been typed?
(A) She's not my type.
(B) We didn't have time to type it.
(C) It's too little.

43. Who has a black ink pen?
   (A) Here, you can use my pen.
   (B) She opened a black book.
   (C) Blacken the circles completely.

44. Were you born at home?
   (A) No, I was born in a hospital.
   (B) The barn is behind the house.
   (C) I was carried home.

45. What's for breakfast?
   (A) It's usually at 6:30.
   (B) We're having cold cereal and fruit.
   (C) I'm hungry.

46. How many pages are in the book?
   (A) He's six years of age.
   (B) All the pages are white.
   (C) There are about three hundred pages.

47. Whose briefcase is on the desk?
   (A) The briefcase belongs to the new lawyer.
   (B) The briefcase is under the desk.
   (C) The desk should be closer to the stairs.

48. Who earned the most money last year?
   (A) The money is earning interest.
   (B) The manager earned the most.
   (C) The students learned English last year.

49. When will dinner be served?
   (A) The guests were served roast beef.
   (B) We ate in the diner.
   (C) It'll be served at 7:30.

50. Which bus should we take?
   (A) Take the number 14 bus.
   (B) We took the first one.
   (C) He should talk to us.

## PART III

51. *Man* Would you type this letter for me?
*Woman* Of course, but can it wait until after lunch?
*Man* Yes, as long as it's mailed this evening.

52. *Woman A* Is the car too big for that space?
*Woman B* No, I think you can park there.
*Woman A* I hope so. It's hard to find parking here.

53. *Man A* When will the new phones be installed?
*Man B* They promised us by Wednesday before noon.
*Man A* Last week they said Monday afternoon.

54. *Woman* I need twelve dozen ball-point pens.
*Man* Do you want any specific color?
*Woman* Yes, give me five dozen red, six dozen blue, and a dozen black.

55. *Man* The doctor told me to stay home from work today.
*Woman* Well, I hope you're feeling better tomorrow.
*Man* Me, too. I'm not used to being sick.

56. *Woman* Is it time for the news yet?
*Man* Almost. I'll turn on the TV in a few minutes.
*Woman* Turn it on now so we don't miss the beginning.

57. *Man* The meal was delicious. You're a great cook.
*Woman* You hardly touched a thing. Have some more dessert.
*Man* No, thank you. I already had two pieces of cake.

58. *Woman* Did you buy a new car?
*Man* I had to. I got tired of walking.
*Woman* Now you'll get tired of traffic.

59. *Man* The cleaning staff will be in this evening.
*Woman* How often do they come, once a week?
*Man* Our offices are cleaned every night.

60. *Woman* You should have these figures checked.
*Man* The accountant already looked them over.
*Woman* I'm not sure that these sums balance.

61. *Woman A* You must learn to relax. Take a vacation. Play some golf.
*Woman B* I'd like to take your advice, doctor, but I have to go to work.
*Woman A* If you keep this up, you may never work again.

62. *Man A* Why don't we have lunch together next week?
*Man B* That will be great. I'm not free on Wednesday or Friday.
*Man A* Let's have lunch on Monday then.

63. *Man* Spring is my favorite season. I love the cool rains.
*Woman* Me, too. I really dislike the summer months.
*Man* I can't stand the heat and humidity.

64. *Woman* If it keeps raining, they'll cancel the baseball game.
*Man* We can always go to a movie or play table tennis.
*Woman* It would have been our first night game with the new lights.

65. *Man* Are you ready to go yet? I've got my raincoat on.
*Woman* Help me find my boots and umbrella, will you?
*Man* We're going to miss the bus if you don't hurry.

66. *Woman* Where are the pencils?
*Man* I keep a dozen in my top drawer.
*Woman* I only need two, thank you.

67. *Man* How much more time do we have left?
*Woman* We have another forty-five minutes.
*Man* Good. We should finish in about twenty or thirty minutes.

68. *Man* Do you live by the police station?
*Woman* No, I live on Mountain View Street by the school.
*Man* Oh, that's right. I pass your house on my way to work.

69. *Man* Did you read the paper this morning?
*Woman* Neither today's nor yesterday's. I didn't have time to buy it.
*Man* You should have it delivered.

70. *Man A* May I help you?
*Man B* Yes, I'd like to try on this pair of shoes.
*Man A* Of course. This pair is on sale today, too.

71. *Man* I'm really tired. I didn't get to bed until eleven.
*Woman* What time did you get up?
*Man* Four. I usually get eight hours of sleep. Last night I got five.

72. *Woman A* Did you see the headlines in the paper?
*Woman B* I never read the front page.
*Woman A* You only read the sports section, right?

73. *Man* I'm afraid I'm going to have to pull that tooth out.
*Woman* I probably should brush more often.
*Man* After every meal. You should take better care of your teeth.

74. *Woman* I can't stay late tonight. I have to be home at six.
*Man* Are you having company for dinner?
*Woman* No, but I'm expecting a call from overseas.

75. *Man* What did the thief take?
*Woman* He took my purse, my watch, and my keys.
*Man* You're lucky you weren't hurt.

76. *Woman* The watch is $640 plus tax.
*Man* I'll take it. Do you take credit cards?
*Woman* Of course. Would you like the watch gift wrapped?

77. *Man* I've been here for three hours. The plane was due hours ago.
*Woman* Did they say when it was expected?
*Man* It should land in about a half hour.

78. *Woman A* Is there a dining car on the train?
*Woman B* No, but there is a club car where you can get sandwiches.
*Woman A* I hope they serve coffee.

79. *Man* We can't play golf in weather like this.
*Woman* You have an umbrella, don't you?
*Man* My shoes, my clubs, everything will get all wet in the rain.

80. *Man A* The photocopier never works.
*Man B* The office manager called the repairperson. She'll be here any minute.
*Man A* My secretary fixed it himself last time.

## PART IV

**Questions 81 through 83** refer to the following advertisement.

Office Supplies, Inc., announces fantastic savings. The doors open at 8 A.M. tomorrow and our biggest sale of the year begins. Everything in our store is reduced by 50 percent from Thursday through Saturday; three big days. The sale ends Saturday at 6 P.M.

**Questions 84 and 85** refer to the following weather report.

Yesterday morning's weather will be with us again today. More freezing rain with a chance of snow late this evening. The weekend forecast is looking up, though with this low pressure system moving out. We should expect sunny skies and temperatures as high as the 50's.

**Questions 86 through 88** refer to the following news item.

The electric company warns citizens that the demand for electricity may exceed the supply. Air conditioners and fans are in constant use during the hot summer. This increase in demand for electricity may cause power failures.

**Questions 89 and 90** refer to the following recorded announcement.

Please excuse this short delay. Due to our low bargain fares, our agents are busy with other callers. Please stay on the line, and an airline representative will be with you shortly.

**Questions 91 through 93** refer to the following special announcement.

Good afternoon. I want to welcome you all to our management improvement luncheon. The catering staff here at the Club always makes our noon events special. Today's speaker, Mr. Margalis, worked as management trainer for the last twenty years before he retired. Now he only works in his garden.

**Questions 94 and 95** refer to the following business report.

This area is for authorized personnel only. You must have a special pass to enter the area. Passes may be obtained at the Security Office upon presentation of a valid driver's license.

**Questions 96 and 97** refer to the following advertisement.

Are you unemployed? Are you looking for part-time work? Do you have office skills that would be useful in a doctor's office, a law firm, or an advertising agency? Call Temps Company and let our agents find you a job that matches your qualifications.

**Questions 98 through 100** refer to the following weather report.

Good morning. It's 8:00 in the Windy City. This is Dan Richards with your early morning weather report. Don't forget to take your umbrella to work with you today. Right now it looks like a nice day, and the skies are clear. But dark clouds are moving in, and rain showers are expected this afternoon.

# TAPESCRIPT
# PRACTICE TEST TWO

## PART I

Example:

(A) They're looking out the window.
(B) They're having a meeting.
(C) They're eating in a restaurant.
(D) They're moving the furniture.

1. (A) He's standing behind a taxi.
(B) He's opening a cabinet.
(C) He's carrying a trunk.
(D) He's washing a car.

2. (A) Nothing is on the table.
(B) A necklace is in her hands.
(C) The woman is writing at her desk.
(D) Curtains cover the window.

3. (A) They're looking at the paintings.
(B) They're painting a picture.
(C) They're having their picture taken.
(D) They're taking a picture.

4. (A) The crew prepares for the event.
(B) The technician adjusts the equipment.
(C) The plumber fixes the sink.
(D) The mail carrier sorts the post.

5. (A) Forty people are at the counter.
(B) The phone is on the wall.
(C) The desk clerk assists the guests.
(D) The waiters are serving the customers.

6. (A) They're entering the restaurant.
(B) They're talking on the phone.
(C) They're traveling to Thailand.
(D) They're printing the menu.

7. (A) He's making a presentation.
(B) He's handing out presents.
(C) He's putting on his jacket.
(D) He's training his horses.

8. (A) The man is wearing a jacket.
(B) The birds are on the fence.
(C) The pictures are hung on the wall.
(D) Cars are parked in the lot.

9. (A) The man is walking alone.
(B) Two pupils are studying.
(C) The woman is wearing pants.
(D) The couple is taking a walk.

10. (A) The film is in focus.
(B) The man is carrying a tape recorder.
(C) The camera is on a tripod.
(D) The video store is next door.

11. (A) The poodle is wet.
(B) The chairs are empty.
(C) Children swim in the water.
(D) The pool is crowded.

12. (A) The worker ascends the stairs.
(B) The gas tank in the car is full.
(C) The cargo ship sank.
(D) The letter came in the mail.

13. (A) He's rubbing his knee.
(B) He's climbing the stairs.
(C) He's looking at a microscope.
(D) He's wearing a microphone.

14. (A) The gardeners are planting a tree.
(B) The fire fighters are filling their buckets.
(C) The workers are checking the equipment.
(D) The dentists are cleaning their drill.

15. (A) The flight attendants are getting off the plane.
(B) The pie ought to be ready to take out.
(C) The pilots are preparing to take off.
(D) The musicians are tuning their instruments.

16. (A) Trees are behind the statue.
(B) The butter is golden.
(C) Flowers are in the vase.
(D) The offers are overdue.

17. (A) The hotel guest is talking to the room clerks.
(B) The manager is showing the guest her room.
(C) The housekeeper is making the bed.
(D) The manager is checking the menu.

18. (A) The welders are wearing uniforms.
(B) The waders are in the water.
(C) The couple is by a cart.
(D) The laundress is wetting the dress.

19. (A) The oven operates with gas.
(B) Two men are making repairs.
(C) Both women are sitting down.
(D) Their tools are put away.

20. (A) He's trying on a hat.
(B) He's typing his work order.
(C) He's adding oil to his car engine.
(D) He's standing among the oil drums.

## PART II

Example:

Good morning, John. How are you?
(A) I am fine, thank you.
(B) I am in the living room.
(C) My name is John.

21. Where are the stamps?
(A) The post office is closed.
(B) The stamps are in the top drawer.
(C) The letter was not stamped.

22. Why did you leave work so early?
(A) Because you worked so late.
(B) I am always the first person here.
(C) I left early to go to the doctor.

23. What is your first chore today?
(A) I'm thirsty, too.
(B) First, I'll open the mail.
(C) Today is a short workday.

24. How often do you take a vacation?
(A) I took one of them.
(B) Four to five times an hour.
(C) I take a vacation twice a year.

25. Whose coffee cup is this?
(A) That cup is his.
(B) This is good coffee.
(C) Yes, I like coffee.

26. Will we be on time?
(A) Yes, actually we are early.
(B) No, I don't have a watch.
(C) No, he came at 4:30.

27. How well do you speak Chinese?
(A) She's feeling better.
(B) I know only a few words.
(C) We love Chinese food.

28. Why didn't you study for the test?
(A) They are good students.
(B) Because it was a test.
(C) I was too tired to study.

29. What are they going to do tomorrow?
(A) We are playing golf now.
(B) They plan to stay home tomorrow.
(C) He said he'll go the day after.

30. Where is the ticket counter?
(A) She counted five tickets.
(B) I lost my ticket.
(C) It's on the ground floor.

31. What's for lunch?
(A) Around the corner.
(B) At noon.
(C) Beef and noodles.

32. Would you like sugar in your coffee?
(A) Yes, please. Three spoonfuls.
(B) Yes, there is sugar on the table.
(C) The coffee is hot.

33. How many movies do you see each month?
(A) I'll see that movie next month.
(B) I moved overseas.
(C) About four. I usually go once a week.

34. Which chair is more comfortable?
(A) You should put the chair next to the table.
(B) The brown chair is very comfortable.
(C) We don't care any more.

35. When are we going to take inventory?
(A) It's usually taken in June.
(B) We took him with us.
(C) He invented a substitute.

36. Who rented the apartment upstairs?
(A) The renters moved out.
(B) There are stairs in the apartment.
(C) A young couple rented it.

37. What did the hotel clerk say?
(A) I stayed at the hotel.
(B) He said no rooms were available.
(C) The clerk filed the letters.

38. How did you find a computer programmer?
(A) I advertised for one in the paper.
(B) The computer is on the desk.
(C) We watched the program.

39. Where is the bus stop?
(A) The bus is always late.
(B) Most of us got off the bus.
(C) The bus stops at the corner.

40. When was the package mailed?
(A) He packed it yesterday.
(B) It was mailed last week.
(C) The mail comes in the morning.

41. Where should the employees park?
(A) Our picnic is in the park.
(B) We work after dark.
(C) Employees must park their cars in the street.

42. How much money did the company earn last year?
   (A) We made three hundred thousand dollars.
   (B) Money earns interest during the year.
   (C) We spent a lot of money.

43. When can we take a coffee break?
   (A) Usually we can take one whenever we want.
   (B) We bought coffee and bread.
   (C) The coffeepot broke yesterday.

44. Who turned off the photocopier?
   (A) We copied the photos.
   (B) I turned it off when I finished.
   (C) The photographer turned in the photos.

45. Which room is for nonsmokers?
   (A) Smoking is not allowed anywhere in the library.
   (B) The rooms are full of smoke.
   (C) No one is in the room.

46. How large is the auditorium?
   (A) It can seat 500 people.
   (B) My video player is larger.
   (C) The auditorium is often closed.

47. How many bags can I take on the plane?
   (A) Take the bag next to mine.
   (B) There are two planes.
   (C) You can take only one.

48. Did you buy your plane ticket yet?
   (A) I'm going by jet.
   (B) Yes, I bought it this morning.
   (C) No one has complained yet.

49. What kind of insurance do you have?
   (A) We have health insurance.
   (B) The insurance agent is very kind.
   (C) Because it is necessary.

50. How long does it take to travel from New York to Tokyo?
   (A) None of us likes to travel.
   (B) In big cities, we take the subway.
   (C) It takes fourteen hours by plane.

## PART III

51. *Man* Make a turn at the next light.
*Woman* Are you sure? I don't remember this street.
*Man* You drive the car. I'll read the map.

52. *Woman* I'll leave your place around 5:30. My plane is at 7:00.
*Man* You should leave earlier. Rush hour starts at 5:00.
*Woman* OK. I'll leave at 4:00.

53. *Man* Do you have any medicine for a cold?
*Woman* Yes, they're in aisle B, next to the toothpaste.
*Man* I looked there, but I didn't see any.

54. *Man* How much money do you have?
*Woman* I have about forty dollars.
*Man* Can you lend me ten until tomorrow?

55. *Woman A* Hurry. The bank closes at 2 P.M.
*Woman B* We have thirty minutes to get there. What's your rush?
*Woman A* I just want to be sure that I get there before it closes.

56. *Woman* Have you seen my coat?
*Man* Isn't it in the hall closet?
*Woman* No, I must have left it in the office with my umbrella.

57. *Man A* Turn the channel to the news, please.
*Man B* I want to watch the end of the game.
*Man A* It's my TV so turn the channel.

58. *Woman* I don't like westerns or murder movies. They're too violent.
*Man* Isn't there a comedy playing?
*Woman* No, just war stories and murder mysteries.

59. *Woman A* Call everyone and tell them Monday's meeting is postponed.
*Woman B* Have you set a new date for the meeting?
*Woman A* Let's try for the end of the week on Friday.

60. *Woman* I'm sorry I'm late, but I ran out of gas.
*Man* You should take the bus or get up earlier and walk.
*Woman* I took the bus yesterday and was even later.

61. *Man* I have to pay taxes every three months.
*Woman* I pay quarterly, too.
*Man* I wish it was only once a year.

62. *Man* I left my glasses on your desk.
*Woman* Here, take my keys. My office is locked.
*Man* OK. Hold my briefcase, and I'll meet you at the car.

63. *Man* Do you think she types fast enough?
*Woman* Considering the broken typewriter, very fast.
*Man* Plus, she keeps her desk neat and clean.

64. *Woman* Does your new job begin in June or July?
*Man* Actually, I won't begin until August.
*Woman* If it's that late, you should wait until September.

65. *Man* It sure is hot today. You could fry an egg on the sidewalk.
*Woman* It's usually cooler this time of year.
*Man* Since I sell ice cream, this heat's good for business.

66. *Woman* Where did you buy your suit?
*Man* I bought it in Hong Kong. The shoes, shirt, and tie I already had.
*Woman* That tie and shirt look great with it.

67. *Man* This house has two bedrooms, and it's in your price range.
*Woman* Has the kitchen been renovated?
*Man* Yes, the kitchen and baths are newly painted.

68. *Woman* It's noon. Let's eat and start again at two.
*Man* The reports are due at five o'clock. We can't finish in three hours.
*Woman* Well, then, let's take a shorter lunch break.

69. *Man* How many passengers are on board?
*Woman* There are seventy-two plus three flight attendants.
*Man* We'll be taking off in two minutes. Put on your seat belt.

70. *Woman* The light in here is too dim to read. I can't see.
*Man* Why don't you use brighter bulbs?
*Woman* There weren't any more on the shelf.

71. *Man* Do you think the bed is too close to the window?
*Woman* If we moved it, it would be too close to the dresser.
*Man* Then let's move the dresser closer to the TV.

72. *Man A* We designed the building in the postmodern style.
*Man B* But we also considered the surrounding buildings.
*Man A* Yes, we wanted our building to be a part of the landscape.

73. *Man* I usually swim four miles three times a week.
*Woman* I swim every day but only for twenty minutes.
*Man* That's not swimming; that's bathing.

74. *Woman* I'm going hiking in the mountains for my vacation.
*Man* You're not going to lie around reading on a sunny beach?
*Woman* I'm tired of lazy vacations by the sea.

75. *Woman* Take off your shoes before coming inside.
*Man* Why? They're not dirty.
*Woman* Maybe not, but I just washed the floor. Leave them outside.

76. *Woman* How much food did you buy?
*Man* Enough to last all week.
*Woman* But we're leaving tomorrow for a two-week vacation.

77. *Man* Fill out this application. In ink, please.
*Woman* Are there any jobs open now?
*Man* Not at the moment, but I will call you when there are.

78. *Woman* Shall I trim your beard?
*Man* No, thanks, just cut my hair.
*Woman* Not too short, right?

79. *Woman A* We have four buses to take people from the hotel to the convention.
*Woman B* One bus should leave every fifteen minutes; it takes five minutes to load and ten minutes to get there.
*Woman A* That sounds like a good schedule. The bus could make the round trip in thirty minutes.

80. *Woman* I love to walk through the park at dawn.
*Man* I prefer noon. I don't like to get up so early.
*Woman* I always go to bed before midnight so I can get up early.

## PART IV

**Questions 81 through 83** refer to the following news item.

The City Hall will open on Saturday this week so citizens can file their tax forms. The Revenue Office will be open from 8 A.M. to noon only. Long lines are expected, so be early to avoid them.

**Questions 84 through 86** refer to the following announcement.

If you need ground transportation, please follow the blue signs for rental cars and hotel shuttles. Follow the red signs for access to public transportation, including the subway, city buses, and airport shuttles to other terminals. If you have left your car in an airport parking lot, follow the green signs for a parking shuttle.

**Questions 87 through 89** refer to the following special announcement.

I hope you all enjoyed your lunch on this beautiful Friday. We want to thank the Barcly Hotel for sponsoring our monthly luncheons. Our guest speaker this afternoon will be Dr. Jenny Chang, the author of the best-selling novel *Politics Isn't a Crime.*

**Questions 90 and 91** refer to the following business report.

All employees are required to wear an identification badge. All visitors must be accompanied at all times by employees with IDs. Visitors without escorts will be removed from the building by security personnel.

**Questions 92 and 93** refer to the following advertisement.

Spartan Golf Club announces the opening of its newest golf course. The modern course designed by professional golfers is only fifteen minutes from the city center. Only a few memberships are available, so visit our downtown officc soon.

**Questions 94 and 95** refer to the following weather report.

It's perfect beach weather today. The sun is shining, and it's going to be hot, hot, hot. So take advantage of those ocean breezes and enjoy the sun and surf.

**Questions 96 and 97** refer to the following news item.

A local man died recently and left his entire estate to his dog. Man's best friend inherited over two million dollars. The deceased man had no wife or children.

**Questions 98 through 100** refer to the following recorded announcement.

The Office of Motor Vehicles is open Monday through Friday. If you want to renew your driving license, you must come between the hours of noon and 4 P.M. If you want to get a new license or take a driving test, you may come anytime between 8 A.M. and 4 P.M.

# TAPESCRIPT PRACTICE TEST THREE

## PART I

Example:

(A) They're looking out the window.
(B) They're having a meeting.
(C) They're eating in a restaurant.
(D) They're moving the furniture.

1. (A) The man is fishing.
(B) The sea is salty.
(C) The fish are for sale.
(D) The snow is turning to ice.

2. (A) They're carrying a basket.
(B) They're picking vegetables.
(C) They're cleaning the aisle.
(D) They're selling uniforms.

3. (A) The train does not stop at this station.
(B) The people are getting off the train.
(C) The workers are out of stationery.
(D) No one is wearing a hat.

4. (A) He's using a knife and fork.
(B) He's operating heavy equipment.
(C) He's shredding paper.
(D) He's driving to work.

5. (A) The bottles are inside the cabinets.
(B) The woman is in front of the sink.
(C) The woman is putting a knife on the shelf.
(D) The grocery store is full of goods.

6. (A) The women are on the stairs.
(B) The typist is typing a memo.
(C) The choir is singing a song.
(D) The clock is on the wall.

7. (A) The food is on a cart.
(B) The women are playing cards.
(C) The shop is closed on Tuesday.
(D) The groceries are in the refrigerator.

8. (A) The tables are set outdoors.
(B) The guests are at the tables.
(C) The picnic is on the lawn.
(D) The chairs are stacked against the wall.

9. (A) The architect is designing the church.
(B) The woman is praying by the wall.
(C) The painter is painting the scene.
(D) The runner is panting from the race.

10. (A) The man is pointing the way.
(B) The directions are written clearly.
(C) The appointment is only temporary.
(D) The signpost is a guide for the motorist.

11. (A) The cars are parked in the lot.
(B) There are many bees in the park.
(C) The barking dog does not bite.
(D) The cars are being assembled.

12. (A) He's carving a statue.
(B) He's dusting the railing.
(C) He's cleaning the floor.
(D) He's rubbing his shoulder.

13. (A) The interior decorators are arranging the chairs.
(B) The furniture polishers are waxing the table.
(C) The men are listening to the speaker.
(D) The delegates are leaving the conference.

14. (A) The car is being manufactured.
(B) The windows are being cleaned.
(C) The radio is being installed.
(D) The line is being drawn.

15. (A) They're playing horseshoes.
(B) They're watching the monitors.
(C) They're buying a television set.
(D) They're looking through a catalogue.

16. (A) It's time to go.
(B) The clock strikes the hour.
(C) The watches are on the wall.
(D) The man watches the band.

17. (A) The technicians test their telescopes.
(B) The scientists work in the laboratory.
(C) The physicians perform an operation.
(D) The soldiers clean their uniforms.

18. (A) A few people sit at the counter.
(B) The desert is cool at night.
(C) There are three clocks on the wall.
(D) The postcards are in the mail.

19. (A) The electrician installs a lamppost.
(B) The street is full of pedestrians.
(C) The architects are redesigning the building.
(D) The buses are parked on the sidewalk.

20. (A) The curtains are shut.
(B) The housekeeper makes the beds.
(C) The hotel room is ready for occupancy.
(D) The dining room tables are occupied.

## PART II

Example:

Good morning, John. How are you?
(A) I am fine, thank you.
(B) I am in the living room.
(C) My name is John.

21. What time is she coming?
(A) It's six o'clock now.
(B) She'll be here any minute.
(C) She is combing her hair.

22. Where is the bank?
(A) The check is in the mail.
(B) It's next to the post office.
(C) The banquet is at the hotel.

23. When are you leaving for work?
(A) I'll leave after breakfast.
(B) I plan to retire next month.
(C) I've been working for ten years.

24. Who is on the telephone?
(A) That's Maria talking to her mother.
(B) It's my phone.
(C) I told everyone last week.

25. Why are we taking a bus?
(A) All of us have gone once.
(B) It's cheaper than a taxi.
(C) We walk too much.

26. What type of music is this?
(A) I didn't find any mistakes.
(B) She uses an electric typewriter.
(C) It's classical music.

27. How many oranges do you want?
(A) About five of us ordered wine.
(B) Give me half a dozen, please.
(C) I made arrangements for fifty people.

28. Where were you yesterday?
(A) You were gone yesterday.
(B) I was home all day.
(C) I'm going tomorrow.

29. Which of these books haven't you read?
(A) I haven't read the ones in French.
(B) I only read in the evening.
(C) Here are the books you must read.

30. What day did the guest arrive?
(A) The day after tomorrow.
(B) She arrived yesterday.
(C) You'll never guess who called.

31. When will the performance begin?
(A) The foreman will begin working tomorrow.
(B) The performance is too long.
(C) It always begins a few minutes late.

32. How often do we need to change the oil in the car?
(A) Every 6 months or every 5,000 miles.
(B) I changed it last week.
(C) I want to change the color of my car.

33. Who received the package in the mail?
(A) He looks young for his age.
(B) The receptionist opened the mail.
(C) The package was for me.

34. Can your secretary type this letter for me?
(A) I prefer handwritten letters.
(B) My secretary will send you a letter.
(C) He's too busy to type it now.

35. How many chairs are around the table?
(A) The four of us will sit down.
(B) There are only two chairs.
(C) The table is round.

36. What is the purpose of your visit?
(A) I'm responding to your job announcement.
(B) We visited the purse factory.
(C) Your visit lasted a week.

37. When are you taking a vacation?
(A) I enjoy taking evening walks.
(B) I'll take it in August.
(C) The apartment will be vacant next month.

38. Where is your class meeting?
(A) We're all eating in the cafeteria.
(B) No, it's not made of glass.
(C) The class is meeting in room 300.

39. Is it time for lunch?
(A) No, not yet. Lunch is in about twenty minutes.
(B) This time we'll eat at home.
(C) Please pass the salt.

40. Why is the radio on?
(A) It's on the bookcase.
(B) We want to hear the news.
(C) Because no one is ready.

41. How many pencils are in the drawer?
(A) It's in the bottom drawer.
(B) She's drawing with a pen.
(C) There's about a dozen.

42. Where is the golf course?
   (A) I play golf in the morning.
   (B) The course is two miles from here.
   (C) Because it's near the Gulf of Thailand.

43. When did the plane take off?
   (A) It took off on time.
   (B) Take off that shirt now.
   (C) We'll leave shortly.

44. What is the fastest way to get downtown?
   (A) Traffic is slow during rush hour.
   (B) The tallest building is downtown.
   (C) At this time of day, I'd take the subway.

45. How far is the restaurant from here?
   (A) I'm not hungry.
   (B) It's about two blocks.
   (C) Because it serves good food.

46. Why are you so tired?
   (A) I didn't sleep last night.
   (B) The tire needs air.
   (C) We are required to wear ties at work.

47. Who cleans your office?
   (A) My office is near my home.
   (B) We have a cleaning service come in once a week.
   (C) The windows need cleaning.

48. Where does the bus stop?
   (A) It stops on the corner.
   (B) We shop at the department store.
   (C) The bus comes every half hour.

49. Whose desk is near the window?
   (A) My desk is by the door.
   (B) The one by the window is Bob's desk.
   (C) I'll close the window.

50. What shall we do first?
   (A) I was the last one here.
   (B) I need a towel.
   (C) Let's clean up the office first.

## PART III

51. *Woman* What kept you? I've been waiting on this corner for twenty minutes.
*Man* I'm sorry. I had to get gas.
*Woman* You should have planned ahead.

52. *Woman A* There are only twelve chairs. We'll need five more.
*Woman B* You mean six more. There'll be eighteen of us.
*Woman A* OK. I'll get another six chairs.

53. *Man* Did you park the car in the lot next door?
*Woman* No, I parked in the garage across the street.
*Man* That's better than parking it on the street.

54. *Man A* This line isn't moving. I wonder if there's a problem.
*Man B* Yes, the ticket seller can't make change.
*Man A* We'll miss the movie at this rate.

55. *Woman* Can you wait for me while I see if the store is open?
*Man* This is a taxi, lady, not your limousine.
*Woman* Please. I'll pay you for waiting.

56. *Woman* Put the ladder in the garage next to the paint cans.
*Man* What should I do with the bucket and brushes?
*Woman* Put those in the garage, too.

57. *Woman A* How high should the pictures be?
*Woman B* The center should be about fifty-seven inches from the floor.
*Woman A* That seems low to me. Let's hang them at sixty-two inches.

58. *Man* Do you have my hammer?
*Woman* No, you should keep track of your tools.
*Man* You're right. On my last job, someone ran off with my saw.

59. *Man* Sit still. You're rocking the boat.
*Woman* I'm bored. I don't like fishing.
*Man* I suppose you'd rather be back at the office.

60. *Woman* I only have ten more pages to go.
*Man* You'd better hurry. We leave in thirty minutes.
*Woman* At two minutes a page, I'll finish in twenty minutes.

61. *Man* Before you step up to the tee, take one practice swing.
*Woman* And I'll keep my eye on the ball.
*Man* Right, and don't throw your golf club.

62. *Woman* This play is really boring. Who told us to come see it?
*Man* Well, we don't have to stay to the end.
*Woman* That's right. Let's leave now before I fall asleep.

63. *Man A* Can you cash this check, please?
*Man B* Do you have an account with this bank?
*Man A* No, but I have one with one of your branches.

64. *Woman* This morning I sorted through my clothes and threw all the old ones out.
*Man* Are you moving soon?
*Woman* The moving van is coming tomorrow, but I'll leave tonight.

65. *Man* You shouldn't feed the pigeons bread.
*Woman* Where else are they going to find food?
*Man* They don't look hungry. Besides, pigeons breed diseases.

66. *Woman* Have you ever worked in sales?
*Man* Yes, I've worked in retail sales for eight years.
*Woman* You must have some experience dealing directly with customers, then.

67. *Man* You two go in your car. You can follow me.
*Woman* OK. Don't drive too fast.
*Man* I'll drive really slowly, so you won't get lost.

68. *Man A* What kind of crops do you grow here?
*Man B* This is a small farm, so we grow mostly vegetables.
*Man A* Yes, I didn't see any orchards or flowers anywhere.

69. *Man* I'll plant the trees and the flowers next week.
*Woman* And you should cut the grass, too.
*Man* Of course, and I'll trim the bushes.

70. *Woman* Over four thousand people are coming to the dinner.
*Man* Last year's attendance was half that many.
*Woman* We've raised between fifteen and twenty thousand dollars for charity.

71. *Woman* I'm sorry I didn't call you last week.
*Man* Were you sick this time, or did you lose my number again?
*Woman* Well, the simple reason is that it slipped my mind.

72. *Woman* I've worked here since I was sixteen years old. My entire life, it seems.
*Man* It was your father's business, wasn't it?
*Woman* Actually, it's been a family business for four generations.

73. *Woman* Can you lend me a stamp?
*Man* For a domestic or an overseas letter?
*Woman* Domestic, but it's for a postcard.

74. *Woman* Did you watch TV last night?
*Man* No, did I miss a good program?
*Woman* Yes, there's one on every Wednesday night at 6:00.

75. *Man* Leave the dishes on the table. I'll clean them later.
*Woman* The dinner was delicious. I really appreciated the invitation.
*Man* It's always good to have an appreciative dinner guest.

76. *Woman* Don't get me wet. I don't want to swim.
*Man* Come on. I'll race you across the pool.
*Woman* Not me. The water's too cold.

77. *Man* I can't wait. At 2 P.M. my plane leaves.
*Woman* What time are you leaving for the airport?
*Man* I have to be there at noon, so I'll have to leave here at 11:30 A.M.

78. *Woman* Have you finished that magazine yet?
*Man* It's a very long, but interesting article.
*Woman* At the rate you're reading, you'll never finish.

79. *Woman A* How many potatoes do we need? Five or ten pounds?
*Woman B* The recipe says we need seven.
*Woman A* Then we'll have to get one ten-pound bag.

80. *Man* Is this elevator going up or down?
*Woman* Up. What floor, please?
*Man* I need the home furnishings department on seven, please.

## PART IV

**Questions 81 and 82** refer to the following weather announcement.

It's another hot, humid summer day. Chance of seasonal showers late this afternoon.

**Questions 83 and 84** refer to the following recorded announcement.

Hello. Dr. Miller's office hours are from 8:30 A.M. to 4 P.M., Monday through Thursday. The office is closed on Friday. If you have a dental emergency, please call 555-3212.

**Questions 85 and 86** refer to the following special announcement.

Ladies and Gentlemen, may I have your attention, please. Would you please gather your personal belongings and leave the restaurant at once. I'm sorry for the inconvenience, but there is a small fire in the kitchen.

**Questions 87 through 89** refer to the following business report.

Attention, please. Attention, please. All personnel will report to the south lawn for morning exercises. Supervisors will accompany their work teams. The exercise session will begin at 10:30 and end at 11:00.

**Questions 90 and 91** refer to the following advertisement.

Rent-a-Computer lets you rent a computer by the day, month, or year. We carry all brands of computers and all models. Tell us your needs, and we will help you find a computer. Short-term leasing is available, too.

**Questions 92 and 93** refer to the following news item.

An earthquake was recorded in the northern islands of Japan today. No one was hurt and there was little damage to property.

**Questions 94 and 95** refer to the following announcement.

Friendly Skies Airlines announces the departure of Flight 58 to Honolulu and San Francisco. All passengers should proceed through Passport Control and go immediately to gate 16.

**Questions 96 through 98** refer to the following business report.

Employee parking is permitted on the second and third levels of the parking structure. Yellow spaces are reserved for management; blue spaces are for all other employees. Red spaces are for maintenance vehicles. Employees or visitors parking in red spaces will have their cars towed.

**Questions 99 and 100** refer to the following announcement.

On your visit, you will see the Monument of Independence. On your left is the United Nations Building, our next stop. Please stay with your guide and be back on the bus by two o'clock.

# TAPESCRIPT
# PRACTICE TEST FOUR

## PART I

Example:

(A) They're looking out the window.
(B) They're having a meeting.
(C) They're eating in a restaurant.
(D) They're moving the furniture.

1. (A) She's wearing protective clothing.
(B) She's buying a new hat.
(C) She's storing food in jars.
(D) She's dressing for a party.

2. (A) The water glass is empty.
(B) The swimmers are racing.
(C) The man is cleaning the pool.
(D) The guest is relaxing by the pool.

3. (A) The man is pulling his suitcases.
(B) The woman is behind the man.
(C) The couple is getting out of the car.
(D) The bags are being weighed.

4. (A) The basket is for laundry.
(B) The boys are playing basketball.
(C) Two balls are close together.
(D) The bowling alley has two lanes.

5. (A) The cord is being cut.
(B) The telephone booth is on the corner.
(C) The woman is on the phone.
(D) The tourist is studying the map.

6. (A) The panes are in the frames.
(B) The planes are at their gates.
(C) The trains are in the station.
(D) The cranes are on the wharf.

7. (A) The ferry crosses the water.
(B) The passengers board at the pier.
(C) The sailboat is in the harbor.
(D) The tanker is in dry-dock.

8. (A) This is a first draft.
(B) They enjoy rafting.
(C) A light is above the table.
(D) The artist is sketching.

9. (A) He's trying to catch a mouse.
(B) He's waiting on the corner.
(C) He's changing sweaters.
(D) He's working at his computer.

10. (A) The tourists are on the bus.
(B) The woman is behind the counter.
(C) The directions are in the brochure.
(D) The information is in the directory.

11. (A) They're in a waiting area.
(B) They're in an operating room.
(C) They're on a factory floor.
(D) They're on a loading dock.

12. (A) The jazz club is long and dark.
(B) The man is collecting stamps.
(C) The orchestra is tuning up.
(D) The musician is playing for money.

13. (A) The seamstress is making an alteration.
(B) The waitress is taking an order.
(C) The actress is auditioning for a part.
(D) The politician is introducing herself.

14. (A) They're looking for a light.
(B) They're lighting a fire.
(C) They're fighting a fire.
(D) They're watering the garden.

15. (A) They're setting the table.
(B) They're writing on the board.
(C) They're discussing an issue.
(D) They're adding sugar to their coffee.

16. (A) She's measuring an angle.
(B) She's reaching for the controls.
(C) She's answering a question.
(D) She's boarding the plane.

17. (A) He's pouring a cup of coffee.
(B) He's emptying his pockets.
(C) He's spilling the liquid.
(D) He's brewing a pot of coffee.

18. (A) The customers are waiting for a table.
(B) The people are reading their newspapers.
(C) The library is open at night.
(D) The menus are being printed.

19. (A) The window is being washed.
(B) The film is about to begin.
(C) The buckets are in the store.
(D) The washing machine is outside.

20. (A) The shelves are empty.
(B) The closet is full of shoes.
(C) The man is running.
(D) The shoes line the wall.

## PART II

Example:

Good morning, John. How are you?
(A) I am fine, thank you.
(B) I am in the living room.
(C) My name is John.

21. What time will the bank open?
(A) It opens at 8 A.M.
(B) The door is open.
(C) The bank has a large clock.

22. Where did you park the car?
(A) The day before yesterday.
(B) I bought a new car.
(C) In the parking lot.

23. How often do you watch TV?
(A) My watch needs to be repaired.
(B) I watch the news every evening.
(C) The TV is in the living room.

24. Why are you walking so quickly?
(A) Sue talks very fast.
(B) I'm late for a meeting.
(C) They enjoy walking.

25. Who may I say is calling?
(A) My name is Ralph Smith.
(B) You are calling my mother.
(C) You didn't tell me who called.

26. When do you expect your visitor?
(A) Her visit was too short.
(B) He should arrive any minute.
(C) I will visit there next week.

27. Whose car shall we take?
(A) It is shallow.
(B) We took the bus.
(C) Let's take my car.

28. How hungry are you?
(A) Not very, but I could eat.
(B) I've never been to Hungary.
(C) Because I haven't eaten.

29. Which letter will you answer first?
(A) I'll mail the letter tomorrow.
(B) This is my last envelope.
(C) I'll answer the first one I received.

30. Do I have any messages?
(A) Yes, your wife called at noon.
(B) I had a massage.
(C) No one has seen us for ages.

31. Why is the ground wet?
(A) He hasn't grown up yet.
(B) It rained all morning.
(C) Because it's round.

32. Where are the invoices?
(A) They're in the files.
(B) Her voice is low.
(C) The invoice is paid.

33. Why don't you take a vacation?
(A) I'll take them with me.
(B) I'm too busy at work.
(C) I take public transportation.

34. What color will you paint the walls?
(A) I think green is a good color.
(B) Because he painted it blue.
(C) He read the poster on the wall.

35. Do any of you like sugar with your coffee?
(A) He doesn't like cigars.
(B) We all like sugar with our coffee.
(C) Sugar is very sweet.

36. How much time will it take to finish the building?
(A) The architect thinks about three more months.
(B) The building is thirty stories high.
(C) We'll be here about six o'clock.

37. Whose newspaper is on the table?
(A) The table is by the window.
(B) It's our new table.
(C) That newspaper belongs to me.

38. Did the mail come yet?
(A) No, we'll eat later.
(B) Yes, the mail is on your desk.
(C) Nobody came this morning.

39. What was the last speech about?
(A) It lasted about ten minutes.
(B) The speaker discussed management.
(C) The first speech was very interesting.

40. When did the train arrive?
(A) It arrived on time at 6:40.
(B) It rained all night.
(C) They came by train.

41. Why are you working late?
(A) You never work at night.
(B) Because my work is finished.
(C) I have to finish this report.

42. Where should the applicants wait?
   (A) Let them sit in my office.
   (B) We applied for a job here.
   (C) They waited for over an hour.

43. Can you recommend a good hotel?
   (A) I don't have a reservation.
   (B) That's not good enough.
   (C) I like the new hotel by the river.

44. Which do you prefer, a pen or a pencil?
   (A) My pencil needs sharpening.
   (B) I prefer to write with a pen.
   (C) This pen writes well.

45. How many employees do you have?
   (A) I have nine employees.
   (B) My employees work very hard.
   (C) Because we pay well.

46. Where did you leave your coat?
   (A) I left it on the bus.
   (B) I bought my coat last year.
   (C) Leave your coat at the door.

47. When will the weather get warmer?
   (A) They'll get her one tomorrow.
   (B) Whenever she wants.
   (C) Not until summer.

48. Who is copying the report?
   (A) The reporter asked the questions.
   (B) The clerk is making five copies.
   (C) The copyright date is 1996.

49. Is your chair comfortable?
   (A) No, it is very uncomfortable.
   (B) Yes, the chairman is available.
   (C) He's neither fair nor capable.

50. How far is your office from here?
   (A) Not bad, thank you.
   (B) It's only about a mile.
   (C) I can hear very well.

## PART III

51. *Man* Have you finished with the sports section?
*Woman* Here, you can have all the newspaper.
*Man* How could you have read it so quickly?

52. *Woman* The driver will meet you at the gate.
*Man* What kind of car will he be driving?
*Woman* He has a large black limousine.

53. *Man* Where do you keep the paper cups?
*Woman* They're in the cabinet above the sink.
*Man* I looked there. I think you're out of cups.

54. *Woman* How many children do you have?
*Man* I have one boy and two girls.
*Woman* That's a good number. I have four.

55. *Man* Is your husband a doctor?
*Woman* No, he trained to be an architect, but he's working for the city.
*Man* I studied to be a lawyer, but I never practiced law.

56. *Woman A* This flashlight won't work. Maybe it needs new batteries.
*Woman B* I'm sure it does. The ones inside are really old.
*Woman A* OK. What size do we need? I'll get some batteries this afternoon.

57. *Man* You're not allowed to smoke in the dining room or in the lounge.
*Woman* Can we smoke in our offices?
*Man* No, you can only smoke outside.

58. *Woman* Checkout time is at noon, Mr. Smith.
*Man* OK. Could you send someone for my bags?
*Woman* Yes, sir. Will you need a taxi to the airport?

59. *Man* I'm sorry I was late. My bus was late again.
*Woman* That's the second time this week.
*Man* I'll take an earlier one tomorrow.

60. *Woman* Can I borrow your screwdriver?
*Man* It's in my toolbox, but don't forget to return it.
*Woman* I'll give it back to you after lunch.

61. *Woman A* It was so cold my car wouldn't start.
*Woman B* Mine was covered with ice.
*Woman A* We should move to the tropics.

62. *Woman* Could you work until 9:00 tonight?
*Man* No, I have to be home by 8:00.
*Woman* If you stayed until 6:30 or 7:00, you would still make it.

63. *Man* I left your suitcase in the hall.
*Woman* Thanks. I was afraid it was still in the taxi.
*Man* Don't worry. I'll take it upstairs after dinner.

64. *Woman* I've always wanted to sail around the world.
*Man* It would be faster to fly.
*Woman* I don't like to hurry. That's why I like boats.

65. *Man* Can you read the signature on the letter?
*Woman* No, it must be from a doctor. They never write clearly.
*Man* No, it's from the library. My book is overdue.

66. *Man* Is this chair taken?
*Woman* No, it isn't. Please sit down.
*Man* Thanks. All the other chairs are occupied.

67. *Woman* Pete, it's two o'clock. It's the third time you've missed the meeting.
*Man* You should have called me fifteen minutes ago.
*Woman* I tried six times! Your line was busy.

68. *Woman* Did the brochures come from the printers?
*Man* They're in a white box on the floor of the supply room.
*Woman* Good. I need to mail a hundred of them to Singapore.

69. *Man* The company directory is being revised.
*Woman* It's about time. My phone number is listed incorrectly.
*Man* Put your correct number on this form and return it by Friday.

70. *Woman* Have you finished your breakfast?
*Man* No, I'm still eating.
*Woman* Before you go to work, can you drive me to school?

71. *Man* This coffee is too strong.
*Woman* Add more water. That will make it weaker.
*Man* I can't drink it when it is this bitter.

72. *Woman* Go ahead and turn left at the next intersection.
*Man* We can't. It's one way going to the right.
*Woman* Well, now what do we do?

73. *Man A* We'd like a table for two, please.
*Man B* How about one by the window in the nonsmoking section?
*Man A* We'd prefer to eat in the smoking section.

74. *Woman* It's freezing. Your new air conditioner really works.
*Man* I have the system turned down low.
*Woman* It really circulates the air. It's like a refrigerator in here.

75. *Woman A* Let's play that song again.
*Woman B* We've rehearsed it enough. Let's take a break.
*Woman A* The concert is tomorrow. We need more practice.

76. *Woman* Watch out for that hole in the road!
*Man* They need to resurface this street.
*Woman* Every spring we get more and more holes.

77. *Man* I need a long-sleeved shirt.
*Woman* Yes, sir. What size and what color?
*Man* I take a 16 neck and a 36 sleeve. The color should be white or blue.

78. *Woman A* We have enough cups for everyone at the party.
*Woman B* I bought napkins, spoons, and forks.
*Woman A* Now, I hope the cake arrives in time.

79. *Man* We've waited half an hour for you.
*Woman* I'm sorry. I left over two hours ago.
*Man* Yesterday you were forty-five minutes late.

80. *Woman* We always start our vacation the first week of August.
*Man* Do you take the whole month?
*Woman* Yes, two or three weeks is not enough.

## PART IV

**Questions 81 and 82** refer to the following weather report.

The Weather Center at the airport reported at noon that the airport is closed this morning due to heavy fog. The fog will lift by early evening, and planes will be allowed to take off and land at that time.

**Questions 83 and 84** refer to the following special announcement.

The express train from Washington to New York leaves Monday through Friday at 6:50 A.M. and arrives in Penn Station in New York at 9:30 A.M. The two-hour forty-minute trip is nonstop.

**Questions 85 through 87** refer to the following recorded message.

The City Convention Bureau reports that all hotels are full for the period of August 15 through August 30. We regret the inconvenience. At the end of this message, you may leave your name and phone number to be put on a waiting list. If a room becomes available, we will contact you.

**Questions 88 through 90** refer to the following announcement.

Thank you for your report, Ms. Johnson. It's 10:30 now. Before we continue with the board meeting and the question-answer period, why don't we take a coffee break? We'll resume in fifteen minutes.

**Questions 91 and 92** refer to the following news item.

Flood waters have risen over twenty feet since Monday. Thousands of families have been evacuated. Fortunately, there has been no loss of life, but property damage is in the millions.

**Questions 93 and 94** refer to the following advertisement.

Carlos's Painting and Decorating can make your home look like new. You choose the colors, and we supply the painters. Ask your neighbors; they probably use us.

**Questions 95 and 96** refer to the following special announcement.

Ladies and Gentlemen, this is your captain speaking. Because of the large number of planes waiting to take off, twenty-five to be exact, we can expect to sit on the runway for a good fifteen minutes or so. I ask you all to be patient, and we'll be airborne soon.

**Questions 97 and 98** refer to the following recorded announcement.

Hello. You have reached the Center for the Performing Arts. Tonight in the small Concert Hall is the Young Musicians Recital at 8 P.M. In the large Concert Hall is the New Company Orchestra at 7:30. For ticket information, please call between the hours of 4 and 6 P.M.

**Questions 99 and 100** refer to the following news item.

All shipping came to a stop today when two tankers crashed into the side of the Panama Canal. This is the third shipping accident this month. Authorities will clear the canal within days.

# ANSWER KEY

# ANSWER KEY
# PRACTICE TEST ONE

## PART I

1. (A) The plane is being fueled. Choice (B) is incorrect because the plane's fuel tank may be low, but the plane is not flying low. Choice (C) confuses the similar sounds *plan* with *plane* and *add more guests* with *add more gas*. Choice (D) confuses the similar sounds *playing* and *plane*.

2. (C) The technician is looking at the gauges and dials to check how the systems are functioning. Choices (A), (B), and (D) are out of context.

3. (B) The hotel clerk is looking down. Choice (A) confuses *the hotel is on the corner* with *the pictures and clock in the corner of the room.* Choice (C) confuses the prepositions *on* and *in* and the similar sounds *counter* with *corner.* Choice (D) is incorrect because there are no customers in the picture.

4. (C) The man is bending over the box. Choice (A) confuses *going fishing* and *looking at fish.* Choice (B) confuses the prepositions *at* and *in* and the similar sounds *locks* and *box.* Choice (D) confuses the similar sounds *dish* and *fish.*

5. (A) The woman and child are walking down the sidewalk. Choice (B) is incorrect because they are looking in opposite directions, not at each other. Choice (C) is incorrect because they are walking, not dancing, in the street. Choice (D) confuses the similar sounds *movie* and *in motion.*

6. (B) The speaker is in front of the room. Choice (A) is incorrect because the audience is sitting in the room listening to the speaker, not leaving the room. Choice (C) is out of context; they are in a conference room, not on the lawn. Choice (D) is incorrect because there are plants in the room, but the room is not a lobby.

7. (D) The people are shaking hands. Choice (A) confuses *rubbing their fingers* and *shaking hands.* Choice (B) confuses *arm wrestling* and *shaking hands.* Choice (C) confuses the similar sounds *band* and *hand.*

8. (D) The trainer is in front of the chart. Choice (A) confuses the similar sounds *conductor* with *instructor* and the similar words *train* with *trainer.* Choice (B) confuses the similar words *entertainer* and *trainer;* the trainer is standing by the television, not appearing on television. Choice (C) associates *teacher* with *trainer* and is incorrect because the man is not behind a desk.

9. (C) The bus's storage bins are open. Choices (A) and (B) are out of context. Choice (D) is incorrect because the bins, not the boxes, are empty.

10. (A) The man is preparing food. Choice (B) confuses *sawing a board* and *cutting bread.* Choice (C) confuses *changing his shirt* and *wearing a shirt.* Choice (D) confuses *cutting his hair* and *cutting bread.*

11. (D) The people are taking an escalator down to the next level. Choice (A) confuses *riding a tram* with *riding an escalator.* Choice (B) confuses the similar sounds *fight* and *flight (of stairs).* Choice (C) is incorrect because they are taking the escalator to the next floor, not running across the floor.

12. (B) Smoke is coming from the chimney. Choice (A) confuses *fireplace* and *chimney.* Choice (C) is incorrect because there is smoke coming from the chimney, not fire coming from a skyscraper. Choice (D) confuses the similar words *fired* (to be terminated) and *fire* (burning flames) by associating *fire* with *smoke.*

13. (C) The workers are at their stations. Choice (A) confuses the similar words *assembly* (meeting) and *assembly line.* Choice (B) confuses the similar sounds *walking* and *working.* Choice (D) confuses the similar words *plant* (botanical) and *plant* (factory).

14. (A) The men are sitting side by side. Choice (B) confuses *buying a record* and *being in a recording studio.* Choice (C) confuses *building a studio* and *working in a recording studio.* Choice (D) is out of context.

15. (A) The man is reading a newspaper in an airplane. Choice (B) is incorrect because, except for the chair the man is in, all the chairs are empty. Choice (C) associates *pilot* with *airplane* and the *pilot light* with *light coming in the windows.* Choice (D) is incorrect because the man is sitting down, but he is only one passenger.

16. (C) The woman is painting a picture. Choice (A) confuses the similar sounds *faint* and *paint.* Choice (B) confuses the similar words *brushing* (her hair) and *(paint)brush.* Choice (D) confuses *discussing art* and *creating art.*

17. (B) The people are having a discussion. Choice (A) is incorrect because there is a coffee cup, but no one is drinking. Choice (C) is incorrect because there is a picture behind them, but they are not painting. Choice (D) is incorrect because there is a calculator on the table, but they are not using it.

18. (A) The man is pushing a hand truck. Choice (B) is incorrect because the boxes are on a hand truck, not on a shelf. Choice (C) is incorrect because there might be produce in the boxes on the hand truck, but there is no produce on display. Choice (D) is incorrect because the picture shows a man behind a hand truck, not a horse behind a cart.

19. (B) The waiter is clearing the table. Choice (A) confuses the similar sounds *buying an umbrella* and *by an umbrella.* Choice (C) is something a waiter would do but is not what he's doing in the picture. Choice (D) confuses the similar sounds *restroom* and *restaurant.*

20. (D) The man is standing on the train platform. Choice (A) confuses the similar sounds *new* and *view.* Choice (B) confuses the similar words *newspaper stand* and *standing on the platform.* Choice (C) confuses *car tracks* with *train tracks.*

## PART II

21. (A) *Let's sit in the front row* is a way of answering the questions of *where to sit.* Choice (B) confuses the similar words *sat* and *sit* and uses the prepositional phrase of place *in the back,* which does not answer the question. Choice (C) answers *what.*

22. (B) *All trains on Track 1 go there* answers *which train.* Choice (A) repeats *New York* but does not answer the question. Choice (C) repeats the words *goes* and *train* but does not answer *which train.*

23. (A) *It costs thirty dollars* answers *how much.* Choices (B) and (C) repeat the word *suit* but do not answer *how much.*

24. (C) *My secretary took the message* answers *who took it.* Choices (A) and (B) repeat the words *phone* and *telephone* but do not answer the question.

25. (A) *I'll have dinner about 6 P.M.* answers *what time* with the future meaning of the present progressive *are eating.* Choice (B) associates *dined* with *dinner.* Choice (C) repeats the word *dinner* but does not answer the question.

26. (C) *Yes, it came an hour ago* answers *has the mail arrived* by providing a time. Choice (A) confuses the similar sounds *jet* and *yet.* Choice (B) confuses the similar sounds *failed* and *mail.*

27. (B) *It's too hot in here* answers *why.* Choice (A) confuses the opposites *closed* and *open.* Choice (C) associates *windmill* and *wind* with *window.*

28. (B) *I'm expecting my aunt* answers *who are you expecting.* Choice (A) confuses the similar sounds *suspected* and *expecting.* Choice (C) confuses the similar sounds *suspected* and *expecting.*

29. (A) *It's at the end of the hall* answers *where.* Choices (B) and (C) repeat the word *accountant* but do not answer the question.

30. (B) *There are about fifteen* answers *how many.* Choice (A) repeats the word *class* but does not answer the question. Choice (C) repeats the word *students* but does not answer the question.

31. (C) *She only reads business magazines* answers *which magazines does she read.* Choice (A) uses the word *magazine* but does not answer *which.* Choice (B) confuses the past pronunciation of *read* with the present pronunciation of *read.*

32. (A) *I'm going tomorrow* answers *when.* Choice (B) uses the word *leaving* but is not appropriate because the subject is still second person. Choice (C) uses the word *Hawaii* but does not answer the question.

33. (B) *No, it won't* answers *will it be finished on time.* Choice (A) associates *five o'clock* with *time.* Choice (C) confuses the similar sounds *reporter* and *report.*

34. (A) *Because* usually states a reason that answers a *why* question. Choice (B) confuses the similar sounds *get* (receive) and *get up* (awake). Choice (C) repeats the word *early* but is in the past tense.

35. (C) *No, I'd prefer salad* is a polite response to the request. Choice (A) confuses the similar sounds *thinner* and *dinner*. Choice (B) answers *when did you have dinner.*

36. (A) *I learned when I was young* answers *when.* Choice (B) repeats the word *swim* but is in the present tense. Choice (C) confuses the similar words *learned* and *learn* but does not answer the question.

37. (B) *About three thousand dollars* answers *how much.* Choice (A) uses *because,* which usually answers a *why* question. Choice (C) repeats the word *car* but does not answer the question.

38. (C) *Because* usually states a reason that answers a *why* question. Choice (A) uses *shirt* but does not answer *why.* Choice (B) confuses the homonyms *change* (coins) and *change* (to substitute).

39. (C) *Western film* is a genre of movies. Choice (A) confuses the word *about* (near a time) and *about* (concerning). Choice (B) confuses the similar sounds *moved* and *movie.*

40. (B) *In the hall closet* answers *where are the supplies.* Choice (A) confuses the similar words *supplies* (verb) and *supplies* (noun). Choice (C) confuses *offices* and *office supplies.*

41. (A) *She left at noon* answers *when* the doctor left. Choice (B) confuses the similar sounds *docked* and *doctor.* Choice (C) confuses the similar words *left* (remaining) and *leave* (to depart).

42. (B) *We didn't have time to type it* answers *why* the letter was not typed. Choice (A) confuses the homonyms *type* (kind) and *typed* (to write on a computer/typewriter). Choice (C) confuses the similar sounds *little* and *letter.*

43. (A) *Here, you can use my pen* is a response to the request for a pen. Choices (B) and (C) use *black* and *blacken* but do not answer the request.

44. (A) *No, in a hospital* answers the *yes/no* question. Choice (B) confuses the similar sounds *barn* and *born.* Choice (C) associates *carried* with *born*'s homonym *borne.*

45. (B) *Cold cereal and fruit* answers *what.* Choice (A) answers *when is breakfast.* Choice (C) answers *why.*

46. (C) *About three hundred pages* answers *how many.* Choice (A) confuses the similar sounds *age* and *page.* Choice (B) answers *what color are the pages.*

47. (A) *The briefcase belongs to the new lawyer* answers *whose briefcase.* Choice (B) confuses the similar sounds *under* and *on the.* Choice (C) does not answer the question.

48. (B) *The manager earned the most* answers *who.* Choice (A) uses the related words *money* and *earning* but does not answer the question. Choice (C) confuses the similar sounds *earned* and *learned.*

49. (C) *At 7:30* answers *when will dinner be served.* Choice (A) repeats the word *served* but does not answer *when.* Choice (B) associates *diner* with *dinner.*

50. (A) *Take the number 14 bus* advises the questioner correctly. Choice (B) uses the past tense. Choice (C) confuses the similar sounds *talk* and *take.*

## PART III

51. (C) The woman is a typist because the man asks her to type something. Choice (A) confuses *mailed this evening* with *mail carrier.* Choice (B) associates *lunch* with *waitress.* Choice (D) is not mentioned.

52. (A) They are going to park a car. Choice (B) confuses the similar sounds *race* and *space.* Choice (C) confuses the similar words *park* (recreational place) with *park* (to leave an automobile somewhere). Choice (D) is not mentioned.

53. (C) The woman states *Wednesday before noon.* Choices (A) and (D) are not mentioned. Choice (B) is what was promised last week.

54. (D) She is ordering twelve dozen pens. Choice (A) is the number of black pens. Choice (B) is the number of red pens. Choice (C) is the number of blue pens.

55. (B) The man is sick. Choice (A) does not answer the question. Choice (C) confuses the similar sounds *full* and *feeling*. Choice (D) associates *house* with *home*.

56. (A) The speakers are going to watch the news. Choice (B) confuses *watch* (timepiece) with *watch* (to look at). Choice (C) confuses the similar sounds *tea* and *TV*. Choice (D) confuses the similar words *begin* and *beginning*.

57. (A) The speakers are talking at a dinner table. Choice (B) confuses the similar sounds *desert* and *dessert*. Choice (C) is impossible because they are eating. Choice (D) associates *bakery* with *cake*.

58. (D) The man bought a car. Choices (A) and (B) associate *sweater* and *shoes* with *walking*. Choice (C) confuses the similar words *tire* (wheel of a car) with *tired* (weary).

59. (A) The offices are cleaned every night. Choice (B) is mentioned but is not correct. Choice (C) is not mentioned. Choice (D) is contradicted by *only*.

60. (A) The woman is concerned about the balance. Choice (B) confuses *accountant is not ready* with *accountant already*. Choice (C) confuses the similar sounds *sons* and *sums*. Choice (D) confuses the similar words *check* (noun) and *check* (verb).

61. (B) A physician is giving advice. Choice (A) associates *travel agent* with *take a vacation*. Choice (C) is out of context. Choice (D) associates *golfer* with *play some golf*.

62. (A) They are having lunch on Monday. Choices (B) and (D) are days that the man is not free. Choice (C) is not mentioned.

63. (B) They can't stand the heat. Choices (A) and (C) are mentioned as things they do like. Choice (D) confuses the similar words *standing* (gerund) and *can't stand* (verb).

64. (B) The game will be canceled if it continues to rain. Choice (A) confuses *players* with *play table tennis*. Choices (C) and (D) confuse *nighttime* and *lights* with the fact that this game will be the first *night game* with *new lights*.

65. (A) They have to hurry or they will miss the bus. Choice (B) associates *raining* with *umbrella* and *raincoat*. Choice (C) confuses *lost her raincoat* with *got my raincoat on*. Choice (D) confuses *umbrella won't open* with *find my umbrella*.

66. (B) The woman needs two pencils. Choices (A) and (C) are not mentioned. Choice (D) confuses the fact that he *has a dozen in his top drawer* with *twelve*.

67. (C) They have another forty-five minutes. Choices (A) and (B) are how long it will take them to finish. Choice (D) is an addition of *twenty* and *thirty*.

68. (A) The woman lives by the school. Choice (B) is the place the man asks her if she lives near. Choice (C) confuses *by a mountain* with *Mountain View Street*. Choice (D) confuses *where the man goes to work* with *the woman's house*.

69. (B) She didn't have the time to buy a paper. Choice (A) associates *money* with *buy*. Choice (C) associates the man's suggestion to *have it delivered* with *delivered on time*. Choice (D) confuses *yesterday's instead* with *neither today's nor yesterday's*.

70. (D) The speakers are in a shoe store. Choice (A) confuses the homonyms *sailboat* and *sale*. Choice (B) associates and confuses *fruit store* and *pear* (fruit) with the homonym *pair* (two of a kind). Choice (C) confuses the homonyms *of course* and *golf course*.

71. (C) He usually gets eight hours of sleep. Choice (A) is the time he awoke today. Choice (B) is the number of hours he slept last night. Choice (D) is the time he went to bed the previous night.

72. (C) They are talking about a newspaper. Choice (A) confuses *sports event* with *sports section*. Choice (B) associates *book* with *read*. Choice (D) confuses the similar sounds *long line* with *headline* (newspaper).

73. (A) The man is a dentist because he is going to pull that tooth out. Choice (B) confuses the similar sounds *take care of* with *caretaker*. Choice (C) associates *waiter* with *meal*. Choice (D) confuses *brush salesperson* with *brush more often* (one's teeth).

74. (D) *She's getting an overseas phone call* answers *why*. Choice (A) is not mentioned. Choice (B) confuses the similar sounds *sick* and *six*. Choice (C) is what the man assumes but is not correct.

75. (B) They are talking about a robbery. Choice (A) associates *shopping trip* with the items *purse* and *watch*. Choice (C) associates *accident* with *hurt*. Choice (D) is not mentioned.

76. (A) The woman is a salesperson. Choice (B) confuses *tax lawyer* with *plus tax*. Choice (C) confuses *cardplayer* with *credit card*. Choice (D) associates *shipping clerk* with *wrapped*.

77. (B) *In thirty minutes* is the same as *in about a half hour*. Choice (A) is not mentioned. Choice (C) confuses *one hour* with *hours*. Choice (D) is how long the man has been there.

78. (D) The phrases *dining car, club car,* and *on the train* show they are talking on a train. Choice (A) associates *coffee shop* with *coffee*. Choice (B) confuses *diner* with *dining car*. Choice (C) associates *restaurant* with *dining car, sandwiches,* and *coffee*.

79. (D) *It's raining* is the reason *why they can't play golf*. Choice (A) confuses the question of *having an umbrella* with *having only one umbrella*. Choices (B) and (C) confuse *clubs* and *shoes* with the fact that they will get wet.

80. (A) They are expecting a repairperson to fix the photocopier. Choice (B) confuses *photographer* with *photocopier*. Choice (C) is who fixed the photocopier last time. Choice (D) is who called the repairperson.

## PART IV

81. (B) The company's name is Office Supplies, Inc. Choice (A) confuses *office space* with *office supplies*. Choice (C) associates *down pillows* with *reduce*, by taking the word *down* out of context. Choice (D) confuses the homonyms *sailboats* with *sale*.

82. (B) The sale lasts from Thursday through Saturday. Choices (A) and (C) are not mentioned. Choice (D) confuses eight days with 8 A.M.

83. (C) The sale ends Saturday at 6 P.M. Choice (A) is when the sale begins. Choice (B) is the middle of the sale. Choice (D) is not mentioned.

84. (A) Yesterday's weather was rainy. Choice (B) is not mentioned. Choices (C) and (D) are the forecasts for the weekend.

85. (A) It might snow this evening. Choices (B) and (C) are not mentioned. Choice (D) is when the weather will be sunny.

86. (D) This news item is a warning about electrical demand exceeding supply. Choices (A), (B), and (C) are incorrect because the first sentence uses the verb *warn,* and there is no overt analysis, review, or correction.

87. (B) Summer is when this would be heard because it is in the present tense and *hot summer months, air conditioners,* and *fans* are all mentioned. Choice (A) is incorrect because it is not in the future tense. Choices (C) and (D) are both incorrect because the tense is present.

88. (A) When excessive use exceeds supply, then a power failure occurs. Choices (B) and (C) repeat the words *demand* and *supply* but are the opposite of what causes failure. Choice (D) uses the word *fans* but *poor quality* is not mentioned as a reason for power failure.

89. (D) Potential travelers are listening to this announcement. Choices (A) and (C) are those who are busy. Choice (B) associates *callers* and *on the line* with *telephone line technicians*.

90. (A) *All the agents are busy* answers *why*. Choice (B) associates *late* with *delay*. Choice (C) uses *fares* but is the opposite of what is stated. Choice (D) associates *strike* (picket line) with *on the line*.

91. (B) Managers are attending the management improvement luncheon. Choice (A) associates *teachers* with the fact that *Mr. Margalis was a trainer*. Choice (C) confuses the fact that *they are at a luncheon* with *waiters*. Choice (D) confuses Mr. Margalis's *work in his garden* with *gardeners*.

92. (B) Mr. Margalis is a retired manager trainer. Choice (A) is the opposite of what he is. Choice (C) confuses *speechless* with the fact that he is giving a speech. Choice (D) is incorrect because he worked for the last twenty years, meaning he is not young.

93. (C) It is a luncheon so *a dining hall* is the logical choice. Choice (A) associates his *gardening* with *a garden.* Choice (B) associates *office* with *management.* Choice (D) confuses the similar sounds *train* (locomotive with cars) and *trainer* (one who teaches).

94. (A) A special pass is needed to enter. Choice (B) uses the word *authorized,* but *pass* is not mentioned. Choice (C) confuses *secure* with *security.* Choice (D) confuses *hunting license* and *driver's license.*

95. (C) Passes may be obtained at the Security Office. Choice (A) confuses the similar words *secure* and *security.* Choice (B) is *who may enter* but is not *who can issue passes.* Choice (D) uses the word *license,* but there is no mention of *bureau.*

96. (B) Part-time work is mentioned in the second sentence. Choices (A), (C), and (D) are not mentioned.

97. (D) Office skills are required. Choice (A) confuses *law degree* with *law firm.* Choice (B) associates *medical diploma* with *doctor's office.* Choice (C) confuses *advertising experience* with *advertising agency.*

98. (A) The time is 8:00 in the morning. Choices (B), (C), and (D) are not mentioned.

99. (D) *Don't forget to take your umbrella* is the advice given. Choices (A), (B), and (C) are not mentioned.

100. (B) *Clear skies* is how the weatherperson describes the current situation. Choices (A) and (C) are the expectations for the afternoon. Choice (D) is a euphemism for Chicago, the Windy City.

## PART V

101. (A) *In* is the correct preposition meaning *involved* or *sharing.* Choice (B) is impossible because *with* means *in the company of* and two companies cannot be one. Choice (C) means *originating from a source.* Choice (D) means *going in one side and coming out the other.*

102. (C) *Because* is a subordinate conjunction showing cause and effect with an expected result. Choice (A) is a subordinate conjunction showing a conditional. Choices (B) and (D) are relative pronouns.

103. (D) *Had been* is the correct past perfect verb for a past unreal condition in an *if* clause. Choice (A) is the past tense. Choice (B) is the simple present. Choice (C) is the present perfect

104. (B) *Payable* is the shorter substitution for the relative clause *which are paid.* Choice (A) uses the past participle and cannot come after the causative verb *make.* Choice (C) uses the present participle and cannot come after the causative verb *make.* Choice (D) uses the simple present.

105. (C) The paired conjunction/adverb *both...and* is correct. Choices (A), (B), and (D) cannot be paired with *both.*

106. (B) *Although* is the correct subordinate conjunction showing unexpected result. Choice (A) shows expected result. Choice (C) continues the same idea. Choice (D) shows expected result.

107. (C) *At* is the correct preposition for a specific time. Choice (A) means *by a certain time.* Choice (B) is incorrect for a specific time. Choice (D) is an article.

108. (A) *Therefore* is the correct adverb transition word showing an expected result. Choices (B), (C), and (D) all show unexpected result.

109. (C) *Deliver* is the correct form of the verb after the causative verb *had.* Choice (A) is the present participle. Choice (B) is the infinitive. Choice (D) is the past participle.

110. (B) *Start* is the correct verb to show habitual aspect with *usually.* Choice (A) suggests an action started in the past. Choice (C) suggests an action happening right now. Choice (D) suggests an action starting in the past and progressing up to now.

111. (D) *Turned down* is the correct two-word verb showing rejection. Choice (A) means *discovered.* Choice (B) means *started a flow.* Choice (C) means *rejected.*

112. (C) *Had to buy* shows past necessity to complement the unexpected result from *even though*. Choices (A) and (D) are present tense and not parallel with *was* in the previous clause. Choice (B) shows past certainty.

113. (D) *Since* is the correct subordinate conjunction showing cause and effect. Choice (A) shows cause and effect but would need present tense in the main clause to be parallel. Choice (B) is incorrect because of the present perfect use of *have become* in the main clause. Choice (C) means *although* or *during*.

114. (B) *Step down* is the logical choice meaning *retire*. Choice (A) means *leave a room or building*. Choice (C) means *go down from a higher place*. Choice (D) means *go in one side and come out another*.

115. (C) *After* is the correct subordinate conjunction showing a logical time relationship. Choice (A) shows cause and effect. Choice (B) expresses opposition. Choice (D) means *till that time and no longer*.

116. (B) *Interest* is the correct noun modifying *rates*. Choice (A) is the present participle. Choice (C) is the past participle. Choice (D) is the simple present third-person verb.

117. (A) *Put off* is the logical choice because it means *postpone*. Choice (B) means *set with*. Choice (C) means *clothe*. Choice (D) means *cause to do* or *connect on a phone*.

118. (C) *See* is the correct present tense verb in a future, adverbial time clause. Choice (A) is the future tense and impossible in an adverbial time clause. Choice (B) is the present progressive and *see* is usually a stative verb. Choice (D) is the present perfect progressive and *see* is usually a stative verb.

119. (A) The correct word order places *ever* before the verb in a negative command using the auxiliary *do*. Choices (B) and (C) incorrectly use *never* with the auxiliary *do*. Choice (D) incorrectly places *ever* after *accept*.

120. (B) *When* is the correct subordinate conjunction expressing *at the same time*. Choices (A) and (C) show opposition. Choice (D) is a preposition.

121. (A) *With* is the correct preposition showing association. Choices (B), (C), and (D) are all impossible with the verb *collaborate*.

122. (B) *Limited* is the correct second conditional verb. Choice (A) is the present participle. Choice (C) is the third conditional. Choice (D) is the present progressive.

123. (A) *Raise* is the correct infinitive. Choice (B) suggests some action that began in the past. Choices (C) and (D) suggest some progression.

124. (A) *Checked* is the correct choice with the causative verb *want*. Choice (B) adds an unnecessary *be*. Choice (C) is the present participle. Choice (D) is not correct with the causative verb *want*.

125. (D) *Therefore* shows cause and effect with an expected result. Choices (A) and (B) show opposition. Choice (C) is illogical because it needs a specific example of what she has done.

126. (C) *Representing* is the correct participle which is a reduced modifying phrase. Choice (A) is a noun. Choice (B) is a noun referring to a person. Choice (D) is a noun plus preposition and would be correct if it had a *the* before *representative* and commas around *Mr. James* to make it nonrestrictive.

127. (C) Adverbs of definite frequency may appear at the end of a clause. Choices (A), (B), and (D) all incorrectly place the adverb.

128. (D) *And* is the correct coordinate conjunction meaning *in addition to*. Choices (A) and (B) are not coordinate conjunctions and cannot be followed by a phrase. Choice (C) shows opposition.

129. (A) *While* expresses the idea of *during*. Choices (B), (C), and (D) all show cause and effect.

130. (B) *In* is the correct preposition for a city. Choices (A), (C), and (D) are all illogical prepositions of place.

131. (A) *Competitors* is the plural object of the preposition referring to people. Choice (B) is a noun that cannot follow *one of*. Choices (C) and (D) are both adjectives.

132. (C) *Decision* is the noun and subject of the sentence. Choices (A), (B), and (D) are all adjectives and cannot be subjects.

133. (A) *In* is the correct preposition for a city. Choices (B), (C), and (D) are all prepositions of place.

134. (C) *Findings* means *results.* Choice (A) is a creature that has been found. Choice (B) is the plural of something found. Choice (D) is the past tense of *find.*

135. (D) *Suspected* is the correct past tense verb to agree with *staff.* Choices (A) and (B) are both nouns. Choice (C) is an adjective.

136. (C) *Look up* means *to search for in a reference book.* Choice (A) means *to overlook.* Choice (B) means *to be careful.* Choice (D) means *to rely upon.*

137. (B) *Considered* is the correct passive of the verb. Choices (A) and (C) are both adjectives. Choice (D) is the active, simple present form of the verb.

138. (D) The simple past of the verb is necessary because of the particular past time reference *a year ago.* Choice (A) is the simple present. Choice (B) is the present progressive. Choice (C) is the present perfect.

139. (C) *Awarded* is the correct simple past for a particular time in the past. Choice (A) is the present participle. Choice (B) is the past perfect and suggests a time further back in the past. Choice (D) is the simple present and suggests something habitual.

140. (A) *Spend* is the correct verb form to follow the causative verb *had.* Choice (B) is the infinitive. Choice (C) is the simple past. Choice (D) is the present participle.

## PART VI

141. (C) The superlative *most* is necessary to show it is number one of many. *More* just makes a comparison between two things. Choice (A) is a correct prepositional phrase. Choice (B) is a correct two-word verb. Choice (D) is a correct noun.

142. (B) The verb *decided* takes the infinitive *to make.* Choice (A) is a correct preposition and modifier. Choice (C) is a correct pronoun. Choice (D) is a correct verb.

143. (C) The modal *would* is necessary because the main verb is in the past tense. Choice (A) is a correct relative pronoun. Choices (B) and (D) are correct nouns.

144. (A) *Total amount* needs the definite article *the* before it to show specificity. Choice (B) is a correct noun. Choice (C) is a correct prepositional phrase. Choice (D) is a correct verb.

145. (D) The time reference *yesterday* means that the main verb must be in the past, *disappointed.* Choice (A) is a correct adverb. Choice (B) is a correct noun and verb. Choice (C) is a correct noun phrase.

146. (D) The past perfect auxiliary *had* is necessary because the thinking occurred before finding the location. Choice (A) is a correct verb. Choice (B) is a correct noun. Choice (C) is a correct pronoun.

147. (C) The subject *result* is a singular noun which requires the verb *has had.* Choice (A) is a correct preposition. Choice (B) is a correct noun. Choice (D) is a correct preposition.

148. (A) When using *should* as a conditional, it takes sentence initial position, *Should the director.* Choice (B) is a correct infinitive. Choice (C) is a correct infinitive. Choice (D) is a correct noun.

149. (B) The verb *stop* takes the gerund *interviewing* when the meaning is not *in order to.* Choice (A) is a correct verb. Choice (C) is a correct relative pronoun plus auxiliary verb and negative adverb. Choice (D) is a correct infinitive.

150. (C) The subject *series* agrees with the verb *has been.* Choice (A) is a correct definite article plus adjective. Choice (B) is a correct noun plus conjunction. Choice (D) is a correct preposition plus article.

151. (A) The subject is *intelligence.* Choice (B) is a correct noun plus verb. Choice (C) is a correct demonstrative plus noun. Choice (D) is a correct adverb.

152. (B) The participle is *given* with no *are.* Choice (A) is a correct noun. Choice (C) is a correct noun. Choice (D) is a correct adverb.

153. (C) An employee can *pick up* a paycheck. Choice (A) is a correct preposition. Choice (B) is a correct conjunction. Choice (D) is a correct noun.

154. (C) The past perfect *had transferred* is necessary because the transferring occurred before the discovering. Choice (A) is a correct noun phrase. Choice (B) is a correct adverb plus adjective. Choice (D) is a correct preposition plus article and adjective.

155. (C) In a relative clause, the verb comes after the subject, *the product had.* Choice (A) is a correct adjective plus noun. Choice (B) is a correct relative pronoun. Choice (D) is a correct verb plus preposition.

156. (C) The adjective comparison is *as easy as.* Choice (A) is a correct conjunction and pronoun. Choice (B) is a correct article plus adjective. Choice (D) is a correct noun.

157. (A) The subject *Board* agrees with *is.* Choice (B) is a correct prepositional phrase. Choice (C) is a correct noun. Choice (D) is a correct article.

158. (C) The verb *are considering* takes the gerund *refinancing.* Choice (A) is a correct subordinate conjunction and pronoun. Choice (B) is a correct adverb and verb. Choice (D) is a correct noun and preposition.

159. (C) The modal *could* is not parallel with the present tense, *is that.* Possible modal auxiliaries are *can, should, ought to,* etc. Choice (A) is a correct article plus adjective. Choice (B) is a correct preposition. Choice (D) is a correct infinitive.

160. (D) *Union* needs the indefinite article *a* preceding it. Choice (A) is a correct nonreferential *there* plus *to be.* Choice (B) is a correct relative pronoun. Choice (C) is a correct verb.

## PART VII

161. (D) A clerk in a clothing store would apply for this job because he or she would need two years' experience in the clothing industry. Choice (A) associates *engineer* with *professional.* Choice (B) associates *real estate agent* with *sales.* Choice (C) associates *professor* with *college degree.*

162. (C) A college degree is required; however, a master's degree is not. Choices (A) and (B) are both mentioned in the announcement. Choice (D) is the same as *excellent communication skills.*

163. (D) This information would most likely appear in a newspaper. Choice (A) confuses *university catalogue* with the requirement of a *college degree.* Choice (B) associates *telephone* with *communication.* Choice (C) associates *tourist guide* with *the Pacific Rim area.*

164. (A) This article is about the harm of excessive packaging. Choice (B) confuses the reference to compact discs with the main idea. Choice (C) confuses the reference to garbage dumps with the main idea. Choice (D) confuses the reference to environmentalists with the main idea.

165. (B) Products are packaged to make them more attractive. Choice (A) is contradicted by *it does not protect the goods.* Choice (C) confuses the similar sounds *consumption* with *consumer.* Choice (D) associates *environmental* with *environmentalists.*

166. (B) The excessive wrapping ends up in the trash, which then ends up in the nation's garbage dumps. Choice (A) is what environmentalists would like to happen to the wrapping. Choices (C) and (D) are contradicted by *end up in the garbage dumps.*

167. (B) *Color Crown makes four-color separations* is their specialization. Choice (A) confuses *selling computers* with *support all types of computers.* Choice (C) confuses *producing magazines* with *publishing.* Choice (D) confuses *furniture* with *desktop publishing.*

168. (A) These companies have *plans to merge.* Choices (B) and (C) are not mentioned. Choice (D) confuses *separating* with *four-color separation.*

169. (C) Four-color separations are used for printing. Choice (A) associates *computing* with *computers.* Choice (B) confuses the similar words *merging* and *plans to merge.* Choice (D) confuses *dying* and *four-color.*

170. (C) This table compares the number of commuters and students who ride the bus. Choice (A) is not mentioned. Choice (B) confuses *means of transportation* with *bus.* Choice (D) confuses the similar sounds *drivers* and *riders.*

171. (B) July had the most commuters. Choice (A) has the highest number of student riders. Choices (C) and(D) have lower numbers of riders.

172. (D) The buses were used least in December. Choices (A), (B), and (C) have higher numbers of riders.

173. (D) The main focus of this report is to discuss the results of a postal increase. Choice (A) confuses *postal commission* with *postal rates.* Choices (B) and (C) are mentioned but are not the main subject of the report.

174. (A) The direct-marketing companies say the proposed postal rate increase will hurt their industry and drive some of them into bankruptcy. Choice (B) would not be affected. Choice (C) associates *postal employee* with *postal rates;* postal employees might be slightly affected by complaining customers. Choice (D) might not buy as many stamps, but since stamp collecting is a hobby and not a business, they wouldn't be as affected as direct-mail companies.

175. (C) Most direct-marketing companies use third class. Choice (A) confuses *book rate* and *catalogue.* Choice (B) confuses *first-class* with *the rise in first-class postage rates.* Choice (D) is the possible rise of third-class postage.

176. (B) A catalogue house is a direct-marketing company, meaning that they market their products directly to the consumer by mail instead of advertising with a third party. Choice (A) confuses *postal client* with *postal rate.* Choice (C) associates *financially stable company* with *bankruptcy.* Choice (D) is incorrect because catalogue houses use third-class mail.

177. (A) Safety is the main focus of this passage. Choices (B), (C), and (D) are all mentioned but are individual components of the overall message of safety.

178. (D) One-Call is the number that individuals call in order to locate pipelines before digging. Choice (A) associates *call* with *telecommunications.* Choice (B) associates *excavating* with *digging.* Choice (C) is who should call One-Call before digging.

179. (C) They coordinate emergency readiness in case of a leak and/or fire. Choice (A) is what pipeline companies want to prevent. Choice (B) associates *drilling* with *petroleum.* Choice (D) is what controls/monitors pipeline conditions.

180. (D) An alarm is sounded if there is any sudden change in pressure. Choice (A) is a normal part of the pipeline process because valves can be closed in the case of a leak. Choice (B) could possibly lead to a leak later on. Choice (C) is what happens after a leak has been detected.

181. (B) An oil industry marketing firm would publish this information to show that all oil/pipeline companies are working to ensure safety. Choice (A) is too broad a forum for such specific information. Choice (C) would publish something more specific to the outbreak of fires. Choice (D) would list its name as a form of advertising, yet there are no specific oil company names in this information.

182. (A) The Royal Inn is the most expensive with a standard rate of $250 and a weekend rate of $215. Choices (B), (C), and (D) are all less expensive.

183. (B) Under Benefits, the Royal Inn has full breakfast listed. Choices (A) and (C) have no mention of a breakfast. Choice (D) has only a continental breakfast.

184. (A) The Palmer House is the least expensive, with a standard rate of $135 and a weekend rate of $75. Choices (B), (C), and (D) are all more expensive.

185. (D) Yamakura Cororation is a communications electronics firm. Choice (A) confuses *Southeast Asia* with *Southeast Asian markets.* Choice (B) confuses *overseas travel* with *overseas production.* Choice (C) associates *exports* with *imports.*

186. (A) Yamakura plans to manufacture its telephone equipment in Singapore. Choice (B) is not mentioned. Choice (C) may be true but is not mentioned in the announcement. Choice (D) associates *import duties* with *imports,* but there is no mention of low duties in Singapore.

187. (B) An increase of 100 percent is equal to double. Choices (A), (C), and (D) are all not equal to double.

188. (A) This chart is used to identify and solve a problem if the TV does not work. Choice (B) confuses *TV program* with *TV*. Choices (C) and (D) are not mentioned.

189. (B) For an all-white picture, **What to do** suggests *adjust brightness control.* Choice (A) associates *turn down the volume* with *sound heard.* Choice (C) is what one should do if there is no picture. Choice (D) is the advice if there is a picture but no sound.

190. (D) For no picture and noise, **What to do** suggests *adjust tuning*. Choice (A) is not mentioned. Choice (B) needs the volume turned up or the earphones disconnected. Choice (C) needs the brightness control adjusted.

191. (A) No one owes money because Ms. Tomkins has already paid for the book. Choice (B) has already paid. Choice (C) is who keeps sending "Payment Due" notices. Choice (D) associates *author* with *book.*

192. (C) The date on the check was October 13. Choice (A) is when the letter was written. Choice (B) is not mentioned. Choice (D) is when China Books canceled the check.

193. (A) Ms. Tomkins received two notices and sent two letters, but only paid once. Choices (B) and (C) are mentioned. Choice (D) is true also because, although the company keeps sending her notices, they did cancel the back of her check, which means they received payment.

194. (C) This report is about the "paperless office." Choice (A) confuses *selling computers* and *using computers*. Choice (B) associates *desktop publishing* with *computers*. Choice (D) is mentioned but is not the main focus.

195. (A) The "paperless office" was supposed to reduce paper usage, which would help preserve resources and improve the world's solid-waste disposal problem. Choice (B) might have been true at first, but was not the intention. Choices (C) and (D) are not mentioned.

196. (B) This information would appear in the classified section of a medical periodical. Choices (A) and (C) are too general for such specific information. Choice (D) would not have an advertisement so medically oriented.

197. (B) Supervising research would be a responsibility of the chief of a public health clinic. Choices (A) and (D) are too general for a medical professor. Choice (C) is not mentioned.

198. (B) Medical board certification is required. Choice (A) is not mentioned. Choice (C) confuses *clinical nutrition training experience* with *the need to develop clinical nutrition programs.* Choice (D) is not mentioned.

199. (D) *Abstracts of published articles* is not mentioned. Choices (A), (B), and (C) are all mentioned as requirements.

200. (A) Since this is the job of an assistant professor, it would be logical that a medical school professor would apply. Choices (B), (C), and (D) would not have the specific training necessary.

# ANSWER KEY
# PRACTICE TEST TWO

## PART I

1. (A) The man is standing behind the taxi. Choice (B) confuses the similar sounds *cabinet* and *taxi cab.* Choice (C) confuses the similar words *trunk* (a large box) and *trunk* (of a car). Choice (D) is not what the man is doing.

2. (C) The woman is writing at her desk. Choice (A) is incorrect because there is a lot of stuff on the table. Choice (B) is incorrect because a necklace is around her neck, not in her hands. Choice (D) is incorrect because there are no curtains on the windows.

3. (A) The people are attending an opening at an art gallery. Choice (B) uses the associated words *painting* and *picture,* but the statement does not match the action. Choices (C) and (D) use the associated word *picture* but in the context of photography.

4. (B) The technician is adjusting the equipment. Choices (A) and (C) are out of context. Choice (D) confuses the similar sounds *mail* and *male.*

5. (C) The desk clerk is assisting the guests. Choice (A) confuses the similar sounds *forty* and *four.* Choice (B) is incorrect because the phone is on the counter, not on the wall. Choice (D) is out of context.

6. (A) The people are entering a restaurant. Choice (B) is incorrect because there is a public phone on the wall, but no one is using it. Choice (C) confuses *traveling to Thailand* and the *Thai* restaurant sign. Choice (D) associates *menu* with *restaurant.*

7. (A) The man is making a presentation. Choice (B) confuses the similar sounds *presents* and *presentation.* Choice (C) confuses the similar sounds *jacket* and *pocket.* Choice (D) confuses *training horses* and *conducting a training session.*

8. (D) Cars are parked in the parking lot. Choice (A) is incorrect because the man is carrying a jacket, not wearing it. Choice (B) is incorrect because there are no birds on the fence. Choice (C) confuses *pictures on the wall* and *the painted building.*

9. (D) The man and woman are taking a walk. Choice (A) is incorrect because the man is with a woman. Choice (B) is a correct association but is out of context. Choice (C) is incorrect because the woman is wearing a skirt, not pants.

10. (C) The camera is on a three-legged stand, called a tripod. Choice (A) confuses *the film is in focus* and *focusing the camera.* Choice (B) is incorrect because the man is not carrying anything. Choice (D) associates *video store* with camera.

11. (B) The chairs are empty. Choice (A) confuses the similar sounds *poodle* and *pool.* Choices (C) and (D) are incorrect because the pool is empty.

12. (A) The worker is going up the stairs. Choice (B) confuses *a gas tank in a car* and *an oil storage tank.* Choice (C) confuses the similar sounds *sank* and *tank.* Choice (D) confuses the similar sounds *letter* and *ladder.*

13. (D) The man is wearing a microphone. Choice (A) is incorrect because his hand is on his knee, but he's not rubbing his knee. Choice (B) is incorrect because his leg is up, but he's not climbing stairs. Choice (C) confuses the similar sounds *microscope* and *microphone.*

14. (C) The workers are checking the equipment. Choices (A), (B), and (D) are out of context.

15. (C) The pilots are preparing for takeoff. Choice (A) confuses *flight attendants* with *pilots* and *get off* with *take off.* Choice (B) confuses the similar sounds *pie ought* with *pilot* and *take out* with *take off.* Choice (D) confuses *musical instruments* and the plane's *instrument panel.*

16. (A) There are trees behind the statue. Choice (B) confuses the similar sounds *butter* and *Buddha* and associates *gold* with this type of statue. Choice (C) is incorrect because the flowers are in the ground, not in a vase. Choice (D) confuses the similar words *offers* and *offerings.*

17. (A) The hotel guest is talking to the room clerks. Choices (B), (C), and (D) are correct relationships but are out of context.

18. (C) The wedding couple is standing by a cart. Choice (A) confuses the similar sounds *welders* and *wedding*. Choice (B) confuses the similar sounds *waders* and *wedding*. Choice (D) confuses the similar sounds *wetting the dress* and *wedding dress*.

19. (B) Two men are making repairs. Choice (A) confuses *gas used to operate an oven* and *the inflammable gas sign*. Choice (C) is incorrect because one of the men is kneeling and the other is standing. Choice (D) is incorrect because their tools are laid out around them, not put away.

20. (D) The worker is surrounded by oil drums. Choice (A) uses the associated word *hat* for *hard hat*. Choice (B) suggests he may be looking at his work orders, but he is not typing them. Choice (C) uses the associated word *oil*.

## PART II

21. (B) *In the top drawer* answers *where*. Choice (A) associates *post office* with *stamps*. Choice (C) confuses the similar words *stamped* and *stamps*.

22. (C) *To go to the doctor* answers *why did you leave early*. Choice (A) confuses the opposites *late* and *early* and uses the word *because*, which often is used in a response to a *why* question. Choice (B) confuses *arriving early* and *leaving early*.

23. (B) *First I'll open the mail* answers *what is your first chore*. Choice (A) confuses the similar sounds *thirst(y)* and *first*. Choice (C) confuses the similar sounds *short* with *chore* and *workday* with *today*.

24. (C) *Twice a year* answers *how often*. Choice (A) incorrectly answers in the past tense. Choice (B) is not realistic.

25. (A) *That cup is his* answers *whose coffee cup is this*. Choice (B) repeats the word *this* but does not answer the question. Choice (C) answers *do you like coffee*.

26. (A) *Yes, actually we are early* answers *will we be on time*. Choice (B) associates *watch* with *time*. Choice (C) confuses the similar sounds *he* and *we* and associates *4:30* with *time*.

27. (B) *I only know a few words* answers *how well do you speak Chinese*. Choice (A) answers *how does she feel*. Choice (C) confuses *Chinese food* and *the Chinese language*.

28. (C) *I was too tired* answers *why didn't you study*. Choice (A) confuses the similar sounds *students* and *study*. Choice (B) repeats the word *test* but does not answer the question.

29. (B) *They plan to stay home* answers *what are they going to do tomorrow*. Choice (A) answers *what are they doing now*. Choice (C) confuses *the day after* and *tomorrow*.

30. (C) *On the ground floor* answers *where*. Choice (A) repeats the word *ticket* and confuses the similar sounds *counted* with *counter*. Choice (B) answers *where is your ticket*.

31. (C) *Beef and noodles* answers *what's for lunch*. Choice (A) answers *where*. Choice (B) answers *when*.

32. (A) *Yes, please* is a polite response to the question. Choice (B) answers *is there sugar*. Choice (C) repeats the word *coffee* but does not answer the question.

33. (C) *About four* answers *how many*. Choice (A) answers *when will you see that movie*. Choice (B) confuses the similar sounds *moved* with *movies* and *overseas* with *see*.

34. (B) *The brown chair* answers *which chair*. Choice (A) confuses the similar sounds *table* and *(comfor)table*. Choice (C) confuses the similar sounds *care* and *chair*.

35. (A) *In June* answers *when*. Choice (B) uses a form of the verb *take (took)* but does not answer the question. Choice (C) confuses the similar sounds *invented* and *inventory*.

36. (C) *A young couple* answers *who rented the apartment*. Choice (A) confuses the similar words *renters* and *rented*. Choice (B) confuses the similar words *stairs* and *upstairs*.

37. (B) *He said no rooms were available* answers *what did the hotel clerk say*. Choice (A) confuses the similar sounds sounds *stay(ed)* and *say*. Choice (C) uses the word *clerk* out of context.

38. (A) *I advertised for one in the paper* answers *how did you find a computer programmer*. Choice (B) associates *computer* with *computer program* and answers *where is the computer*. Choice (C) confuses *program* and *programmer*.

39. (C) *At the corner* answers *where is the bus stop.* Choice (A) repeats the word *bus* but does not answer the question. Choice (B) confuses *got off the bus* with *bus stop.*

40. (B) *Last week* answers *when was the package mailed.* Choice (A) confuses the similar sounds *packed* and *package.* Choice (C) answers *when does the mail come.*

41. (C) *In the street* answers *where should the employees park.* Choice (A) confuses the similar words *park* (place for recreation) and *park* (to put a car in a parking spot). Choice (B) confuses the similar sounds *dark* and *park.*

42. (A) *Three hundred thousand dollars* answers *how much money.* Choice (B) repeats many of the words used in the question but does not answer the question. Choice (C) confuses the opposites *spent* and *earned.*

43. (A) *Whenever we want* answers *when.* Choice (B) confuses the similar sounds *bread* and *break.* Choice (C) confuses the similar words *broke* (smashed to pieces) and *break* (a short break from work).

44. (B) *I turned it off* answers *who turned off the photocopier.* Choice (A) confuses the similar words *copied the photos* and *photocopier.* Choice (C) confuses the similar sounds *photographer* and *photocopier* and the phrases *turned in* and *turned off.*

45. (A) *Smoking is not allowed anywhere* is a way of saying *all rooms are for nonsmokers,* which answers *which room.* Choice (B) confuses the similar words *smoke* and *(non)smokers.* Choice (C) confuses the similar sounds *no one* and *(non)smokers.*

46. (A) *It can seat 500 people* answers *how large is the auditorium.* Choice (B) uses the similar word *larger* out of context. Choice (C) confuses the questions *how often* and *how large.*

47. (C) *Only one* answers *how many.* Choice (A) answers *which bag can I take.* Choice (B) answers *how many planes can I take.*

48. (B) *Yes, ...this morning* answers *did you buy your plane ticket yet.* Choice (A) confuses the similar sounds *jet* and *yet.* Choice (C) confuses the similar sounds *(com)plained* and *plane.*

49. (A) *Health insurance* answers *what kind of insurance do you have.* Choice (B) associates *insurance agent* with *health insurance.* Choice (C) answers *why do you have insurance.*

50. (C) *Fourteen hours by plane* answers *how long does it take.* Choice (A) answers *do you like to travel.* Choice (B) associates *big cities* with *New York* and *Tokyo* and *the subway* with *travel.*

## PART III

51. (B) *Turn at the next light* and *you drive the car* are things that are said in a car. Choice (A) confuses *light store* and *traffic light* and the similar sounds *store* and *sure.* Choice (C) associates *library* with *map.* Choice (D) is not possible.

52. (A) The woman will leave at 4:00. Choice (B) is when rush hour starts. Choice (C) is the first time the woman mentions; she later changes her mind. Choice (D) is when her plane leaves.

53. (D) The man wants to buy medicine for his cold. Choice (A) is what the cold medicine is next to. Choice (B) confuses the similar sounds *TV* and *aisle B.* Choice (C) confuses *new glasses* and *didn't see any.*

54. (B) The man asks for ten dollars. Choice (A) is not mentioned. Choice (C) confuses the similar sounds *thirty* and *forty.* Choice (D) is how much money the woman has.

55. (B) It is 1:30 because they have thirty minutes before the bank closes at 2:00. Choice (A) is not mentioned. Choice (C) is when the bank closes. Choice (D) is thirty minutes after the bank closes.

56. (C) The woman asks if the man has seen her coat. Choice (A) is where the man thinks the coat is. Choice (B) is where the woman thinks she must have left it. Choice (D) is what her coat was with.

57. (B) The speakers are watching TV. Choice (A) confuses the similar words *watch* (a thing that tells time) and *watch* (to look at). Choice (C) associates *reading the (news)paper* with *news.* Choice (D) confuses *playing a game* and *watching the game.*

58. (A) The man asks if there are any comedies playing. Choice (B) is one of the movies playing. Choices (C) and (D) are movies they don't like.

59. (D) The meeting will be held at the end of the week on Friday. Choice (A) is when the meeting was originally scheduled. Choices (B) and (C) are contradicted by *the end of the week on Friday.*

60. (D) The woman was late today because she ran out of gas. Choices (A) and (B) confuse *slept late* and *walked slowly* with the man's suggestions to get up earlier and walk. Choice (C) is what she did yesterday.

61. (C) The speakers pay their taxes every three months, or quarterly. Choice (A) is how often the man wishes he had to pay taxes. Choice (B) confuses the similar sounds *two* and *too.* Choice (D) confuses *four months* with *quarterly.*

62. (B) The man left his glasses on the desk in the woman's office. Choice (A) confuses *his desk* and *her desk.* Choice (C) confuses *in his briefcase* and *hold my briefcase.* Choice (D) confuses *in the car* and *I'll meet you at the car.*

63. (A) The speakers are talking about a typist. Choice (B) associates *a typewriter repairperson* with the *broken typewriter.* Choice (C) is out of context. Choice (D) confuses *a cleaning person* and *keeping a neat and clean desk.*

64. (C) The man starts work in August. Choices (A) and (B) are when the woman thought he started. Choice (D) is when the woman suggests he should start.

65. (A) The man likes the hot weather because he sells ice cream and the heat is good for business. Choice (B) is contradicted by *the heat.* Choice (C) confuses the similar sounds *ice skating* and *ice cream.* Choice (D) associates *hungry* with *egg* and *ice cream.*

66. (C) The man bought a suit. Choices (A), (B), and (D) he already had.

67. (C) The man is showing the woman a house, so he is a real estate agent. Choice (A) associates *cook* with *kitchen.* Choice (B) associates *construction worker* with *renovation.* Choice (D) associates *painter* with the newly painted kitchen and baths.

68. (D) The reports are due at five o'clock. Choice (A) is what time it is now. Choice (B) is when the woman wants to start working on them again. Choice (C) confuses *three o'clock* and *three hours.*

69. (B) The reference to *flight attendants* tells us the conversation takes place on a plane. Choice (A) confuses the similar sounds *train* and *plane.* Choice (C) associates *clothing store* with *(seat) belt.* Choice (D) confuses *hospital attendants* and *flight attendants.*

70. (C) The woman can't read because the light is too dim. Choices (A), (B), and (D) are not mentioned.

71. (A) The speakers mention a bed and a dresser, which are pieces of furniture found in a bedroom. Choice (B) confuses the similar sounds *clothes* and *close,* by associating *closet* with *clothes.* Choices (C) and (D) are contradicted by the references to *bed* and *dresser.*

72. (C) The speakers design buildings. Choice (A) associates *office workers* with *building.* Choice (B) confuses *building superintendents,* who maintain buildings, and *architects,* who design buildings. Choice (D) associates *gardeners* with *landscape.*

73. (B) The man swims three times a week. Choice (A) is contradicted by *three times a week.* Choice (C) confuses *four times a week* and *four miles.* Choice (D) is how often the woman swims.

74. (A) The woman is going hiking in the mountains for her vacation. Choices (B), (C), and (D) are what the man asks if she will do.

75. (B) The woman wants the man to take off his shoes. Choice (A) is what the woman just did and the reason she wants him to take off his shoes. Choice (C) confuses *polish his shoes* and *the shoes are not dirty.* Choice (D) confuses *leave the house* and *leave his shoes outside.*

76. (B) The speakers are leaving tomorrow. Choice (A) is contradicted by *we're leaving tomorrow.* Choice (C) confuses *at the end of the week* and *enough to last all week.* Choice (D) confuses *in two weeks* with *a two-week vacation.*

77. (A) The woman is filling out a job application. Choice (B) confuses *telephoning someone* with *I will call you.* Choice (C) confuses *filling up a car* and *filling out an application* and the similar sounds *car* and *call.* Choice (D) confuses *opening a door* and *job openings.*

78. (B) The woman is a barber. Choice (A) confuses the similar sounds *banker* and *barber*. Choice (C) confuses *tree trimmer* with *shall I trim your beard.* Choice (D) confuses the similar sounds *dressmaker* and *hairdresser,* by associating *hairdresser* with *barber.*

79. (C) One bus should leave every fifteen minutes. Choice (A) is how long it takes to load the bus. Choice (B) is how long it takes to get there. Choice (D) is how long the round trip should take.

80. (A) The woman loves to walk through the park at dawn. Choice (B) is what the man prefers. Choice (C) confuses *early in the evening* and *getting up early in the morning.* Choice (D) is the time the woman likes to go to bed.

## PART IV

81. (A) The Revenue Office in City Hall will be open from 8 A.M. to noon on Saturday. Choices (B), (C), and (D) are contradicted by the information given.

82. (B) Tax forms must be filed. Choices (A), (C), and (D) are not documents that would be filed with the Revenue Office.

83. (C) Long lines are expected, so people should come early to avoid them. Choice (A) confuses *refund* and *revenue.* Choice (B) confuses *become citizens* and *citizens can file.* Choice (D) confuses the similar words *files* (documents) and *file* (to register).

84. (D) The reference to an airport parking lot indicates that this announcement would be heard at an airport. Choices (A) and (B) are mentioned as destinations. Choice (C) associates *airplane* with *airport.*

85. (A) Passengers should follow the blue signs for rental cars. Choice (B) is for public transportation. Choice (C) is for parking shuttles. Choice (D) confuses the similar sounds *yellow* and *follow.*

86. (B) Passengers who have left their cars in an airport parking lot should follow the green signs for a parking shuttle. Choices (A) and (C) are mentioned as methods of public transportation. Choice (D) is not mentioned.

87. (B) The speaker hopes everyone enjoys their lunch and then introduces the guest speaker, which indicates that the speech will be heard after lunch. Choice (A) is contradicted by *I hope you have enjoyed your lunch.* Choice (C) confuses *next month* and *monthly luncheons.* Choice (D) confuses *next Friday* and *on this beautiful Friday.*

88. (B) The luncheons are monthly. Choice (A) confuses *every Friday* and *the day this luncheon is being held.* Choices (C) and (D) are contradicted by *monthly.*

89. (D) Dr. Chang is the author of a best-selling novel. Choices (A) and (B) confuse *politician* and *criminal* with the title of her book. Choice (C) associates *saleswoman* with *best-selling.*

90. (A) Visitors must be accompanied by employees with IDs. Choice (B) confuses *permission of security personnel* and *removed by security personnel.* Choice (C) is how employees must appear at all times. Choice (D) is not mentioned.

91. (A) All employees are required to wear an identification badge. Choice (B) is not likely. Choices (C) and (D) do not need to have an ID, but they do need to be with an employee with an ID.

92. (B) Spartan Golf Club announced the opening of its newest golf course. Choice (A) confuses the similar sounds *Civic Center* and *city center.* Choice (C) is where golfers can apply for memberships. Choice (D) confuses the similar sounds *residential* and *professional.*

93. (D) Club memberships are being offered. Choices (A), (B), and (C) are not mentioned.

94. (A) It's perfect beach weather. Choices (B), (C), and (D) are not mentioned.

95. (C) The sun is shining. Choices (A), (B), and (D) are not mentioned.

96. (D) The man's estate was worth over two million dollars. Choice (A) is contradicted by *two million dollars.* Choice (B) confuses the opposites *under* and *over.* Choice (C) confuses *a million* and *two million.*

97. (C) The man left his entire estate to his dog. Choices (A) and (B) are contradicted by *left his entire estate to his dog.* Choice (D) confuses *his best friend* and *man's best friend.*

98. (D) The office is open Monday through Friday. Choices (A), (B), and (C) are contradicted by *Monday through Friday*.

99. (A) Renewal of driver's licenses are done in the afternoon between the hours of noon and 4:00 P.M. Choices (B) and (C) are done from 8:00 A.M. to 4:00 P.M. Choice (D) is not something that would be done at the Office of Motor Vehicles.

100. (B) The office closes at 4:00. Choice (A) is when they start taking customers who want to renew their licenses. Choices (C) and (D) are not possible because the office closes at 4:00.

## PART V

101. (A) Adverbs of indefinite frequency may appear before the main verb. Choices (B), (C), and (D) are not possible positions for indefinite frequency adverbs.

102. (C) *Depend on* is a two-word verb. Choices (A), (B), and (D) do not follow *depend*.

103. (B) *Nonetheless* is a conjunction that indicates an unexpected result. Choice (A) indicates a substitution. Choice (C) indicates sequence. Choice (D) indicates an unexpected result but must be followed by a noun phrase.

104. (D) *Operating* forms part of the title *chief operating officer*. Choice (A) is a noun referring to people. Choice (B) is an adjective but is not used in this title. Choice (C) is a noun that refers to things.

105. (C) *And* is a coordinating conjunction that links items equally. Choice (A) eliminates both items. Choice (B) is usually paired with *neither*. Choice (D) indicates a choice between items.

106. (B) To *run out of* something means *you do not have any more*. Choice (A) means *to meet unexpectedly*. Choice (C) is confused with *run out of*. Choice (D) means *to use up*.

107. (C) *While* is a subordinate conjunction that indicates simultaneous action. Choices (A) and (B) indicate cause and effect. Choice (D) indicates purpose.

108. (C) *Of all* indicates that one item is being singled out from a group. Choice (A) indicates direction away. Choice (B) indicates similarity. Choice (D) indicates an exception.

109. (A) *During* is a preposition that indicates a period of time. Choice (B) indicates association. Choice (C) indicates location. Choice (D) indicates direction toward.

110. (B) *For example* indicates that one item is an instance of another. Choices (A) and (D) indicate unexpected results. Choice (C) indicates alternative points.

111. (C) Someone else will sign the invoice, so the past participle is used. Choice (A) is a noun referring to a name that has been signed. Choice (B) is a verb. Choice (D) is a gerund.

112. (C) Adverbs of indefinite frequency may appear after forms of the verb *be*. Choices (A), (B), and (D) are not possible positions for indefinite frequency adverbs.

113. (B) The past participle *based* completes the verb *will be based on*. Choice (A) is an adjective. Choice (C) is a gerund. Choice (D) is a noun referring to a thing.

114. (A) *Were* is the form of *be* used in the *if* clause of unreal conditions. Choices (B), (C), and (D) are not the form of *be* used in unreal conditions.

115. (D) *To stand up to* means *to support your point of view against others*. Choice (A) means *to support a cause* and is not followed by *to*. Choice (B) indicates position or attitude and is not followed by *to*. Choice (C) means *to associate yourself with others for a cause* and is not followed by *to*.

116. (B) Future perfect tense indicates a future action that will occur before another future action. Choice (A) is the passive form of the future. Choice (C) is the present tense. Choice (D) is the past tense.

117. (D) *Housing market* is a business term. Choice (A) refers to a certain kind of pigeon. Choice (B) is a past participle. Choice (C) is a noun referring to a thing.

118. (C) *Besides* indicates an additional supporting point. Choice (A) indicates association. Choice (B) indicates cause and effect. Choice (D) indicates result.

119. (A) *Because* indicates cause and effect. Choice (B) indicates an unexpected result. Choice (C) is a conditional. Choice (D) indicates time sequence.

120. (C) Adverbs of definite frequency may appear at the end of a clause. Choices (A), (B), and (D) are adverbs of indefinite frequency.

121. (B) *Successor* means *a person who follows another in a job or role.* Choice (A) is an adjective. Choice (C) is a noun referring to a thing. Choice (D) is an adjective indicating sequence.

122. (D) Adverbs of indefinite frequency can appear between the auxiliary and the main verb. Choices (A), (B), and (C) are not appropriate positions for indefinite frequency adverbs.

123. (D) *Have been satisfied* is the passive form of the present perfect tense, which indicates an action that started in the past and continues to the present. Choice (A) is the present tense. Choice (B) is the present perfect (active form). Choice (C) is the present perfect progressive.

124. (C) *Either . . . or* is a paired conjunction. Choices (A), (B), and (D) are not paired with *either.*

125. (B) *Composed of* is a two-word verb that indicates composition. Choices (A), (C), and (D) do not complete the verb.

126. (D) *Take on* means *to accept a challenge.* Choice (A) means *to leave.* Choice (B) means *to remove.* Choice (C) means *to remove from someone's possession.*

127. (C) *Employees* is a noun that refers to the people who work for a business. Choice (A) is a noun that refers to a thing. Choice (B) is a verb. Choice (D) is a gerund.

128. (A) *Despite* indicates an unexpected result. Choice (B) indicates cause and effect. Choice (C) indicates association. Choice (D) indicates similarity.

129. (C) *Financial* is an adjective that modifies *affairs.* Choice (A) is a noun that refers to a thing. Choice (B) is a gerund. Choice (D) is a past participle.

130. (D) *Already* is an adverb of indefinite frequency indicating a completed action and may appear between the auxiliary and the main verb. Choice (A) indicates an ongoing situation. Choice (B) is an adverb of definite frequency. Choice (C) indicates an action that has not taken place at the time indicated.

131. (C) *And* is a conjunction that links items equally. Choice (A) indicates a contrast between items. Choice (B) is usually paired with *neither.* Choice (D) indicates cause and effect.

132. (B) *Take over* means *to obtain control of.* Choice (A) means *to leave.* Choice (C) means *to bring something to a person or place.* Choice (D) means *to remove.*

133. (A) *But* is a conjunction that indicates a contrast between items. Choice (B) links items equally. Choice (C) indicates association. Choice (D) indicates contrast but links clauses, not phrases.

134. (B) *If* can indicate a possible situation. Choice (A) indicates simultaneous action. Choice (C) indicates an unexpected result. Choice (D) adds an idea.

135. (C) *On* is used with specific dates. Choice (A) indicates time or location. Choice (B) is an article. Choice (D) is used with dates only to indicate a limit on a time span, *from April 28 to May 1.*

136. (A) *Advertising costs* describes the cost of providing advertisements. Choice (B) is a noun referring to things. Choice (C) *advertised costs* refers to costs that have been advertised. Choice (D) is a verb.

137. (C) *Drops in (quarterly) profits* is a business expression. Choice (A) might be used to indicate the level of the drop. Choice (B) might be used to indicate the starting point of the drop, *dropped from two million to one million.* Choice (D) indicates association.

138. (D) *Founded* means *established* or *started.* Choice (A) *was found* means *was located.* Choice (B) is an adjective. Choice (C) is the simple form of the verb *find.*

139. (B) *Nevertheless* indicates an unexpected result. Choice (A) adds additional information. Choice (C) indicates an example. Choice (D) indicates simultaneous action.

140. (D) Ms. Alva will write the press release so the simple form *write* is used. Choice (A) is the present tense. Choice (B) is the infinitive. Choice (C) is the gerund.

## PART VI

141. (C) An indirect question follows subject-verb order: *where the meeting was being held.* Choice (A) is a correct infinitive. Choice (B) is a correct subordinate conjunction. Choice (D) is a correct verb.

142. (B) The verb must agree with the singular subject *opportunity: The opportunity for promotions has increased.* Choice (A) is a correct preposition. Choice (C) is a correct adverb. Choice (D) is a correct verb.

143. (C) The pronoun must agree with the noun *information: if you have questions about it.* Choice (A) is a correct verb. Choice (B) is a correct conditional. Choice (D) is a correct verb.

144. (B) The oil prices are falling, so the present participle is required: *rapidly falling oil prices.* Choice (A) is a correct adverb. Choice (C) is a correct infinitive. Choice (D) is a correct conjunction.

145. (A) Singular count nouns must be used with an article: *the book where visitors sign in.* Choices (B) and (C) are correct verbs. Choice (D) is a correct preposition.

146. (B) The present perfect is required: *should have been taken.* Choice (A) is a correct comparative. Choice (C) is a correct noun. Choice (D) is a correct noun phrase.

147. (C) The modal must be consistent with the time expressed: *that she would promote her administrative assistant before the end of last year.* Choice (A) is a correct noun phrase. Choice (B) is a correct relative pronoun. Choice (D) is a correct noun phrase.

148. (A) The present participle should be used to describe *repair job: a repair job costing over $3,000.* Choice (B) is a correct adverb. Choice (C) is a correct verb. Choice (D) is a correct article.

149. (D) Equal comparisons require *as* on both sides of the adjective: *not as impressive as.* Choice (A) is a correct conjunction. Choices (B) and (C) are correct verbs.

150. (A) Singular count nouns must be used with an article: *after the press conference.* Choice (B) is a correct noun phrase. Choice (C) is a correct noun. Choice (D) is a correct adjective.

151. (A) Verbs are modified by adverbs: *the newly established advertising agency.* Choice (B) is a correct verb. Choice (C) is a correct adjective. Choice (D) is a correct infinitive.

152. (B) The subject should not be repeated: *The downtown store is definitely luxurious.* Choices (A) and (C) are correct adjectives. Choice (D) is a correct adverb.

153. (C) The verb must agree with the singular subject *background: a background in economics which is considered critical.* Choice (A) is a correct article. Choices (B) and (D) are correct noun phrases.

154. (B) Adverbs usually precede adjectives in a group of modifiers: *the specially developed program.* Choice (A) is a correct prepositional phrase. Choices (C) and (D) are correct adverbs.

155. (B) The verb *admitted to* is followed by the gerund: *admitted to offering an estimate.* Choice (A) is a correct noun. Choices (C) and (D) are correct prepositional phrases.

156. (B) A pronoun must agree with the noun it refers to: *the size of the building and its proximity.* Choice (A) is a correct noun phrase. Choice (C) is a correct verb. Choice (D) is a correct adjective.

157. (B) *Than* is used in comparative forms: *worth more than education.* Choice (A) is a correct relative pronoun. Choice (C) is a correct verb. Choice (D) is a correct adverb.

158. (C) *Expect* is followed by the infinitive: *they had expected to know the results.* Choice (A) is a correct noun phrase. Choice (B) is a correct conjunction. Choice (D) is a correct noun.

159. (B) The verb must agree with the singular subject *result: The result of the evaluations and recommendations shows.* Choice (A) is a correct noun. Choice (C) is a correct comparative. Choice (D) is a correct prepositional phrase.

160. (A) When used as a conditional, *should* precedes the subject: *Should the manager receive a telephone call from Tokyo.* Choice (B) is a correct verb. Choice (C) is a correct prepositional phrase. Choice (D) is a correct pronoun.

## PART VII

161. (D) This is a list of local restaurants. Choice (A) is incorrect because price ranges are included but not the actual prices. Choice (B) confuses *people* and *the names of the restaurant*. Choice (C) associates *countries* with *USA*.

162. (B) The phone number for Ovid's is 555-6821. Choice (A) is the number for Nathan's USA. Choice (C) is the number for Papa's Kitchen. Choice (D) is the number for Peking Palace.

163. (A) Papa's Kitchen is the only restaurant listed with low prices. Choices (B), (C), and (D) have moderate or high prices.

164. (C) One Devonshire Gardens is a hotel. Choice (A) confuses *garden* and *the name of the hotel*. Choice (B) is contradicted by the references to a hotel. Choice (D) is included in the cost of the room.

165. (C) A superior double room was reserved. Choice (A) confuses a *single* and *one superior double room*. Choice (B) confuses *twin* with *double*. Choice (D) is not mentioned.

166. (D) Dinner is not included in the price of the room. Choices (A), (B), and (C) are all included in the price of the room.

167. (A) Mr. Peterman faxed his reservation. Choices (B), (C), and (D) are contradicted by *thank you for your confirmation fax*.

168. (D) A large law firm is hiring an accountant. Choice (A) confuses *a computer company* and *computer experience*. Choice (B) associates *accounting office* with *accountant*. Choice (C) confuses *advertising agency* and *job advertisement*.

169. (C) A law degree is not mentioned as a qualification. Choices (A), (B), and (D) are mentioned.

170. (B) An accountant would probably be most interested in an accounting position. Choice (A) associates *lawyer* with *law firm*. Choice (C) associates *a computer science major* with *computer experience*. Choice (D) associates *personnel director* with *supervisory experience*.

171. (C) The Assistant Controller will supervise a 7-person department. Choices (A) and (B) are the minimum number of years of supervisory experience desired. Choice (D) is the number of years of accounting experience desired.

172. (B) Applicants should have 2 or 3 years of supervisory experience. Choice (A) is not mentioned. Choice (C) is the number of people the Assistant Controller will supervise. Choice (D) is the number of years of accounting experience desired.

173. (A) This letter would be found in a microwave manual. Choices (B) and (C) are contradicted by *in this manual*. Choice (D) confuses *design store* and *product is designed to give you many years of trouble-free operation*.

174. (B) A microwave oven was purchased. Choice (A) associates *globe* and *the world*. Choice (C) repeats the word *operation* but is used out of context. Choice (D) comes free with the product purchased.

175. (D) With proper use, the product is designed to give many years of trouble-free operation. Choice (A) might be offered if the oven gives the owner trouble but is not mentioned. Choice (B) is probably hoped for by the consumer but is not a requirement for trouble-free operation. Choice (C) is not mentioned.

176. (B) The user must follow the instructions in the manual. Choices (A) and (C) are not mentioned. Choice (D) confuses *redesign the kitchen* andthe *design of the product*.

177. (D) The press release is about the Summer Consumer Electronics Show. Choice (A) is where the show will be held. Choice (B) confuses *Chicago's convention centers* and *the McCormick Convention Center in Chicago*. Choice (C) is who will be at the show.

178. (A) Thirteen hundred manufacturers will exhibit. Choice (B) is not mentioned. Choice (C) confuses *13,000* and *1,300*. Choice (D) is the number of electronics retailers and distributors expected to attend.

179. (A) Manufacturers will exhibit the latest high-technology equipment. Choice (B) associates *distribution network* and *distributors*. Choice (C) associates *retail outlets* and *retailers*. Choice (D) confuses *shelving samples* and *products will appear on retailers' shelves*.

180. (D) People would contact Metropolitan to get a loan. Choice (A) is not possible. Choice (B) associates *stock* with *financial services* and *investor*. Choice (C) confuses *getting a loan* and *loaning money*.

181. (C) Financing for hospitalization is not mentioned. Choices (A), (B), and (D) are mentioned.

182. (B) These TV listings feature business programs. Choices (A) and (D) are not mentioned. Choice (C) associates *Travelogues* with *World View*.

183. (A) Business Today begins at 2:00 P.M. Choice (B) begins at 1:00 P.M. Choice (C) begins at 4:00 P.M. Choice (D) begins at 11:30 A.M.

184. (D) Someone who wants to invest would probably watch Making Money on Channel 20. Choices (A), (B), and (C) are stations that are airing shows that would not be as helpful as Making Money, Channel 20's successful personal investing show.

185. (B) On Tuesday there will be a lecture on CD-ROM. Choice (A) associates *price* with *cost*. Choice (C) associates *lunch* with *seating* and *reservation*. Choice (D) confuses *sales presentations* and *lecture on CD-ROM*.

186. (D) The session is for people who are unfamiliar with CD-ROM. Choice (A) is incorrect because computer specialists probably have experience with CD-ROM. Choice (B) would not be interested. Choice (C) would not need a layperson's introduction.

187. (A) Seating is limited to thirty people. Choices (B), (C), and (D) are contradicted by *seating is limited to thirty*.

188. (B) This is a job announcement. Choice (A) associates *government* with *national*. Choice (C) confuses *television listing* and *providing TV service*. Choice (D) confuses *publicity for the opening of the National Career Center* and *job openings*.

189. (D) A computer specialist would be most interested in computer programming and analyst positions. Choices (A), (B), and (C) would be interested in working with a company that provides TV, radio, and marketing services but not in the computer openings.

190. (A) Ms. Makestos is looking for a job. Choice (B) is incorrect because she currently doesn't have a job. Choice (C) is not likely, since she is applying for a job in Greece. Choice (D) confuses *applying to school* and *working during her summer vacations*.

191. (A) Mr. Denikos's company is located in Athens, Greece. Choice (B) is where Ms. Hogan's company is. Choice (C) is the name of the street that International Films is on. Choice (D) confuses the similar sounds *London* and *Hogan*.

192. (B) Ms. Makestos worked at International Films during her summer vacations for the last three years. Choices (A) and (C) are contradicted by *during her summer vacations for the last three years*. Choice (D) is incorrect because she only worked during the summers.

193. (C) This is a letter of recommendation. Choice (A) is contradicted by the compliments given by Ms. Makestos. Choice (B) confuses *a job inquiry* with *a letter of support for Ms. Makestos's job application*. Choice (D) confuses *a request for information* and *call if you need further information*.

194. (A) This form would most likely be seen on a computer monitor. Choice (B) confuses *movie screen* and *computer screen*. Choice (C) associates *phone book* with *e-mail address*. Choice (D) is contradicted by *Moscow Daily Home Page found on the Internet*.

195. (D) All subscriptions are honored with a money-back guarantee. Choice (A) is true regardless of whether the subscriber is satisfied or not. Choice (B) is incorrect because if the subscriber wasn't satisfied with the subscription, he or she wouldn't want to continue receiving the publication. Choice (C) is not mentioned.

196. (C) The newspaper supports charities that deal with environmental concerns. Choices (A), (B), and (D) are not mentioned.

197. (C) Subscribers can pay by check or credit card. Choice (A) is contradicted by the numerous currencies offered as payment methods. Choices (B) and (D) are not mentioned.

198. (C) On-the-job training is the most common form of training. Choice (A) describes off-the-job training. Choice (B) confuses *ineffective* and *efficiency*. Choice (D) is not mentioned.

199. (A) On-the-job training is similar to an apprenticeship. Choice (B) is the opposite of on-the-job training. Choice (C) confuses *a supervisory position* and *an employee learns from his or her supervisor*. Choice (D) confuses *a company benefit* with *training being a benefit to the employee and the company.*

200. (A) The purpose of training is to improve the employee's efficiency. Choices (B) and (C) are not mentioned. Choice (D) is a result of a well-trained employee.

# ANSWER KEY
# PRACTICE TEST THREE

## PART I

1. (C) The fish are for sale. Choice (A) is incorrect because the man is putting ice on the fish, not fishing. Choice (B) confuses the similar sounds *salty* and *sale.* Choice (D) confuses *turning to ice* and *putting ice on the fish.*

2. (A) The two women walking up the train aisle are selling food from a basket. Choice (B) assumes one would pick vegetables and place them in the basket. Choice (C) correctly states their location but not their activity. Choice (D) correctly states their activity *(selling)* and describes what they are wearing *(uniforms),* but they are not selling uniforms.

3. (B) The people are getting off the train. Choice (A) is incorrect because the train is stopped at the station. Choice (C) confuses the similar sounds *workers* and *walkers* and *stationery* and *station.* Choice (D) is incorrect because they are all wearing hats.

4. (B) The man is operating a forklift, which is heavy equipment. Choice (A) confuses the similar sounds *fork* and *forklift.* Choice (C) talks about what the man is lifting. Choice (D) confuses the similar sounds *work* and *forklift.*

5. (B) The woman is in front of the sink. Choice (A) is incorrect because the bottles are on the shelf, not inside the cabinet. Choice (C) is incorrect because she's using the knife, not putting it on the shelf. Choice (D) is incorrect because the shelves, not the grocery store, are full of goods.

6. (D) The clock is on the wall. Choice (A) is incorrect because no one is on the stairs. Choices (B) and (C) are out of context.

7. (A) The food is on a cart. Choice (B) confuses the similar sounds *cards* and *cart.* Choice (C) cannot be determined from the picture. Choice (D) is incorrect because the groceries are on a cart, not in a refrigerator.

8. (A) The tables are set outdoors. Choice (B) is incorrect because no one is at the tables. Choice (C) associates *picnic* with *outdoors.* Choice (D) is incorrect because the chairs are at the tables, not stacked against the wall.

9. (C) The woman is painting a church scene. Choice (A) confuses *designing a church* and *painting a church.* Choice (B) associates *praying* with *church.* Choice (D) confuses the similar sounds *panting* and *painting.*

10. (A) The man is pointing the way. Choice (B) is incorrect because the man is giving directions orally, not in written form. Choice (C) confuses the similar sounds *appointment* and *pointing.* Choice (D) is incorrect because the man, not a signpost, is the guide for the motorist.

11. (A) The cars are parked in long, curved rows in the parking lot. Choice (B) confuses the similar words *park* (place for outdoor recreation) and *park* (to put a car into a space). Choice (C) confuses the similar sounds *barking* and *parking.* Choice (D) uses the associated word *cars* but is out of context.

12. (B) The cleaner is using a rag to dust the railing. Choice (A) is incorrect because he is standing by a statue, not carving one. Choice (C) uses the associated word *clean,* but he is cleaning the railing, not the floor. Choice (D) uses the associated word *rub,* but he is rubbing the railing, not his shoulder.

13. (C) The men are listening to the speaker. Choices (A) and (B) are out of context. Choice (D) is incorrect because they are not leaving the conference room.

14. (A) The car is being manufactured. Choices (B) and (C) might be done later but are not being done now in the picture. Choice (D) confuses the similar words *line* and *(assembly) line.*

15. (B) The men are watching the monitors while participating in a video conference. Choice (A) confuses *playing horseshoes* and *the horseshoe-shaped table.* Choice (C) confuses *buying a television* and *watching the monitors.* Choice (D) is out of context.

16. (C) The watches are on the wall. Choice (A) associates *time* with *watch*. Choice (B) associates *clock* with *watch*. Choice (D) confuses the similar words *watches* (looks at) and *watches* (apparatus that tells time) and *band* (musical group) and *band* (watch band).

17. (B) The equipment, the uniforms, and the environment suggest people, probably scientists, in a laboratory. Choice (A) confuses *telescopes* and *microscopes*. Choice (C) uses the associated word *physicians;* the people could be doctors in uniform, but they are not performing an operation. Choice (D) uses the associated word *uniforms*.

18. (A) A few people are seated at the counter. Choice (B) confuses the similar sounds *desert* and *dessert*. Choice (C) is incorrect because there is only one clock on the wall. Choice (D) is incorrect because the postcards are on the rack, not in the mail.

19. (B) The street has been closed off so only pedestrians and cycles can use it. Choices (A), (C), and (D) are out of context.

20. (C) This spacious, resort hotel room is clean and ready for the next guest. Choices (A), (B), and (D) are out of context.

## PART II

21. (B) *She'll be here any minute* answers *what time is she coming*. Choice (A) answers *what time is it*. Choice (C) confuses the similar sounds *combing* and *coming*.

22. (B) *Next to the post office* answers *where*. Choice (A) associates *check* with *bank*. Choice (C) confuses the similar sounds *banquet* and *bank*.

23. (A) *After breakfast* answers *when*. Choice (B) answers *when will you retire*. Choice (C) answers *how long have you been working*.

24. (A) *Maria* answers *who*. Choice (B) confuses the similar sounds *who is* and *whose*. Choice (C) confuses the similar sounds *everyone* and *who is one*.

25. (B) *It's cheaper* answers *why* by providing a reason. Choice (A) confuses the similar sounds *us* and *bus*. Choice (C) confuses the similar sounds *much* and *bus*.

26. (C) *Classical* answers *what kind of music is this*. Choice (A) confuses the similar sounds *mistake* and *music*. Choice (B) confuses the similar words *typewriter* and *type* (kind).

27. (B) *Half a dozen* answers *how many*. Choice (A) answers *how many ordered wine*. Choice (C) confuses the similar sounds *arrangements* and *oranges*.

28. (B) *I was home all day* answers *where were you*. Choice (A) repeats the words *you, were,* and *yesterday* but does not answer the question. Choice (C) answers *when are you going*.

29. (A) *The ones in French* answer *which of these books haven't you read*. Choice (B) answers *when do you read*. Choice (C) answers *which books should I read*.

30. (B) *Yesterday* answers *what day did the guest arrive*. Choice (A) answers *when will the guest arrive*. Choice (C) confuses the similar sounds *guess* and *guest*.

31. (C) *It always begins a few minutes late* answers *when will the performance begin*. Choice (A) confuses the similar sounds *foreman* and *performance*. Choice (B) repeats the word *performance* but does not answer the question.

32. (A) *Every 6 months* answers *when*. Choice (B) answers *when did you change it*. Choice (C) confuses *change the color of the car* and *change the oil in the car*.

33. (C) *The package was for me* answers *who received the package*. Choice (A) confuses the similar sounds *age* and *(pack)age*. Choice (B) answers *who opened the mail*.

34. (C) *He's too busy* is a polite response to the request. Choice (A) answers *which type of letters do you prefer*. Choice (B) confuses *send a letter* and *type a letter*.

35. (B) *There are only two chairs* answers *how many*. Choice (A) associates *sit down* with *chairs*. Choice (C) confuses the similar sounds *round* and *around*.

36. (A) *I am responding to your job announcement* answers *what is the purpose of your visit*. Choice (B) confuses the similar sounds *purse* and *purpose*. Choice (C) answers *how long*.

37. (B) *In August* answers *when.* Choice (A) confuses *taking walks* and *taking a vacation.* Choice (C) confuses the similar sounds *vacant* and *vacation.*

38. (C) *In room 300* answers *where.* Choice (A) confuses the similar sounds *eating* and *meeting.* Choice (B) confuses the similar sounds *glass* and *class.*

39. (A) *No, not yet* answers *is it time for lunch.* Choice (B) associates *eat* with *lunch* and answers where. Choice (C) associates *pass the salt* with *lunch.*

40. (B) *We want to hear the news* answers *why* by providing a reason. Choice (A) answers *where is the radio.* Choice (C) confuses the similar sounds *ready* and *radio.*

41. (C) *About a dozen* answers *how many.* Choice (A) answers *where.* Choice (B) confuses the similar sounds *drawing* with *drawer* and *pen* with *pencil.*

42. (B) *Two miles from here* answers *where.* Choice (A) answers *when do you play golf.* Choice (C) confuses the similar sounds *(be)cause* with *course* and *Gulf* with *golf.*

43. (A) *On time* answers *when did the plane take off.* Choice (B) confuses *the plane's takeoff* and *take off the shirt.* Choice (C) associates *leave* with *take off.*

44. (C) *The subway* answers *what is the fastest way to get downtown.* Choice (A) confuses the opposites *slow* and *fast.* Choice (B) confuses the similar sounds *tallest* and *fastest.*

45. (B) *About two blocks* answers *how far.* Choice (A) associates *hungry* with *restaurant.* Choice (C) associates *serves good food* with *restaurant.*

46. (A) *I didn't sleep last night* answers *why are you so tired.* Choice (B) confuses the similar sound *tire* with *tired* and *air* with *are.* Choice (C) confuses the similar sounds *required* with *tired, wear* with *why are,* and *ties* and *tired.*

47. (B) *A cleaning service* answers *who cleans your office.* Choice (A) answers *where is your office.* Choice (C) confuses *cleaning the windows* and *cleaning the office.*

48. (A) *On the corner* answers *where.* Choice (B) confuses the similar sounds *shop* and *stop.* Choice (C) answers *how often.*

49. (B) *Bob's desk* answers *whose desk.* Choice (A) answers where is your desk. Choice (C) repeats the word *window* but does not answer the question.

50. (C) *Let's clean up the office first* answers *what shall we do first.* Choice (A) confuses the opposites *last* and *first.* Choice (B) confuses the similar sounds *towel* and *shall.*

## PART III

51. (B) The woman is upset because the man didn't plan ahead and was late. Choice (A) is incorrect because he already got gas. Choice (C) is not mentioned. Choice (D) is incorrect because the woman had to wait.

52. (D) They need eighteen chairs. Choice (A) is how many more chairs they'll need. Choice (B) confuses the similar sounds *eight* and *eighteen.* Choice (C) is how many chairs they currently have.

53. (B) The woman parked the car in the garage across the street. Choice (A) is what the man uses for comparison. Choice (C) is where the man thought she parked it. Choice (D) confuses *the lot next door,* which is where she said she did not park.

54. (A) The speakers are waiting to buy movie tickets. Choice (B) confuses *change lines* and *make change.* Choice (C) confuses *solve a problem* and *there's a problem.* Choice (D) is what the ticket seller cannot do.

55. (D) The woman asks the taxi driver to wait for her. Choice (A) is incorrect because she is at the store; she wants to see if it is open. Choice (B) confuses *hire a taxi* and the driver's comment about *not being a limousine.* Choice (C) confuses the similar sounds *door* and *store.*

56. (A) The speakers are putting things away. Choice (B) confuses *painting the garage* and *putting painting materials in the garage.* Choice (C) confuses *climbing a ladder* and *putting the ladder in the garage.* Choice (D) confuses *cleaning the brushes* and *putting the brushes in the garage.*

57. (A) The speakers are hanging pictures. Choice (B) confuses *measuring the children* and *measuring distances to hang the paintings.* Choice (C) confuses *adding two figures* and the measurements mentioned. Choice (D) is out of context.

58. (C) The man mentions his hammer and saw, which are tools used by carpenters. Choice (A) associates *runner* with *track* and *someone ran off with*. Choice (B) confuses the similar sounds *farmer* and *hammer*. Choice (D) associates *judge* with *gavel* by confusing a gavel and a hammer.

59. (B) The conversation takes place in a boat. Choice (A) is where the man thinks the woman would rather be. Choice (C) associates *nursery* with *rocking*. Choice (D) confuses *fish store* and *fishing*.

60. (C) The woman will finish in twenty minutes. Choice (A) is how long it takes her for each page. Choice (B) confuses *ten minutes* and *ten pages*. Choice (D) is when they have to leave.

61. (B) The speakers are playing golf. Choice (A) confuses the similar sounds *tea* and *tee*. Choice (C) confuses the similar sounds *bowl(ing)* and *ball*. Choice (D) confuses the similar words *right* (direction) and *right* (I agree).

62. (A) The speakers are leaving because the play is boring. Choice (B) confuses *the play being over* and *not having to stay to the end*. Choice (C) takes the expression *before I fall asleep*, meaning *this is so boring*, literally. Choice (D) confuses *they were told to leave* and *who told us to come see it*.

63. (B) This conversation takes place in a bank. Choice (A) associates *forest* with *branches* by confusing the similar words *branches* (on a tree) and *branches* (various office locations). Choice (C) associates *river* with *bank*. Choice (D) associates *florist shop* with *branches*.

64. (D) The moving van is coming tomorrow. Choice (A) is when the woman sorted through her clothes. Choice (B) confuses the similar sounds *noon* and *soon*. Choice (C) is when the woman will leave.

65. (B) The man tells the woman she shouldn't feed the pigeons because they breed diseases; the man insinuates that it's not wise to touch them. Choice (A) is not mentioned. Choice (C) is contradicted by *where else are they going to find food*. Choice (D) is not mentioned.

66. (D) The man is talking about his sales experience, so he is probably interviewing for a job. Choice (A) confuses *filing a complaint* and *working directly with customers*. Choice (B) is what he did for eight years. Choice (C) associates *shopping* with *retail store*.

67. (A) The woman is afraid of not being able to follow the man and getting lost. Choice (B) confuses *being followed* and *following the man*. Choice (C) confuses *being afraid of driving fast* and *being afraid the man will drive fast so she won't be able to follow him*. Choice (D) is not mentioned.

68. (C) The conversation takes place on a small farm. Choice (A) is out of context. Choice (B) associates *garden* with *orchards* and *flowers*. Choice (D) confuses the similar sounds *props* and *crops*, by associating *props* with *theatre*.

69. (A) The man is a gardener. Choice (B) associates *banker* with *tree branches* by confusing the similar sounds *branches* and *bushes*. Choice (C) associates *florists* with *flowers*. Choice (D) associates *park ranger* with *planting trees*.

70. (A) This year's attendance has doubled, since last year's attendance was half the amount of this year's. Choices (B) and (C) confuse this year's and last year's attendance. Choice (D) is incorrect because 4,000 people will attend this year.

71. (D) The woman forgot to call the man; it slipped her mind. Choice (A) is not mentioned. Choices (B) and (C) are what the man thought the woman would use as reasons for not calling.

72. (D) The business has been in the family for four generations. Choice (A) is when the woman started working there. Choice (B) confuses the similar sounds *forty* and *four*. Choice (C) confuses *a lifetime* and *my entire life*.

73. (B) The woman wants to borrow a stamp for a postcard. Choice (A) confuses *going overseas* and *a stamp for an overseas letter*. Choice (C) confuses *write a letter* and *send a letter*. Choice (D) confuses *buy a postcard* and *send a postcard*.

74. (C) Since they are talking about a program that was on last night and is on every Wednesday, it must be Thursday. Choice (A) is not possible. Choice (B) is the night the program was aired. Choice (D) is not possible.

75. (A) The woman was a dinner guest. Choice (B) confuses *a chef* and the fact that the man is cooking dinner. Choice (C) is what the man was. Choice (D) associates *dishwasher* with the man's reference to *washing the dishes.*

76. (C) The speakers are at a swimming pool. Choice (A) confuses *shower* and *pool.* Choice (B) confuses *racetrack* and *I'll race you.* Choice (D) is contradicted by the reference to *swimming.*

77. (D) The man's plane leaves at 2:00. Choice (A) is when the man will have to leave for the airport. Choice (B) is when he has to be at the airport. Choice (C) confuses *1:30* and *11:30.*

78. (A) The woman thinks the man is taking too long to read the article. Choice (B) describes the article. Choice (C) confuses *growing taller* and *at the rate he's reading.* Choice (D) is not mentioned.

79. (D) The speakers will get a ten-pound bag of potatoes. Choice (A) confuses one pound and one ten-pound bag. Choice (B) is the amount the man first mentioned. Choice (C) is the amount the recipe calls for.

80. (A) This conversation takes place in an elevator in a department store. Choice (B) confuses *at home* and *home furnishings.* Choice (C) confuses the similar sounds *escalator* and *elevator.* Choice (D) is where the woman wants to go.

## PART IV

81. (B) It's summer. Choices (A), (C), and (D) are contradicted by *it's a hot and humid summer day.*

82. (A) There's a chance of seasonal showers late this afternoon. Choices (B), (C), and (D) are not mentioned.

83. (D) Dr. Miller's office is closed on Friday. Choices (A), (B), and (C) are days the office is open.

84. (A) Someone would call 555-3212 to report a dental emergency. Choices (B), (C), and (D) are not mentioned.

85. (D) This announcement is being heard in a restaurant. Choices (A), (B), and (C) are out of context.

86. (C) The customers are asked to leave because there is a small fire in the kitchen. Choice (A) is not mentioned. Choice (B) confuses *lost their belongings* and *gather your personal belongings.* Choice (D) is not mentioned.

87. (A) All personnel must report to the south lawn for morning exercises. Choices (B), (C), and (D) are all contradicted by *all personnel.*

88. (A) The exercises will last thirty minutes, from 10:30 to 11:00. Choices (B) and (C) are contradicted by *from 10:30 to 11:00.* Choice (D) confuses *all morning* and *morning exercises.*

89. (B) The exercises will take place on the south lawn. Choice (A) confuses *south gym* and *south lawn* and associates *gym* with *exercise.* Choices (C) and (D) are not mentioned.

90. (B) The company rents computers. Choice (A) confuses the similar words *models* (representations of an object) and *models* (brands). Choice (C) confuses *help find stolen computers* and *help you find a computer.* Choice (D) confuses *lease cars* and *lease computers.*

91. (B) The minimum rental period is by the day. Choices (A), (C), and (D) are longer periods of time.

92. (D) The announcement is about an earthquake in Japan. Choice (A) associates *riot* with *personal harm* and *property damage.* Choices (B) and (C) are natural disasters that are not mentioned.

93. (B) There was little damage to property. Choices (A), (C), and (D) are contradicted by *little damage.*

94. (A) Flight departures are heard at an airport. Choice (B) associates *plane* with *airport.* Choice (C) associates *consulate* with *passports.* Choice (D) associates *bus station* with *gate 16.*

95. (B) The plane departs from gate 16. Choice (A) confuses the similar sounds *fifteen* and *sixteen.* Choice (C) is the flight number. Choice (D) confuses the similar sounds *sixty* and *sixteen.*

96. (B) The second and third levels are reserved for employee parking. Choice (A) is contradicted by the two levels mentioned. Choice (C) confuses three levels with the third level. Choice (D) confuses the similar sounds *four* and *for.*

97. (A) Red spaces are for maintenance vehicles. Choice (B) must be parked in the blue spaces. Choice (C) is not mentioned. Choice (D) confuses *spaces for tow trucks* and *cars parked in the wrong spaces being towed.*

98. (A) Yellow spaces are reserved for management. Choice (B) are reserved for employees. Choice (C) is not mentioned. Choice (D) is contradicted by *reserved spaces.*

99. (D) Tourists are listening to the tour guide. Choice (A) associates *politicians* with *the United Nations.* Choice (B) is who would be giving the announcement. Choice (C) associates *diplomats* with *the United Nations.*

100. (C) The tour group is traveling by bus. Choices (A), (B), and (D) are contradicted by *be back on the bus by 2:00.*

## PART V

101. (C) *Consulting firm* is a business term. Choice (A) is a noun referring to a thing. Choice (B) is a noun referring to a person. Choice (D) is a verb.

102. (A) *Count on* means *to depend on.* Choice (B) means *to start counting at a particular point.* Choice (C) means *to include.* Choice (D) means *to total.*

103. (D) A past action that happens after a previous past action is in the simple past tense. Choice (A) is the future tense. Choice (B) is the present tense. Choice (C) is the present perfect.

104. (D) An unreal condition in the present tense may use *could* in the result clause. Choices (A), (B), and (C) are not possible modals for an unreal condition.

105. (A) Someone else will deliver the equipment, so the past participle is used. Choice (B) is the present participle. Choices (C) and (D) cannot follow *want.*

106. (B) *Therefore* indicates a cause-and-effect relationship. Choices (A) and (C) indicate an unexpected result. Choice (D) indicates purpose.

107. (B) *Because of* indicates a cause-and-effect relationship and can be followed by a noun phrase. Choice (A) must be followed by a subject and verb. Choice (C) indicates an unexpected result and must be followed by a subject and verb. Choice (D) must be followed by a subject and verb when indicating a cause-and-effect relationship.

108. (C) *In* is used to indicate time during a month. Choice (A) may be used with *month* but indicates the immediate future. Choice (B) is used with dates. Choice (D) *the* is not used with names of months.

109. (B) Adverbs of definite frequency may appear at the end of a sentence. Choices (A), (C), and (D) are not appropriate positions for definite frequency adverbs.

110. (D) *And* joins items equally. Choice (A) indicates a contrast between items. Choice (B) is usually paired with *nor.* Choice (C) indicates sequence or cause and effect.

111. (C) *In* is used to indicate location within cities. Choice (A) is used with specific time. Choice (B) is an article, not a preposition. Choice (D) indicates direction toward.

112. (C) *Consequently* indicates cause and effect. Choice (A) summarizes previous points. Choice (B) adds additional information. Choice (D) indicates an example.

113. (A) The employees are the ones who are leaving, so the simple form of the verb is used. Choice (B) is the past tense. Choice (C) is the past progressive. Choice (D) is the past tense in the passive form.

114. (A) Present or future possible conditions use present tense in the *if* clause. Choice (B) is required in unreal conditions with be. Choice (C) is the present perfect. Choice (D) is the future.

115. (D) The clients are the ones who seem interested, so the simple form of the verb is used. Choices (A) and (C) are progressive forms, which are rarely used with stative verbs. Choice (B) is the future tense.

116. (C) *Find out* is a two-word verb meaning *to uncover information.* Choices (A), (B), and (D) do not complete the verb.

117. (A) An action that starts in the past and continues to the present uses the present perfect tense. Choice (B) is the past tense. Choice (C) is the present. Choice (D) is the future.

118. (D) A past unreal condition that uses the past perfect in the *if* clause uses *could* or *would* and the present perfect in the result clause. Choice (A) is the past tense. Choice (B) is the future. Choice (C) is the present conditional.

119. (D) Someone else will fax the invoices, so the past participle is used. Choice (A) is the simple form. Choice (B) is the gerund. Choice (C) is passive.

120. (B) *Were* is the form of *be* required for the *if* clause of an unreal condition. Choice (A) is the present tense. Choice (C) is the future. Choice (D) is conditional.

121. (D) *And* joins items equally. Choice (A) indicates a choice among items. Choices (B) and (C) are not coordinating conjunctions.

122. (A) The simple past tense is required. Choice (B) is past tense but does not agree with the singular subject *shortage*. Choice (C) is present perfect. Choice (D) is present perfect and does not agree with *shortage*.

123. (C) *Should be given* indicates an intention or recommendation. Choice (A) is past tense and does not agree with *funds*. Choice (B) requires an active subject. Choice (D) *is given* is present tense and does not agree with *funds*.

124. (A) Someone else will deposit the paychecks, so the past participle is used. Choice (B) is the present participle. Choice (C) is the present tense passive. Choice (D) is the simple form.

125. (B) *Therefore* indicates a cause and effect or a result. Choice (A) indicates an unexpected result. Choice (C) indicates simultaneous occurrence. Choice (D) indicates a contrast.

126. (D) *Throughout* is used to mean many different locations within a city or other area. Choices (A) and (B) may be used with street locations but not with cities. Choice (C) means *concerning*.

127. (A) *Retirement plan* is a business term. Choice (B) is the present participle. Choice (C) is the simple form. Choice (D) is the past participle.

128. (D) *After* indicates a time sequence for events. Choice (A) indicates simultaneous action. Choice (B) indicates cause and effect and is not followed by a subject and verb. Choice (C) indicates simultaneous action but is not followed by a subject and verb.

129. (C) *Already* is an adverb that indicates an action that has taken place sooner than expected. Choice (A) indicates the end of a time limit. Choice (B) means *at any point in time*. Choice (D) is an adjective.

130. (C) *When* indicates a time sequence, especially where one action is influenced by another. Choice (A) is not logical. Choice (B) is not the correct form *as soon as*. Choice (D) cannot be followed by a subject and a verb.

131. (D) *Of* is used to relate portions of time to the whole. Choice (A) indicates direction toward. Choice (B) is used with specific times of day. Choice (C) indicates source or origin.

132. (A) *For example* indicates a specific instance of a more general statement. Choice (B) indicates time sequence. Choices (C) and (D) indicate unexpected results.

133. (D) The employees are the ones who will feel like family, so the simple form of the verb is used. Choice (A) is the present participle. Choice (B) is the present tense singular. Choice (C) is the past tense.

134. (C) Present real conditions may use present tense in the *if* clause. Choice (A) is past tense. Choice (B) is future perfect. Choice (D) is present tense but is an active form.

135. (B) *Will be opening* indicates a future time consistent with *within the next year*. Choice (A) is past tense. Choice (C) is present perfect. Choice (D) is conditional.

136. (D) *Stop by* is a two-word verb that means *to see someone briefly*. Choice (A) means *to interrupt a trip briefly*. Choice (B) means *to stop for a specific purpose* (followed by a noun, as in *stop for gas*). Choice (C) means *stop in order to complete an action*.

137. (A) *Dispute* means *an argument or disagreement.* Choice (B) is the gerund. Choice (C) is an adjective. Choice (D) is a noun referring to a person in a dispute.

138. (C) *Authorized* is an adjective meaning *a dealer who is authorized (to deal with a particular product or service).* Choice (A) is a noun referring to a person. Choice (B) is a noun referring to a thing. Choice (D) is an adjective meaning *dependent upon authority.*

139. (B) *Leave out* is a two-word verb meaning *to omit.* Choice (A) indicates *leaving with a destination in mind.* Choice (C) means *to bequeath a possession.* Choice (D) indicates *leaving a location.*

140. (B) The simple future tense is required. Choices (A) and (D) have stative verbs which are rarely used in the progressive. Choice (C) is the future perfect.

## PART VI

141. (C) The verb must be consistent with the time indicated: *that the bank announced bankruptcy late last week.* Choice (A) is a correct preposition. Choice (B) is a correct relative pronoun. Choice (D) is a correct time expression.

142. (C) Comparatives require the *-er* or *more* form of the adjective: *farther than anyone had anticipated.* Choice (A) is a correct noun phrase. Choice (B) is a correct conjunction. Choice (D) is a correct verb.

143. (A) The infinitive form is required: *advised me to talk to my colleague.* Choice (B) is a correct gerund. Choice (C) is a correct article. Choice (D) is a correct prepositional phrase.

144. (D) *In* rather than *at* should be used with cities: *a new branch of their store in Paris.* Choice (A) is a correct noun phrase. Choice (B) is a correct relative pronoun. Choice (C) is a correct verb.

145. (D) Superlative comparisons require the *-est* or *most* form of the adjective: *held in the most exclusive restaurant downtown.* Choice (A) is subject plus negative verb. Choice (B) is a correct noun phrase. Choice (C) is a correct verb plus preposition.

146. (A) Singular count nouns must be used with an article: *A new shopping mall is being planned.* Choice (B) is a correct preposition. Choice (C) is a correct conjunction. Choice (D) is a correct noun phrase.

147. (B) Indirect questions use subject-verb order: *wanted to know when the last staff meeting was.* Choice (A) is a correct infinitive. Choice (C) is a correct verb. Choice (D) is a correct pronoun.

148. (A) The subject form *I* is required: *that you and I report our findings.* Choice (B) is a correct verb. Choice (C) is a correct noun. Choice (D) is a correct noun phrase.

149. (D) *Who have experience* refers to *engineers and scientists,* not to *positions: engineers and scientists who have experience.* Choice (A) is a correct noun. Choices (B) and (C) are correct verbs.

150. (A) The investors have the opinion so the past participle is used: *The opinion held by most investors.* Choice (B) is a correct quantifier. Choice (C) is a correct verb. Choice (D) is a correct infinitive.

151. (B) The pronoun should agree with *employees: for the employees and their families.* Choice (A) is a correct article. Choice (C) is a correct adverb of frequency. Choice (D) is a correct verb.

152. (C) The verb must agree with the subject: *The editors . . . have agreed to accept advertisements.* Choice (A) is a correct prepositional phrase. Choice (B) is a correct relative pronoun. Choice (D) is a correct noun.

153. (A) *Remarks* should be modified by the adjective *spoken: the executive's spoken remarks.* Choices (B) and (C) form a correct comparative. Choice (D) is a correct noun phrase.

154. (B) Plural nouns that are nonspecified do not require an article: *to send thank-you notes to their customers.* Choice (A) is a correct noun phrase. Choice (C) is a correct prepositional phrase. Choice (D) is a correct noun.

155. (B) *All* refers to the plural *people,* so a plural verb is required: *all the people who are interested.* Choice (A) is a correct pronoun. Choice (C) is a correct prepositional phrase. Choice (D) is a correct verb.

156. (B) The pronoun should agree with *residents: The residents ... need to organize themselves.* Choice (A) is a correct preposition. Choice (C) is a correct noun. Choice (D) is a correct verb.

157. (B) The verb should agree with the subject *group: A group ... has discovered.* Choice (A) is a correct conjunction. Choice (C) is a correct preposition. Choice (D) is a correct verb.

158. (A) The subject should not be repeated: *Total retail sales were estimated.* Choice (B) is a correct comparative. Choice (C) is a correct adjective. Choice (D) is a correct noun.

159. (A) When used as a conditional, *should* precedes the subject: *should the client call.* Choice (B) is a correct conjunction. Choice (C) is a correct infinitive. Choice (D) is a correct prepositional phrase.

160. (B) Items joined by *and* should have the same form: *looking for the perfect location and assessing the needs of their company.* Choice (A) is a correct prepositional phrase. Choice (C) is a correct article. Choice (D) is a correct gerund.

## PART VII

161. (C) The memo is about requesting vacation time. Choices (A), (B), and (D) are not mentioned.

162. (B) All requests for vacation leave must be submitted at least four weeks before one's vacation begins. Choice (A) is not mentioned. Choice (C) confuses *before two weeks* and *approval takes two weeks.* Choice (D) confuses *within two weeks* and *approval takes two weeks.*

163. (A) Approval of the vacation request takes two weeks. Choice (B) should be done four weeks in advance. Choice (C) is not mentioned. Choice (D) associates *boat cruises* with *vacation.*

164. (C) The world population in 1950 was 2.5 billion. Choice (A) confuses *half a billion* and *2.5 billion.* Choice (B) was the population in 1925. Choice (D) confuses *5 billion* and *2.5 billion.*

165. (D) In 1975 the population reached 4 billion. Choice (A) is when the population reached 1 billion. Choice (B) is when the population reached 2 billion. Choice (C) is when the population reached 2.5 billion.

166. (A) In 1900 the population was 1 billion, half of 2 billion. Choices (B), (C), and (D) have populations of over 2 billion.

167. (B) The article is about hiring employees. Choice (A) confuses *reading a newspaper* and *placing job ads in newspapers.* Choice (C) is not mentioned. Choice (D) confuses *going to high school* and *high schools as a source of new employees.*

168. (A) High schools are mentioned as a common source of new employees. Choice (B) is an inside source. Choice (C) confuses the similar sounds *spies* and *high (school).* Choice (D) is not mentioned.

169. (C) Firms also use newspapers to help locate job applicants. Choices (A), (B), and (D) are not mentioned.

170. (B) Virtual Desktop 2.0 is a computer software program. Choice (A) confuses *desk* and *computer desktop.* Choice (C) is where the program prints. Choice (D) associates *TV* with *screen* by confusing *TV screen* and *computer screen.*

171. (A) All programs written for Virtual Desktop have a similar look. Choice (B) confuses the similar sounds *cost* and *DOS.* Choice (C) is not mentioned. Choice (D) confuses *their printers* and *the program prints what you see on the screen.*

172. (B) If several programs are in the computer's memory, it means they're open and the user can easily move from one application to another. Choice (A) is not mentioned. Choice (C) is incorrect because having several programs open at once uses more computer memory. Choice (D) is not mentioned.

173. (C) AeroSys is a Berlin-based company. Choices (A), (B), and (D) are major cities that are not mentioned.

174. (B) AeroSys has made an agreement to provide a satellite system. Choices (A) and (C) are what will be able to communicate with each other. Choice (D) is what will use the communications.

175. (D) Ticketing service is not mentioned. Choices (A), (B), and (C) are all mentioned.

176. (D) Textbooks are not mentioned as part of the program. Choices (A), (B), and (C) are all mentioned as part of the program.

177. (D) Students can work and play with the computer whenever they like. Choices (A), (B), and (C) are contradicted by *whenever they like.*

178. (A) Families of the students are encouraged to get into the act. Choice (B) confuses *actors* and the expression *get into the act* (get involved). Choice (C) confuses the similar sounds *away* and *play*. Choice (D) is not mentioned.

179. (B) The article is about types of communication. Choice (A) associates *marketing* with *communication(s).* Choice (C) is a type of communication. Choice (D) is mentioned but is not the main topic.

180. (A) Words are the most commonly used form of communication. Choices (B), (C), and (D) are not used as much as words.

181. (D) Actions are the most important face-to-face communication. Choices (A), (B), and (C) are effective communication tools for distance.

182. (C) Television is not an example of an action. Choices (A), (B), and (D) are all mentioned.

183. (B) Health care professionals would most likely read this announcement about health care for the elderly. Choice (A) is not likely. Choice (C) associates *word processors* with *computing* and *computerized products*. Choice (D) is not likely.

184. (C) Blood pressure monitors could be a computerized product that monitors health. Choices (A) and (B) are not related to health care. Choice (D) is not a computerized product.

185. (B) The plant was shut down because it was causing unhealthy levels of mercury. Choice (A) confuses *too much trash* and *giant trash incinerator*. Choice (C) is incorrect because changing waste into energy was the plant's purpose. Choice (D) is contradicted by *the environmental agency shutting it down.*

186. (D) The plant function was to turn waste into energy. Choice (A) is something the plant does but not its primary function. Choice (B) is the function of environmental officials. Choice (C) is an unexpected result of the conversion process.

187. (B) The Stummering Corporation has had a problem with absenteeism. Choice (A) is who decided something had to be done. Choice (C) associates *low pay* with *the cash incentive offered.* Choice (D) is not mentioned.

188. (A) The average employee was showing up late three times a week. Choice (B) confuses *fifteen times a week* and *fifteen minutes late.* Choice (C) confuses *three times between January and June* and *three times a week between January and June.* Choice (D) confuses *fifteen times* and *fifteen minutes.*

189. (B) Every worker who was on time would be eligible for a cash award. Choices (A), (C), and (D) might be incentives but are not mentioned.

190. (B) The letter is written to reject a job applicant. Choice (A) was the purpose of Mr. Porter's letter. Choice (C) is something usually asked for before a company makes an applicant a job offer. Choice (D) confuses *to learn about the corporation* and *thank you for your interest in the corporation.*

191. (A) Mr. Porter included his resume with his letter of inquiry. Choices (B) and (C) are not mentioned. Choice (D) is what Mr. Porter's letter was in response to.

192. (C) Mr. Porter is an accountant. Choice (A) is Mr. Simons's position. Choice (B) associates *detective* with *inquiry*. Choice (D) is not mentioned.

193. (D) They received twenty applications from qualified accountants. Choice (A) is the day they received Mr. Porter's letter. Choice (B) is the day the letter was sent. Choice (C) confuses the similar sounds *eleven* and *Allen.*

194. (A) This advertisement is for a subscription to a monthly magazine. Choice (B) is contradicted by *monthly*. Choice (C) associates *calendar* with *1 year*. Choice (D) confuses *office supplies* and *office delivery.*

195. (C) The cover price is $30. Choice (A) confuses *$12* and *12 issues*. Choice (B) is the subscription price. Choice (D) confuses *$60* and *6 weeks*.

196. (C) The first issue will be mailed within 6 weeks. Choices (A), (B), and (D) are contradicted by *6 weeks*.

197. (D) The busiest day is Monday, and the busiest times are 12:00 to 2:00. Choice (A) is when the center is open. Choice (B) is contradicted by *the busiest day is Monday*. Choice (C) is the busiest times but not the busiest days.

198. (A) The center is open from 9:00 A.M. to 5:00 P.M. Monday through Friday. Choice (B) is the busiest day. Choice (C) confuses the conjunction *and* with the preposition *through*. Choice (D) is the busiest times.

199. (B) A new computer system is being sold. Choice (A) associates *adding machine* with *add figures*. Choice (C) associates *ballpoint pen* with the name of the product, *Pen-In-Hand*. Choice (D) is contradicted by *forget about keyboards*.

200. (B) The advantage of the product is that no keyboard is required. Choice (A) is not mentioned. Choice (C) is incorrect because writing is all you do. Choice (D) is contradicted by the fact that you can add figures on the computer.

# ANSWER KEY
# PRACTICE TEST FOUR

## PART I

1. (A) The woman is wearing protective clothing. Choices (B), (C), and (D) are out of context.
2. (C) The man is cleaning the pool. Choice (A) is incorrect because the pool, not the water glass, is empty. Choice (B) associates *swimmers* with *swimming pool*. Choice (D) is incorrect because no one is at the pool.
3. (A) The man is pulling his suitcases. Choice (B) is incorrect because the woman is in front of, not behind, the man. Choice (C) is what they might have done earlier but is not what they're doing now. Choice (D) is incorrect because the bags are being pulled, not weighed.
4. (B) The boys are playing basketball. Choice (A) confuses the similar words *laundry basket* and *basket(ball)*. Choice (C) is incorrect because there is only one ball. Choice (D) confuses the similar sounds *bowl(ing)* and *ball*.
5. (C) The woman is talking on the phone. Choice (A) confuses *the cord being cut* and *the telephone cord* in the picture. Choice (B) is incorrect because the woman is on her office phone, not in a telephone booth. Choice (D) confuses *studying the map* and *the map hanging on the wall*.
6. (B) Planes surround the gates of a satellite terminal at an airport. Choice (A) confuses the similar sounds *pane* and *plane*. Choice (C) confuses the similar sounds *trains* and *planes*. Choice (D) confuses the similar sounds *cranes* and *planes*.
7. (A) The ferry is crossing the water. Choice (B) might be true but is not what is seen in the picture. Choice (C) confuses *a sailboat* with *the ferry*. Choice (D) confuses *a tanker* with *the ferry*, which is moving in the water, not in dry dock.
8. (C) A light is above the drafting table. Choice (A) confuses *first draft* and *drafting table*. Choice (B) confuses the similar sounds *rafting* and *drafting*. Choice (D) is incorrect because there is no one at the table.
9. (D) The man is working at his computer. Choice (A) confuses the similar sounds *mouse* (rodent) and *mouse* (computer peripheral). Choice (B) confuses *waiting on the corner* and *working in the corner*. Choice (C) is incorrect because he's wearing, not changing, a sweater.
10. (B) The woman is behind the counter. Choice (A) confuses *tourists boarding the bus* and *the tourist information sign*. Choice (C) confuses the similar words *directions* and *information*. Choice (D) confuses *information is in the directory* with *the information sign*.
11. (A) The people are in a waiting area. Choices (B), (C), and (D) are out of context.
12. (D) The musician is playing for money. Choice (A) associates *jazz* with *saxophone* and is also incorrect because the man's hair, not the jazz club, is long and dark. Choice (B) confuses *collecting stamps* and *collecting money*. Choice (C) is incorrect because the saxophonist, not the orchestra, might be tuning up.
13. (A) The seamstress is making an alteration. Choice (B) confuses the similar sounds *waitress* and *seamstress*. Choice (C) confuses the similar sounds *actress* and *seamstress*. Choice (D) is out of context.
14. (C) The fire fighters are fighting a fire. Choice (A) is incorrect because they're fighting a fire, not looking for a light. Choice (B) confuses the similar sounds *lighting* and *fighting*. Choice (D) confuses *watering a garden* and *putting water on a fire*.
15. (C) The people sitting around the table are talking about some issues that affect their work. Choice (A) confuses the similar sounds *setting* and *sitting*. Choice (B) uses the associated word *board*. Choice (D) is out of context.
16. (B) The woman is reaching for the controls. Choice (A) is incorrect because she is reaching at an angle, not measuring an angle. Choice (C) associates *answering a question* with *raising her hand*. Choice (D) associates *boarding a plane* with *pilot*.

17. (A) The man is pouring a cup of coffee. Choice (B) confuses the similar sounds *pocket* and *pot*. Choice (C) is incorrect because he is pouring, not spilling, liquid. Choice (D) has already been done.

18. (B) The people are reading newspapers. Choice (A) is incorrect because they are already seated at a table. Choice (C) associates *library* with *reading*. Choice (D) associates *menus* with *restaurant*.

19. (A) The man is washing his windows. Choice (B) associates *film* with the *video sign*. Choice (C) is incorrect because the bucket is on the ground outside of the store. Choice (D) confuses *washing machine* and *washing windows*.

20. (D) The shoes line the wall. Choice (A) is incorrect because the shelves are full, not empty. Choice (B) confuses *closet* with *shelves*. Choice (C) associates *running* with *sneakers*.

## PART II

21. (A) *At 8 A.M.* answers *what time*. Choice (B) confuses *the door* and *the bank*. Choice (C) associates *clock* with *what time*.

22. (C) *In the parking lot* answers *where did you park*. Choice (A) answers *when*. Choice (B) repeats the word *car* but does not answer the question.

23. (B) *Every evening* answers *how often*. Choice (A) confuses the similar words *watch* (noun) and *watch* (verb). Choice (C) answers *where*.

24. (B) *I'm late for a meeting* answers *why* by providing a reason. Choice (A) confuses the similar sounds *talks* and *walks*. Choice (C) answers *why are they walking*.

25. (A) *My name is Ralph Smith* answers *who is calling*. Choice (B) answers *who am I calling*. Choice (C) does not answer the question.

26. (B) *Any minute* answers *when do you expect your visitor*. Choice (A) answers *how long was her visit*. Choice (C) confuses the similar words *visit* and *visitor*.

27. (C) *My car* answers *whose car shall we take*. Choice (A) confuses the similar sounds *shallow* and *shall*. Choice (B) confuses *bus* and *car*.

28. (A) *Not very* answers *how hungry are you*. Choice (B) confuses the similar sounds *Hungary* and *hungry*. Choice (C) answers *why are you hungry*.

29. (C) *The first one I received* answers *which letter will you answer first*. Choice (A) answers *when will you mail the letter*. Choice (B) associates *envelope* with *letter* and confuses the opposites *last* and *first*.

30. (A) *Yes, your wife called* answers the *yes/no* question *do I have any messages*. Choice (B) confuses the similar sounds *massage* and *message*. Choice (C) confuses the similar sounds *ages* and *messages*.

31. (B) *It rained all morning* answers *why is the ground wet*. Choice (A) confuses the similar sounds *grown* with *ground* and *yet* with *wet*. Choice (C) confuses the similar sounds *round* and *ground*.

32. (A) *In the files* answers *where*. Choice (B) confuses the similar sounds *voice* and *invoices*. Choice (C) repeats the word *invoice* but does not answer the question.

33. (B) *I'm too busy* answers *why don't you take a vacation*. Choice (A) answers *why don't you take them*. Choice (C) confuses the similar sounds *transportation* and *vacation*.

34. (A) *Green is a good color* answers *what color will you paint the walls*. Choice (B) answers *why*. Choice (C) confuses the similar words *read* and *red* and does not answer the question.

35. (B) *We all like sugar* answers *do any of you like sugar in your coffee*. Choice (A) confuses the similar sounds *cigars* and *sugar*. Choice (C) repeats the word *sugar* but does not answer the question.

36. (A) *About three more months* answers *how much time will it take*. Choice (B) answers *how high is the building*. Choice (C) answers *when will you be here*.

37. (C) *That newspaper belongs to me* answers *whose newspaper is on the table*. Choice (A) answers *where is the newspaper*. Choice (B) confuses the similar sounds *new* and *news(paper)*.

38. (B) *Yes, the mail is on your desk* answers *did the mail come yet*. Choice (A) answers *did you eat yet*. Choice (C) answers *did anyone come*.

39. (B) *Management* answers *what was the speech about.* Choice (A) answers *how long did the speech last.* Choice (C) confuses the opposites *first* and *last.*

40. (A) *On time at 6:40* answers *when did the train arrive.* Choice (B) confuses the similar sounds *rain* and *train.* Choice (C) answers *how did they arrive.*

41. (C) *I have to finish this report* answers *why are you working late.* Choice (A) associates *night* with *late.* Choice (B) answers *why are you leaving.*

42. (A) *In my office* answers *where.* Choice (B) answers *where did you apply.* Choice (C) answers *how long did they wait.*

43. (C) *I like the new hotel by the river* is a recommendation. Choice (A) confuses the similar sounds *reservation* and *recommendation.* Choice (B) confuses *good enough* and *good hotel.*

44. (B) *I prefer a pen* answers *which do you prefer.* Choice (A) repeats the word *pencil* but does not answer the question. Choice (C) repeats the word *pen* but does not answer the question.

45. (A) *Nine employees* answers *how many employees do you have.* Choice (B) confuses the similar sounds *hard* and *have.* Choice (C) does not answer the question.

46. (A) *On the bus* answers *where.* Choice (B) answers *when did you buy your coat.* Choice (C) answers *where can I leave my coat.*

47. (C) *Not until summer* answers *when will the weather get warmer.* Choice (A) confuses the similar sounds *warmer* and *her.* Choice (B) confuses the similar sounds *whenever* and *weather.*

48. (B) *The clerk* answers *who is copying the report.* Choice (A) confuses the similar words *reporter* and *report.* Choice (C) confuses the similar sounds *copyright* and *copying.*

49. (A) *No, it's very uncomfortable* answers *is your chair comfortable.* Choice (B) confuses the similar sounds *chairman* and *chair* and *available* and *comfortable.* Choice (C) confuses the similar sounds *fair* and *chair* and *capable* and *comfortable.*

50. (B) *Only about a mile* answers *how far.* Choice (A) answers *how do you feel.* Choice (C) confuses the similar words *hear* and *here.*

## PART III

51. (A) The speakers are reading the newspaper. Choice (B) associates *game* with *sports.* Choice (C) confuses *playing sports* and *reading the sports section.* Choice (D) confuses *finishing a puzzle* and *finishing the sports section.*

52. (C) The speakers are talking about the limousine driver. Choice (A) confuses *gatekeeper* and *meet at the gate.* Choice (B) confuses the similar sounds *golfer* and *chauffeur.* Choice (D) confuses *car salesperson* and *limo driver.*

53. (D) The man is looking for paper cups. Choice (A) is not mentioned. Choice (B) is where he looked for the cups. Choice (C) is below the cabinet.

54. (C) The man has one boy and two girls. Choice (A) is how many boys he has. Choice (B) is how many girls he has. Choice (D) is how many children the woman has.

55. (C) The woman's husband is working for the city. Choice (A) is what the man studied to be. Choice (B) is what the woman's husband trained to be. Choice (D) is what the man thought her husband was.

56. (B) The batteries are really old. Choice (A) confuses *they're the wrong size* and *what size do we need.* Choice (C) is contradicted by *the ones inside.* Choice (D) is not mentioned.

57. (D) People are only allowed to smoke outside. Choices (A), (B), and (C) are places they are not allowed to smoke.

58. (A) This conversation takes place in a hotel. Choices (B) and (C) are not likely. Choice (D) confuses *at an airport* and *will you need a taxi to the airport.*

59. (C) The man will take an earlier bus tomorrow. Choice (A) confuses the opposites *later* and *earlier.* Choice (B) is what he is trying to avoid. Choice (D) is not mentioned.

60. (B) The woman borrowed a screwdriver. Choice (A) confuses *money for lunch* and *returning it after lunch.* Choice (C) confuses the similar sounds *paperback* and *give it back.* Choice (D) is where she found the screwdriver.

61. (B) It was so cold that the woman's car wouldn't start. Choice (A) confuses the similar sounds *nice* and *ice*. Choice (C) confuses the similar words *tropical* and *tropics*. Choice (D) is not mentioned.

62. (C) The man has to be home by 8:00. Choices (A) and (B) are the times the woman wants him to stay until. Choice (D) is what time the woman originally wanted him to work until.

63. (B) The man left the suitcase in the hall. Choice (A) associates *dining room* with *dinner*. Choice (C) is where the woman was afraid she left it. Choice (D) is where the man will take it after dinner.

64. (B) The woman has always wanted to sail around the world. Choice (A) confuses *buy a boat* and *sail around the world*. Choice (C) confuses *learn to fly* and *it would be faster to fly*. Choice (D) confuses the similar sounds *worry* and *hurry*.

65. (A) The signature is difficult to read. Choice (B) is what the signature is on. Choice (C) associates a *prescription* with a *doctor's signature*. Choice (D) is what's overdue.

66. (D) The man wants to sit in a chair. Choice (A) is not mentioned. Choice (B) is incorrect because if the man wanted to leave he wouldn't be looking for a place to sit. Choice (C) confuses *remove the chair* with *is this chair taken*.

67. (C) The woman called six times. Choice (A) confuses *two times* and *two o'clock*. Choice (B) is how many times the man has missed a meeting. Choice (D) confuses *fifteen times* and *fifteen minutes*.

68. (B) The brochures are on the floor of the supply room. Choice (A) is where they have to mail a hundred brochures. Choice (C) is where a hundred of them have to go. Choice (D) is where the brochures come from.

69. (D) The woman will put her correct phone number on the form. Choice (A) is the day by which she has to return the form. Choice (B) confuses the similar sounds *company director* and *company directory*. Choice (C) confuses *company name* and *company directory*.

70. (A) The man is still eating his breakfast. Choices (B) and (C) confuse *driving a car* and *going to school* with *can you drive me to school*. Choice (D) is what he will do after he finishes eating.

71. (D) The man can't drink his coffee because it's too strong and bitter. Choice (A) is not mentioned. Choice (B) is what will happen if he adds water to his coffee. Choice (C) is contradicted by *too strong*.

72. (A) The woman wants to turn left at the next intersection. Choice (B) is the way the one-way street goes. Choices (C) and (D) are not mentioned.

73. (C) The speakers are in a restaurant. Choice (A) associates *airplane* with *by the window* and *nonsmoking/smoking section*. Choice (B) associates *furniture store* and *we'd like a table*. Choice (D) confuses *living room* and *dining table*.

74. (A) The speakers are talking about a new air conditioner. Choice (B) is what it feels like in the room. Choice (C) associates *music system* with *I have the system turned down low*. Choice (D) associates *wind* with *it really circulates the air*.

75. (B) The speakers are musicians. Choice (A) confuses the similar sounds *physician* and *musician*. Choices (C) and (D) are not likely.

76. (C) There are many holes in the road. Choice (A) confuses *spring came late* and *every spring we get more holes*. Choice (B) is not mentioned. Choice (D) confuses the similar words *watch* and *watch out*.

77. (D) The man is buying a shirt. Choice (A) is incorrect because the man knows his measurements. Choice (B) confuses *painting a house* and *the color of the shirt*. Choice (C) confuses *long vacation* and *long-sleeved shirt*.

78. (A) The speakers are getting ready for a party. Choice (B) associates *election* with *party* by confusing the similar words *party* (political affiliation) and *party* (a social gathering). Choice (C) confuses the similar sounds *par(ade)* and *par(ty)*. Choice (D) is not mentioned.

79. (A) The man waited half an hour. Choice (B) is how long he had to wait yesterday. Choice (C) is an hour ago. Choice (D) is how long ago the woman left.

80. (D) The woman takes the whole month off for vacation. Choice (A) confuses *one week* and *start vacation the first week of August.* Choices (B) and (C) are not long enough for her vacation.

## PART IV

81. (B) The airport is closed because of heavy fog. Choice (A) confuses *heavy traffic* and *heavy fog.* Choices (C) and (D) are not mentioned.

82. (C) The fog will lift by early evening and planes will be allowed to take off and land then. Choice (A) is when the airport closed. Choice (B) is when the Weather Center reported the airport closing. Choice (D) confuses the opposites *late* and *early.*

83. (A) The train arrives at Penn Station in New York at 9:30 A.M. Choice (B) confuses *2:30* and *2-hour 40-minute trip.* Choice (C) confuses *6:00* and *6:50,* the times the train leaves Washington. Choice (D) confuses *6:15* and *6:50.*

84. (A) The express train is nonstop. Choices (B), (C), and (D) are contradicted by *nonstop trip.*

85. (B) The message states that all hotels are full. Choice (A) might be the reason the hotels are booked, but it is not mentioned. Choice (C) confuses *hotels are closed* and *hotels are full.* Choice (D) associates *long lines* and *waiting list.*

86. (D) Hotels are full for the period of August 15 through August 30. Choices (A), (B), and (C) are contradicted by the period mentioned.

87. (D) People can leave their name and phone number to be put on a waiting list. Choice (A) confuses *mailing list* and *waiting list.* Choice (B) is when the center will call people on the waiting list. Choice (C) confuses *applying for any job available* and *applying for any available rooms.*

88. (C) This announcement is being heard in a meeting room. Choice (A) associates *restaurant* with *coffee break.* Choice (B) associates *school* with *report* and *question-answer period.* Choice (D) associates *train station* with *board* by confusing the similar words *board the train* and *board meeting.*

89. (C) Since it is 10:30 now and the meeting will resume in fifteen minutes, the meeting will resume at 10:45. Choice (A) confuses *10:15* and *fifteen-minute break.* Choice (B) is the current time. Choice (D) is not possible if they only take a fifteen-minute break.

90. (D) The participants just finished listening to Ms. Johnson's report. Choice (A) is what they will do when they come back from the break. Choice (B) is what they will have now. Choice (C) confuses the similar words *resume* (noun) and *resume* (verb).

91. (A) Flood waters have risen over twenty feet. Choice (B) is not mentioned. Choice (C) confuses *more homes than families* and *families have been evacuated from their homes.* Choice (D) confuses *expensive property* and *expensive property damage.*

92. (A) Fortunately, there has been no loss of life. Choice (B) is how many feet the flood waters have risen. Choice (C) is how many families have been evacuated. Choice (D) is the cost of property damage.

93. (B) Carlos paints houses. Choice (A) confuses *build new homes* and *make your home look like new.* Choice (C) associates *design interiors* with *decorating.* Choice (D) confuses *supply servants* and *supply painters.*

94. (B) The ad says *ask your neighbors (for references).* Choice (A) is who clients would want a reference for. Choice (C) associates *decorators* with *decorating.* Choice (D) associates *real estate agents* and *new homes.*

95. (C) Airplane passengers are listening to the pilot. Choice (A) confuses *football captain* and *airline captain.* Choice (B) confuses the similar words *hospital patients* and *be patient.* Choice (D) associates *theater* with *Ladies and Gentlemen.*

96. (B) The captain says they can expect to sit on the runway for a good fifteen minutes or so. Choice (A) confuses *five* and *fifteen.* Choice (C) is the number of planes waiting to take off. Choice (D) confuses the similar sounds *fifty* and *fifteen.*

97. (B) The Center for Performing Arts is a music organization. Choice (A) is not related to the performing arts. Choice (C) associates *youth* and *young.* Choice (D) is not related to the performing arts.

98. (A) Ticket information is available between the hours of 4:00 and 6:00 P.M. Choice (B) confuses *between 4:00 and 8:00,* the time of the Young Musicians Recital, and *between 4:00 and 6:00.* Choice (C) confuses *at 6:00* and *between 4:00 and 6:00.* Choice (D) is when the New Company Orchestra performs.

99. (A) This announcement is about two tankers crashing. Choice (B) confuses *gas tanks* and *tankers.* Choice (C) confuses the similar sounds *civil* and *canal.* Choice (D) confuses the similar sounds *activities* and *accidents.*

100. (C) This is the third shipping accident this month. Choices (A), (B), and (D) are contradicted by *the third.*

## PART V

101. (C) *Cost of living* is a business expression. Choice (A) is a noun but is not used in this expression. Choice (B) is a verb. Choice (D) is the past participle.

102. (A) *To call on* means *to request or visit.* Choice (B) means *to get someone's attention by shouting to them.* Choices (C) and (D) are not two-word verbs.

103. (B) An action that is completed before another past action uses the past perfect tense. Choice (A) is the present tense. Choice (C) is the present participle. Choice (D) is the future tense.

104. (C) A real condition in the present tense can use the present tense in the result clause. Choice (A) is conditional. Choice (B) is the past tense. Choice (D) is the present perfect (conditional).

105. (D) Someone else will install the computers, so the past participle is used. Choice (A) is the future tense (passive). Choice (B) is the present participle. Choice (C) is the simple form.

106. (C) *However* indicates an unexpected result. Choice (A) indicates an unexpected result but is not followed by a subject and verb. Choice (B) indicates a result or consequence. Choice (D) indicates purpose.

107. (C) *Even though* indicates an unexpected result. Choice (A) means *anything.* Choice (B) is an interrogative word. Choice (D) indicates an unexpected result but must begin the result clause.

108. (C) *On* is the preposition used with *conduct research.* Choice (A) means *concerning.* Choice (B) indicates source or origin. Choice (D) means *close to.*

109. (B) Adverbs of definite frequency may appear at the end of a sentence. Choices (A), (C), and (D) are not appropriate positions for definite frequency adverbs.

110. (B) *Or* indicates a choice between items. Choice (A) indicates a contrast between items. Choice (C) is a negative, not a conjunction. Choice (D) is usually paired with *or.*

111. (D) *On* is used with days of the week. Choice (A) indicates source or origin. Choices (B) and (C) are used with location.

112. (C) *Until* indicates a time or action that another action depends upon. Choice (A) is conditional and is not logical in the sentence. Choice (B) indicates a time relationship but is not logical in the sentence. Choice (D) is a relative pronoun.

113. (D) The assistant is the one who signed the memo, so the simple form of the verb is used. Choice (A) is the present participle. Choice (B) is the past participle. Choice (C) is the future tense.

114. (C) Real conditions in the present tense may use present tense in the *if* clause. Choice (A) is the past tense. Choice (B) is the present progressive. Choice (D) is the future.

115. (D) An action that has been happening in the past and is continuing in the present may use the present perfect progressive. Choice (A) is the simple form. Choice (B) is the past tense. Choice (C) is the past perfect tense.

116. (B) *To catch on* means *to become familiar with doing something.* Choices (A), (C), and (D) are not two-word verbs.

117. (D) *Final* is an adjective that modifies *result.* Choice (A) is a verb. Choice (B) is an adverb. Choice (C) is a noun referring to a person.

118. (C) *Go through* means *to complete a transaction.* Choice (A) means *to proceed.* Choice (B) means *to leave a place.* Choice (D) means *to exceed.*

119. (C) Someone else will finish the inventory, so the past participle is used. Choice (A) is the future (passive). Choice (B) is the simple form. Choice (D) is the present participle.

120. (B) *Were* is the form of *be* used in the *if* clause of an unreal condition. Choices (A), (C), and (D) are not used in the *if* clause of an unreal condition.

121. (B) *Not only ... but also* is a paired conjunction. Choices (A), (C), and (D) are not paired with *not only.*

122. (D) An action in progress is indicated by the present progressive; here it is in the passive form. Choice (A) is present progressive (active). Choice (B) is present tense. Choice (C) is the simple form of the verb.

123. (C) *Should* is a modal that indicates obligation or preference. Choices (A) and (D) are forms that indicate completed actions and are not consistent with *in the future.* Choice (B) is the simple form of the verb.

124. (A) The secretaries are the ones who are leaving early, so the simple form of the verb is used. Choice (B) is the present tense. Choice (C) is the present participle. Choice (D) is the past tense.

125. (B) *Therefore* indicates a result or consequence. Choice (A) indicates an unexpected result. Choice (C) indicates a summary of points. Choice (D) indicates a contrast.

126. (C) *One of* distinguishes one item from a group. Choice (A) indicates source or origin. Choice (B) indicates manner. Choice (D) is used in comparisons.

127. (C) *Identification number* is a business term. Choice (A) is a verb. Choice (B) is a noun referring to a thing. Choice (D) is the past participle.

128. (D) *Before* indicates a sequential time relationship. Choice (A) indicates a simultaneous time relationship. Choice (B) indicates a cause and effect. Choice (C) indicates a simultaneous time relationship but is not followed by a subject and verb.

129. (A) Adverbs of definite frequency may appear at the end of a sentence. Choice (B) is an indefinite frequency adverb. Choice (C) is used with completed action. Choice (D) indicates a future time.

130. (B) *In spite of* indicates an unexpected result. Choice (A) must be followed by a subject and verb. Choices (C) and (D) are prepositions.

131. (C) *From ... to* indicates the limits of a time frame. Choices (A) and (B) indicate location. Choice (D) indicates manner.

132. (A) *For example* indicates examples from a generalization. Choice (B) indicates additional information. Choice (C) indicates an unexpected result. Choice (D) indicates a result or consequence.

133. (C) *By* indicates a passive form, so the past participle is required. Choice (A) is the simple form. Choice (B) is the present tense. Choice (D) is the gerund.

134. (A) *Were* is the form of *be* used in the *if* clause of an unreal condition. Choices (B), (C), and (D) are not forms of *be* used in the *if* clause of an unreal condition.

135. (A) Third person present tense is required. Choice (B) is the plural form of the present tense and does not agree with *who.* Choices (C) and (D) are progressive forms, which are rarely used with stative verbs.

136. (C) *To take over* means *obtain control of.* Choice (A) means *remove.* Choice (B) means *carry away.* Choice (D) means *leave.*

137. (B) *Briefing* is a noun that means *a meeting to provide current information.* Choice (A) is an adjective. Choice (C) is an adverb. Choice (D) is a past tense.

138. (C) *Advisable* is a predicate adjective. Choices (A) and (D) are verbs. Choice (B) is a noun.

139. (B) A verb is necessary for the command form. Choice (A) is a noun. Choice (C) is a verb. Choice (D) is a gerund.

140. (A) *Either ... or* is a paired conjunction. Choices (B), (C), and (D) are not paired with *either.*

## PART VI

141. (B) The pronoun must agree with *company: the company and its employees.* Choice (A) is a correct noun phrase. Choice (C) is a correct verb. Choice (D) is a correct preposition.

142. (B) *Consider* is followed by a gerund: *considering setting up.* Choice (A) is a correct verb. Choice (C) is a correct infinitive. Choice (D) is a correct relative pronoun.

143. (D) The pronoun must refer to *people: to find seats for them.* Choice (A) is a correct conjunction. Choice (B) is a correct verb. Choice (C) is a correct noun phrase.

144. (B) *Could* is the past tense form of *can: had finally decided that it could start looking.* Choice (A) is a correct adverb. Choice (C) is a correct preposition. Choice (D) is a correct noun.

145. (A) An article must be used with singular count nouns: *There is an article.* Choice (B) is a correct time expression. Choice (C) is a correct relative pronoun. Choice (D) is a correct prepositional phrase.

146. (A) Noncount nouns that are not specific do not require an article: *rather little attention.* Choice (B) is a correct infinitive. Choice (C) is a correct preposition. Choice (D) is a correct prepositional phrase.

147. (A) Reduced relative clauses do not use auxiliaries: *the city commission, believing in the new transportation system.* Choice (B) is a correct verb. Choice (C) is a correct prepositional phrase. Choice (D) is a correct infinitive.

148. (C) An infinitive is formed with the simple form of the verb: *are often used to help solve.* Choices (A) and (D) are correct nouns. Choice (B) is a correct verb.

149. (A) Singular count nouns must be used with an article: *a local car dealer has been making.* Choices (B) and (C) are correct noun phrases. Choice (D) is a correct verb.

150. (B) A pronoun that is the object of a verb must be in the objective form: *report to Ms. Huang and me.* Choice (A) is a correct noun phrase. Choice (C) is a correct pronoun. Choice (D) is a correct prepositional phrase.

151. (B) A superlative comparison requires *the: is the most motivated.* Choice (A) is a correct noun phrase. Choice (C) is a correct noun. Choice (D) is a correct verb.

152. (B) The noncount noun *information* requires a singular verb: *information which has been collected.* Choice (A) is a correct noun. Choice (C) is a correct verb. Choice (D) is a correct comparative.

153. (A) The director noticed the nervousness, so the present participle is used: *noting the nervousness of the speaker, the director.* Choices (B) and (C) are correct prepositional phrases. Choice (D) is a correct pronoun.

154. (B) Indirect questions use subject-verb word order: *where the personnel office was.* Choice (A) is a correct infinitive. Choice (C) is a correct verb. Choice (D) is a correct prepositional phrase.

155. (A) The pronoun must agree with *vice president: the vice president himself.* Choice (B) is a correct conjunction. Choice (C) is a correct verb. Choice (D) is a correct preposition.

156. (A) The singular noun *committee* requires a singular verb: *The committee has finalized.* Choice (B) is a correct noun. Choice (C) is a correct preposition. Choice (D) is a correct adjective.

157. (B) A relative pronoun is required: *the person who answered the phone.* Choice (A) is a correct article. Choice (C) is a correct adjective. Choice (D) is a correct noun.

158. (A) The past participle is required: *having consulted with his lawyer.* Choice (B) is a correct pronoun. Choice (C) is a correct infinitive. Choice (D) is a correct noun.

159. (A) *Should* used as a conditional precedes the subject: *should the report arrive.* Choice (B) is a correct conjunction. Choice (C) is a correct preposition. Choice (D) is a correct equal comparison.

160. (A) *Are* is not required: *when communicating with the support staff.* Choice (B) is a correct verb. Choice (C) is a correct adjective. Choice (D) is a correct noun phrase.

## PART VII

161. (C) Amsterdam is only an hour away from Paris by air. Choice (A) is an hour and 5 minutes from Paris. Choice (B) is an hour and 20 minutes from Paris. Choice (D) is the farthest city from Paris.

162. (A) Madrid and Paris are 13 hours apart by rail. Choice (B) is 7 hours apart. Choice (C) is the second farthest apart. Choice (D) is 9 hours apart.

163. (B) Frankfurt to Brussels takes 1 hour by air. Choice (A) confuses *rail* and *air* transportation. Choice (C) is incorrect because it takes 5 hours and 30 minutes by rail. Choice (D) confuses *rail* and *air transportation.*

164. (A) The Paris to Madrid flight takes 1 hour and 50 minutes. Choice (B) is the second longest flight. Choices (C) and (D) are flights shorter than 1 hour and 50 minutes.

165. (B) A clerical instructor would be most qualified to instruct a clerical training program. Choice (A) confuses the similar sounds *practical (nurse)* and *(office) practices.* Choice (C) associates *office cleaner* with *office practices.* Choice (D) associates *typist* with *teach typing* and *data entry.*

166. (A) Motivated disabled adults are being taught. Choice (B) is who will do the teaching. Choice (C) associates *office managers* with the *job duties listed.* Choice (D) associates *professional typists* with *teaching typing.*

167. (C) Applicants should send their resumes. Choice (A) confuses *contact the nearest agency* and *the agency seeking an instructor.* Choice (B) is not mentioned. Choice (D) is incorrect because there is no phone number given.

168. (A) The problem is that someone in Mr. Gomez's office keeps turning off the thermostat. Choice (B) is incorrect because there is a thermostat in Mr. Gomez's office. Choice (C) confuses *the other tenants want a thermostat* and *the other tenants are complaining about the heat.* Choice (D) is contradicted by *the tenants complaining about the heat.*

169. (C) *Please do not touch it* means that *it should never be turned off.* Choices (A), (B), and (D) are times when people usually adjust their thermostats.

170. (B) Mr. Gomez should not touch the thermostat. Choice (A) is not mentioned. Choice (C) is incorrect because the other tenants are complaining, not Mr. Gomez. Choice (D) might be wise but is not mentioned.

171. (B) The advertisement is promoting a cleaning kit for white shoes. Choice (A) is what the product keeps clean. Choice (C) confuses *shoe repair* with *shoe polish.* Choice (D) confuses *company supplies* (noun) and *the company that supplies* (verb).

172. (A) The kit is a two-step, two-minute kit. Choice (B) confuses *five minutes* and *five dollars,* the price of the kit with a shoe order. Choice (C) confuses *seven minutes* and *seven dollars,* the cost of the kit. Choice (D) is not mentioned.

173. (D) The Kleen-Kit keeps white shoes clean. Choice (A) confuses the similar sounds *Wright* and *white.* Choice (B) confuses the similar words *finishing* (verb) and *finishes* (noun). Choice (C) confuses *staying handsome* and *white shoes are handsome.*

174. (C) Reinhold Company's earnings rose 15 percent in the first quarter of its fiscal year. Choice (A) is incorrect because the most recent report shows increased earnings. Choice (B) is contradicted by *three straight periods of declining earnings.* Choice (D) confuses *fifteen million dollars* and *fifteen percent.*

175. (C) First-quarter earnings rose 15 percent. Choice (A) confuses *one percent* and *first quarter.* Choice (B) confuses *three percent* and *three straight periods.* Choice (D) confuses the similar sounds *sixteen* and *fifteen.*

176. (A) The memo discusses the company's schedules. Choice (B) is not mentioned. Choice (C) confuses the similar words *observations* (noun) and *observes* (verb). Choice (D) is what is needed to establish different schedules.

177. (C) The company observes a 35-hour workweek. Choice (A) is the day the memo was written. Choice (B) confuses the similar sounds *twenty-five* and *thirty-five.* Choice (D) is a national standard workweek.

178. (B) Individual employees may establish different schedules with their supervisor's approval. Choice (A) is contradicted by *with their supervisor's approval.* Choice (C) may be Mr. Rollins's position. Choice (D) is who asked Ms. Gibbons to remind employees of the company's schedule.

179. (B) The memo is addressed to all employees. Choice (A) confuses *clients reading the memo* and *contracts with clients.* Choice (C) is the subject of the memo. Choice (D) is who wrote the memo.

180. (C) Visitors must be escorted because a number of the company's contracts with clients are of a confidential nature. Choice (A) is not mentioned. Choice (B) is why visitors would come to the office. Choice (D) associates *visitors* with *guests.*

181. (D) Visitors are asked to sign in at the reception desk. Choice (A) is what the receptionist will do. Choice (B) is not permitted. Choice (C) is not mentioned.

182. (B) The receptionist will call the employee's office to let him or her know they have a visitor. Choice (A) is contradicted by *the receptionist will call.* Choice (C) is incorrect because visitors, not employees, must wait in the reception area. Choice (D) is incorrect because employees have to come and escort their guests.

183. (A) Apartment-hotels have characteristics of both apartments and hotels, hence the name *apartment-hotels.* Choice (B) is true for apartment buildings but not hotels. Choice (C) is not mentioned. Choice (D) is true for hotels but not apartment buildings.

184. (C) An engineer on a ten-week project away from home would use an apartment-hotel. Choices (A), (B), and (D) would probably use a hotel for such short stays.

185. (C) The location of apartment-hotels is not mentioned. Choices (A), (B), and (D) are all mentioned.

186. (D) Apartment-hotels are often more cost-effective than standard hotels. Choice (A) confuses the similar sounds *larger* and *longer.* Choice (B) is contradicted by *apartment-hotels are often more comfortable.* Choice (C) is contradicted by *they are run like hotels.*

187. (D) David Bikowski was laid off from his production job. Choice (A) is not mentioned. Choice (B) confuses *being fired* and *being laid off.* Choice (C) is contradicted by the fact that he is staying at his new job, which pays $100 less a week.

188. (A) Mr. Bikowski's new job pays $100 less a week than his old job. Choice (B) confuses *a month* and *a week.* Choice (C) confuses the opposites *more* and *less.* Choice (D) confuses *month* and *week* and the opposites *more* and *less.*

189. (B) Mr. Bikowski stayed at his new job, even though he was called back to the factory, because the new firm is much less stressful. Choice (A) is contradicted by *the new job pays $100 less a week.* Choice (C) is not mentioned. Choice (D) confuses *working close to home* and *finding a new job nearby* and confuses the similar sounds *close* and *chose.*

190. (A) This letter accompanies an evaluation report. Choice (B) confuses *inquire about future job possibilities* and *look forward to working with you again in the future.* Choice (C) associates *future projects* with *working with you again in the future.* Choice (D) associates *payment* with *hired.*

191. (B) The report the consultant prepared for Mr. Thompson was about improving employee performance. Choice (A) is contradicted by *Mr. Thompson's hiring of Ms. Guess to write the report.* Choices (C) and (D) are contradicted by *Mr. Thompson's hiring Guess Consulting to do the project evaluation.*

192. (D) Ms. Guess completed the project, which is enclosed with the letter. Choices (A), (B), and (C) are mentioned.

193. (A) Mr. Thompson must be a lawyer because of the *Esq.* following his name. Choice (B) associates *personnel director* with *employee performance evaluation.* Choice (C) is Ms. Guess's profession. Choice (D) is contradicted by *I enjoyed working with your law firm.*

194. (D) This customer guide would probably appear in a telephone directory. Choice (A) is incorrect because the information might be found in a telephone directory in a telephone booth, not in the telephone booth itself. Choice (B) is not likely. Choice (C) confuses *with a telephone bill* and the billing listing; it is also very unlikely that a telephone bill would be twenty-nine pages long.

195. (C) The list is in alphabetical order. Choice (A) is listing things in order by date. Choices (B) and (D) are not able to be determined.

196. (A) Telephone repair begins on page 3. Choice (B) is choosing a telephone service. Choice (C) is consumer information. Choice (D) is special services.

197. (B) Page 7 contains information on choosing a telephone service. Choice (A) is directory assistance. Choice (C) is consumer information. Choice (D) is area codes.

198. (B) A multifunction watch is being sold. Choice (A) associates *a suitcase* with *Traveller* and *Paris Jewelers*. Choice (C) confuses *a steel band* and *the watch being available in stainless steel*. Choice (D) confuses *a gold ring* and *the watch being available in 18 kt. gold.*

199. (D) The ad says the watch displays all twenty-four time zones. Choice (A) confuses *five time zones* and *five-year international warranty*. Choice (B) confuses the similar sounds *twelve* and *twen(ty)*. Choice (C) confuses *eighteen time zones* and *eighteen karat*.

200. (B) A five-year international limited warranty is offered. Choices (A) and (C) confuse *eighteen months* and *eighteen years* with *eighteen karats*. Choice (D) associates *lifetime* with *tradition* and *since 1928*.

# ANSWER SHEETS

# ANSWER SHEET: Practice Test One

## Listening Comprehension

Part I — Part II — Part III — Part IV

| | Answer | | Answer | | Answer | | Answer | | Answer | | Answer | | Answer | | Answer | | Answer | | Answer |
|---|---|---|---|---|---|---|---|---|---|---|---|---|---|---|---|---|---|---|---|
| | A B C D | | A B C D | | A B C | | A B C | | A B C | | A B C D | | A B C D | | A B C D | | A B C D | | A B C D |
| 1 | Ⓐ Ⓑ Ⓒ Ⓓ | 11 | Ⓐ Ⓑ Ⓒ Ⓓ | 21 | Ⓐ Ⓑ Ⓒ | 31 | Ⓐ Ⓑ Ⓒ | 41 | Ⓐ Ⓑ Ⓒ | 51 | Ⓐ Ⓑ Ⓒ Ⓓ | 61 | Ⓐ Ⓑ Ⓒ Ⓓ | 71 | Ⓐ Ⓑ Ⓒ Ⓓ | 81 | Ⓐ Ⓑ Ⓒ Ⓓ | 91 | Ⓐ Ⓑ Ⓒ Ⓓ |
| 2 | Ⓐ Ⓑ Ⓒ Ⓓ | 12 | Ⓐ Ⓑ Ⓒ Ⓓ | 22 | Ⓐ Ⓑ Ⓒ | 32 | Ⓐ Ⓑ Ⓒ | 42 | Ⓐ Ⓑ Ⓒ | 52 | Ⓐ Ⓑ Ⓒ Ⓓ | 62 | Ⓐ Ⓑ Ⓒ Ⓓ | 72 | Ⓐ Ⓑ Ⓒ Ⓓ | 82 | Ⓐ Ⓑ Ⓒ Ⓓ | 92 | Ⓐ Ⓑ Ⓒ Ⓓ |
| 3 | Ⓐ Ⓑ Ⓒ Ⓓ | 13 | Ⓐ Ⓑ Ⓒ Ⓓ | 23 | Ⓐ Ⓑ Ⓒ | 33 | Ⓐ Ⓑ Ⓒ | 43 | Ⓐ Ⓑ Ⓒ | 53 | Ⓐ Ⓑ Ⓒ Ⓓ | 63 | Ⓐ Ⓑ Ⓒ Ⓓ | 73 | Ⓐ Ⓑ Ⓒ Ⓓ | 83 | Ⓐ Ⓑ Ⓒ Ⓓ | 93 | Ⓐ Ⓑ Ⓒ Ⓓ |
| 4 | Ⓐ Ⓑ Ⓒ Ⓓ | 14 | Ⓐ Ⓑ Ⓒ Ⓓ | 24 | Ⓐ Ⓑ Ⓒ | 34 | Ⓐ Ⓑ Ⓒ | 44 | Ⓐ Ⓑ Ⓒ | 54 | Ⓐ Ⓑ Ⓒ Ⓓ | 64 | Ⓐ Ⓑ Ⓒ Ⓓ | 74 | Ⓐ Ⓑ Ⓒ Ⓓ | 84 | Ⓐ Ⓑ Ⓒ Ⓓ | 94 | Ⓐ Ⓑ Ⓒ Ⓓ |
| 5 | Ⓐ Ⓑ Ⓒ Ⓓ | 15 | Ⓐ Ⓑ Ⓒ Ⓓ | 25 | Ⓐ Ⓑ Ⓒ | 35 | Ⓐ Ⓑ Ⓒ | 45 | Ⓐ Ⓑ Ⓒ | 55 | Ⓐ Ⓑ Ⓒ Ⓓ | 65 | Ⓐ Ⓑ Ⓒ Ⓓ | 75 | Ⓐ Ⓑ Ⓒ Ⓓ | 85 | Ⓐ Ⓑ Ⓒ Ⓓ | 95 | Ⓐ Ⓑ Ⓒ Ⓓ |
| 6 | Ⓐ Ⓑ Ⓒ Ⓓ | 16 | Ⓐ Ⓑ Ⓒ Ⓓ | 26 | Ⓐ Ⓑ Ⓒ | 36 | Ⓐ Ⓑ Ⓒ | 46 | Ⓐ Ⓑ Ⓒ | 56 | Ⓐ Ⓑ Ⓒ Ⓓ | 66 | Ⓐ Ⓑ Ⓒ Ⓓ | 76 | Ⓐ Ⓑ Ⓒ Ⓓ | 86 | Ⓐ Ⓑ Ⓒ Ⓓ | 96 | Ⓐ Ⓑ Ⓒ Ⓓ |
| 7 | Ⓐ Ⓑ Ⓒ Ⓓ | 17 | Ⓐ Ⓑ Ⓒ Ⓓ | 27 | Ⓐ Ⓑ Ⓒ | 37 | Ⓐ Ⓑ Ⓒ | 47 | Ⓐ Ⓑ Ⓒ | 57 | Ⓐ Ⓑ Ⓒ Ⓓ | 67 | Ⓐ Ⓑ Ⓒ Ⓓ | 77 | Ⓐ Ⓑ Ⓒ Ⓓ | 87 | Ⓐ Ⓑ Ⓒ Ⓓ | 97 | Ⓐ Ⓑ Ⓒ Ⓓ |
| 8 | Ⓐ Ⓑ Ⓒ Ⓓ | 18 | Ⓐ Ⓑ Ⓒ Ⓓ | 28 | Ⓐ Ⓑ Ⓒ | 38 | Ⓐ Ⓑ Ⓒ | 48 | Ⓐ Ⓑ Ⓒ | 58 | Ⓐ Ⓑ Ⓒ Ⓓ | 68 | Ⓐ Ⓑ Ⓒ Ⓓ | 78 | Ⓐ Ⓑ Ⓒ Ⓓ | 88 | Ⓐ Ⓑ Ⓒ Ⓓ | 98 | Ⓐ Ⓑ Ⓒ Ⓓ |
| 9 | Ⓐ Ⓑ Ⓒ Ⓓ | 19 | Ⓐ Ⓑ Ⓒ Ⓓ | 29 | Ⓐ Ⓑ Ⓒ | 39 | Ⓐ Ⓑ Ⓒ | 49 | Ⓐ Ⓑ Ⓒ | 59 | Ⓐ Ⓑ Ⓒ Ⓓ | 69 | Ⓐ Ⓑ Ⓒ Ⓓ | 79 | Ⓐ Ⓑ Ⓒ Ⓓ | 89 | Ⓐ Ⓑ Ⓒ Ⓓ | 99 | Ⓐ Ⓑ Ⓒ Ⓓ |
| 10 | Ⓐ Ⓑ Ⓒ Ⓓ | 20 | Ⓐ Ⓑ Ⓒ Ⓓ | 30 | Ⓐ Ⓑ Ⓒ | 40 | Ⓐ Ⓑ Ⓒ | 50 | Ⓐ Ⓑ Ⓒ | 60 | Ⓐ Ⓑ Ⓒ Ⓓ | 70 | Ⓐ Ⓑ Ⓒ Ⓓ | 80 | Ⓐ Ⓑ Ⓒ Ⓓ | 90 | Ⓐ Ⓑ Ⓒ Ⓓ | 100 | Ⓐ Ⓑ Ⓒ Ⓓ |

## Reading

Part V — Part VI — Part VII

| | Answer | | Answer | | Answer | | Answer | | Answer | | Answer | | Answer | | Answer | | Answer | | Answer |
|---|---|---|---|---|---|---|---|---|---|---|---|---|---|---|---|---|---|---|---|
| | A B C D | | A B C D | | A B C D | | A B C D | | A B C D | | A B C D | | A B C D | | A B C D | | A B C D | | A B C D |
| 101 | Ⓐ Ⓑ Ⓒ Ⓓ | 111 | Ⓐ Ⓑ Ⓒ Ⓓ | 121 | Ⓐ Ⓑ Ⓒ Ⓓ | 131 | Ⓐ Ⓑ Ⓒ Ⓓ | 141 | Ⓐ Ⓑ Ⓒ Ⓓ | 151 | Ⓐ Ⓑ Ⓒ Ⓓ | 161 | Ⓐ Ⓑ Ⓒ Ⓓ | 171 | Ⓐ Ⓑ Ⓒ Ⓓ | 181 | Ⓐ Ⓑ Ⓒ Ⓓ | 191 | Ⓐ Ⓑ Ⓒ Ⓓ |
| 102 | Ⓐ Ⓑ Ⓒ Ⓓ | 112 | Ⓐ Ⓑ Ⓒ Ⓓ | 122 | Ⓐ Ⓑ Ⓒ Ⓓ | 132 | Ⓐ Ⓑ Ⓒ Ⓓ | 142 | Ⓐ Ⓑ Ⓒ Ⓓ | 152 | Ⓐ Ⓑ Ⓒ Ⓓ | 162 | Ⓐ Ⓑ Ⓒ Ⓓ | 172 | Ⓐ Ⓑ Ⓒ Ⓓ | 182 | Ⓐ Ⓑ Ⓒ Ⓓ | 192 | Ⓐ Ⓑ Ⓒ Ⓓ |
| 103 | Ⓐ Ⓑ Ⓒ Ⓓ | 113 | Ⓐ Ⓑ Ⓒ Ⓓ | 123 | Ⓐ Ⓑ Ⓒ Ⓓ | 133 | Ⓐ Ⓑ Ⓒ Ⓓ | 143 | Ⓐ Ⓑ Ⓒ Ⓓ | 153 | Ⓐ Ⓑ Ⓒ Ⓓ | 163 | Ⓐ Ⓑ Ⓒ Ⓓ | 173 | Ⓐ Ⓑ Ⓒ Ⓓ | 183 | Ⓐ Ⓑ Ⓒ Ⓓ | 193 | Ⓐ Ⓑ Ⓒ Ⓓ |
| 104 | Ⓐ Ⓑ Ⓒ Ⓓ | 114 | Ⓐ Ⓑ Ⓒ Ⓓ | 124 | Ⓐ Ⓑ Ⓒ Ⓓ | 134 | Ⓐ Ⓑ Ⓒ Ⓓ | 144 | Ⓐ Ⓑ Ⓒ Ⓓ | 154 | Ⓐ Ⓑ Ⓒ Ⓓ | 164 | Ⓐ Ⓑ Ⓒ Ⓓ | 174 | Ⓐ Ⓑ Ⓒ Ⓓ | 184 | Ⓐ Ⓑ Ⓒ Ⓓ | 194 | Ⓐ Ⓑ Ⓒ Ⓓ |
| 105 | Ⓐ Ⓑ Ⓒ Ⓓ | 115 | Ⓐ Ⓑ Ⓒ Ⓓ | 125 | Ⓐ Ⓑ Ⓒ Ⓓ | 135 | Ⓐ Ⓑ Ⓒ Ⓓ | 145 | Ⓐ Ⓑ Ⓒ Ⓓ | 155 | Ⓐ Ⓑ Ⓒ Ⓓ | 165 | Ⓐ Ⓑ Ⓒ Ⓓ | 175 | Ⓐ Ⓑ Ⓒ Ⓓ | 185 | Ⓐ Ⓑ Ⓒ Ⓓ | 195 | Ⓐ Ⓑ Ⓒ Ⓓ |
| 106 | Ⓐ Ⓑ Ⓒ Ⓓ | 116 | Ⓐ Ⓑ Ⓒ Ⓓ | 126 | Ⓐ Ⓑ Ⓒ Ⓓ | 136 | Ⓐ Ⓑ Ⓒ Ⓓ | 146 | Ⓐ Ⓑ Ⓒ Ⓓ | 156 | Ⓐ Ⓑ Ⓒ Ⓓ | 166 | Ⓐ Ⓑ Ⓒ Ⓓ | 176 | Ⓐ Ⓑ Ⓒ Ⓓ | 186 | Ⓐ Ⓑ Ⓒ Ⓓ | 196 | Ⓐ Ⓑ Ⓒ Ⓓ |
| 107 | Ⓐ Ⓑ Ⓒ Ⓓ | 117 | Ⓐ Ⓑ Ⓒ Ⓓ | 127 | Ⓐ Ⓑ Ⓒ Ⓓ | 137 | Ⓐ Ⓑ Ⓒ Ⓓ | 147 | Ⓐ Ⓑ Ⓒ Ⓓ | 157 | Ⓐ Ⓑ Ⓒ Ⓓ | 167 | Ⓐ Ⓑ Ⓒ Ⓓ | 177 | Ⓐ Ⓑ Ⓒ Ⓓ | 187 | Ⓐ Ⓑ Ⓒ Ⓓ | 197 | Ⓐ Ⓑ Ⓒ Ⓓ |
| 108 | Ⓐ Ⓑ Ⓒ Ⓓ | 118 | Ⓐ Ⓑ Ⓒ Ⓓ | 128 | Ⓐ Ⓑ Ⓒ Ⓓ | 138 | Ⓐ Ⓑ Ⓒ Ⓓ | 148 | Ⓐ Ⓑ Ⓒ Ⓓ | 158 | Ⓐ Ⓑ Ⓒ Ⓓ | 168 | Ⓐ Ⓑ Ⓒ Ⓓ | 178 | Ⓐ Ⓑ Ⓒ Ⓓ | 188 | Ⓐ Ⓑ Ⓒ Ⓓ | 198 | Ⓐ Ⓑ Ⓒ Ⓓ |
| 109 | Ⓐ Ⓑ Ⓒ Ⓓ | 119 | Ⓐ Ⓑ Ⓒ Ⓓ | 129 | Ⓐ Ⓑ Ⓒ Ⓓ | 139 | Ⓐ Ⓑ Ⓒ Ⓓ | 149 | Ⓐ Ⓑ Ⓒ Ⓓ | 159 | Ⓐ Ⓑ Ⓒ Ⓓ | 169 | Ⓐ Ⓑ Ⓒ Ⓓ | 179 | Ⓐ Ⓑ Ⓒ Ⓓ | 189 | Ⓐ Ⓑ Ⓒ Ⓓ | 199 | Ⓐ Ⓑ Ⓒ Ⓓ |
| 110 | Ⓐ Ⓑ Ⓒ Ⓓ | 120 | Ⓐ Ⓑ Ⓒ Ⓓ | 130 | Ⓐ Ⓑ Ⓒ Ⓓ | 140 | Ⓐ Ⓑ Ⓒ Ⓓ | 150 | Ⓐ Ⓑ Ⓒ Ⓓ | 160 | Ⓐ Ⓑ Ⓒ Ⓓ | 170 | Ⓐ Ⓑ Ⓒ Ⓓ | 180 | Ⓐ Ⓑ Ⓒ Ⓓ | 190 | Ⓐ Ⓑ Ⓒ Ⓓ | 200 | Ⓐ Ⓑ Ⓒ Ⓓ |

# ANSWER SHEET: Practice Test Two

## Listening Comprehension

Part I — Part II — Part III — Part IV

| | Answer | | Answer | | Answer | | Answer | | Answer | | Answer | | Answer | | Answer | | Answer | | Answer |
|---|---|---|---|---|---|---|---|---|---|---|---|---|---|---|---|---|---|---|---|
| | A B C D | | A B C D | | A B C | | A B C | | A B C | | A B C D | | A B C D | | A B C D | | A B C D | | A B C D |
| 1 | Ⓐ Ⓑ Ⓒ Ⓓ | 11 | Ⓐ Ⓑ Ⓒ Ⓓ | 21 | Ⓐ Ⓑ Ⓒ | 31 | Ⓐ Ⓑ Ⓒ | 41 | Ⓐ Ⓑ Ⓒ | 51 | Ⓐ Ⓑ Ⓒ Ⓓ | 61 | Ⓐ Ⓑ Ⓒ Ⓓ | 71 | Ⓐ Ⓑ Ⓒ Ⓓ | 81 | Ⓐ Ⓑ Ⓒ Ⓓ | 91 | Ⓐ Ⓑ Ⓒ Ⓓ |
| 2 | Ⓐ Ⓑ Ⓒ Ⓓ | 12 | Ⓐ Ⓑ Ⓒ Ⓓ | 22 | Ⓐ Ⓑ Ⓒ | 32 | Ⓐ Ⓑ Ⓒ | 42 | Ⓐ Ⓑ Ⓒ | 52 | Ⓐ Ⓑ Ⓒ Ⓓ | 62 | Ⓐ Ⓑ Ⓒ Ⓓ | 72 | Ⓐ Ⓑ Ⓒ Ⓓ | 82 | Ⓐ Ⓑ Ⓒ Ⓓ | 92 | Ⓐ Ⓑ Ⓒ Ⓓ |
| 3 | Ⓐ Ⓑ Ⓒ Ⓓ | 13 | Ⓐ Ⓑ Ⓒ Ⓓ | 23 | Ⓐ Ⓑ Ⓒ | 33 | Ⓐ Ⓑ Ⓒ | 43 | Ⓐ Ⓑ Ⓒ | 53 | Ⓐ Ⓑ Ⓒ Ⓓ | 63 | Ⓐ Ⓑ Ⓒ Ⓓ | 73 | Ⓐ Ⓑ Ⓒ Ⓓ | 83 | Ⓐ Ⓑ Ⓒ Ⓓ | 93 | Ⓐ Ⓑ Ⓒ Ⓓ |
| 4 | Ⓐ Ⓑ Ⓒ Ⓓ | 14 | Ⓐ Ⓑ Ⓒ Ⓓ | 24 | Ⓐ Ⓑ Ⓒ | 34 | Ⓐ Ⓑ Ⓒ | 44 | Ⓐ Ⓑ Ⓒ | 54 | Ⓐ Ⓑ Ⓒ Ⓓ | 64 | Ⓐ Ⓑ Ⓒ Ⓓ | 74 | Ⓐ Ⓑ Ⓒ Ⓓ | 84 | Ⓐ Ⓑ Ⓒ Ⓓ | 94 | Ⓐ Ⓑ Ⓒ Ⓓ |
| 5 | Ⓐ Ⓑ Ⓒ Ⓓ | 15 | Ⓐ Ⓑ Ⓒ Ⓓ | 25 | Ⓐ Ⓑ Ⓒ | 35 | Ⓐ Ⓑ Ⓒ | 45 | Ⓐ Ⓑ Ⓒ | 55 | Ⓐ Ⓑ Ⓒ Ⓓ | 65 | Ⓐ Ⓑ Ⓒ Ⓓ | 75 | Ⓐ Ⓑ Ⓒ Ⓓ | 85 | Ⓐ Ⓑ Ⓒ Ⓓ | 95 | Ⓐ Ⓑ Ⓒ Ⓓ |
| 6 | Ⓐ Ⓑ Ⓒ Ⓓ | 16 | Ⓐ Ⓑ Ⓒ Ⓓ | 26 | Ⓐ Ⓑ Ⓒ | 36 | Ⓐ Ⓑ Ⓒ | 46 | Ⓐ Ⓑ Ⓒ | 56 | Ⓐ Ⓑ Ⓒ Ⓓ | 66 | Ⓐ Ⓑ Ⓒ Ⓓ | 76 | Ⓐ Ⓑ Ⓒ Ⓓ | 86 | Ⓐ Ⓑ Ⓒ Ⓓ | 96 | Ⓐ Ⓑ Ⓒ Ⓓ |
| 7 | Ⓐ Ⓑ Ⓒ Ⓓ | 17 | Ⓐ Ⓑ Ⓒ Ⓓ | 27 | Ⓐ Ⓑ Ⓒ | 37 | Ⓐ Ⓑ Ⓒ | 47 | Ⓐ Ⓑ Ⓒ | 57 | Ⓐ Ⓑ Ⓒ Ⓓ | 67 | Ⓐ Ⓑ Ⓒ Ⓓ | 77 | Ⓐ Ⓑ Ⓒ Ⓓ | 87 | Ⓐ Ⓑ Ⓒ Ⓓ | 97 | Ⓐ Ⓑ Ⓒ Ⓓ |
| 8 | Ⓐ Ⓑ Ⓒ Ⓓ | 18 | Ⓐ Ⓑ Ⓒ Ⓓ | 28 | Ⓐ Ⓑ Ⓒ | 38 | Ⓐ Ⓑ Ⓒ | 48 | Ⓐ Ⓑ Ⓒ | 58 | Ⓐ Ⓑ Ⓒ Ⓓ | 68 | Ⓐ Ⓑ Ⓒ Ⓓ | 78 | Ⓐ Ⓑ Ⓒ Ⓓ | 88 | Ⓐ Ⓑ Ⓒ Ⓓ | 98 | Ⓐ Ⓑ Ⓒ Ⓓ |
| 9 | Ⓐ Ⓑ Ⓒ Ⓓ | 19 | Ⓐ Ⓑ Ⓒ Ⓓ | 29 | Ⓐ Ⓑ Ⓒ | 39 | Ⓐ Ⓑ Ⓒ | 49 | Ⓐ Ⓑ Ⓒ | 59 | Ⓐ Ⓑ Ⓒ Ⓓ | 69 | Ⓐ Ⓑ Ⓒ Ⓓ | 79 | Ⓐ Ⓑ Ⓒ Ⓓ | 89 | Ⓐ Ⓑ Ⓒ Ⓓ | 99 | Ⓐ Ⓑ Ⓒ Ⓓ |
| 10 | Ⓐ Ⓑ Ⓒ Ⓓ | 20 | Ⓐ Ⓑ Ⓒ Ⓓ | 30 | Ⓐ Ⓑ Ⓒ | 40 | Ⓐ Ⓑ Ⓒ | 50 | Ⓐ Ⓑ Ⓒ | 60 | Ⓐ Ⓑ Ⓒ Ⓓ | 70 | Ⓐ Ⓑ Ⓒ Ⓓ | 80 | Ⓐ Ⓑ Ⓒ Ⓓ | 90 | Ⓐ Ⓑ Ⓒ Ⓓ | 100 | Ⓐ Ⓑ Ⓒ Ⓓ |

## Reading

Part V — Part VI — Part VII

| | Answer | | Answer | | Answer | | Answer | | Answer | | Answer | | Answer | | Answer | | Answer | | Answer |
|---|---|---|---|---|---|---|---|---|---|---|---|---|---|---|---|---|---|---|---|
| | A B C D | | A B C D | | A B C D | | A B C D | | A B C D | | A B C D | | A B C D | | A B C D | | A B C D | | A B C D |
| 101 | Ⓐ Ⓑ Ⓒ Ⓓ | 111 | Ⓐ Ⓑ Ⓒ Ⓓ | 121 | Ⓐ Ⓑ Ⓒ Ⓓ | 131 | Ⓐ Ⓑ Ⓒ Ⓓ | 141 | Ⓐ Ⓑ Ⓒ Ⓓ | 151 | Ⓐ Ⓑ Ⓒ Ⓓ | 161 | Ⓐ Ⓑ Ⓒ Ⓓ | 171 | Ⓐ Ⓑ Ⓒ Ⓓ | 181 | Ⓐ Ⓑ Ⓒ Ⓓ | 191 | Ⓐ Ⓑ Ⓒ Ⓓ |
| 102 | Ⓐ Ⓑ Ⓒ Ⓓ | 112 | Ⓐ Ⓑ Ⓒ Ⓓ | 122 | Ⓐ Ⓑ Ⓒ Ⓓ | 132 | Ⓐ Ⓑ Ⓒ Ⓓ | 142 | Ⓐ Ⓑ Ⓒ Ⓓ | 152 | Ⓐ Ⓑ Ⓒ Ⓓ | 162 | Ⓐ Ⓑ Ⓒ Ⓓ | 172 | Ⓐ Ⓑ Ⓒ Ⓓ | 182 | Ⓐ Ⓑ Ⓒ Ⓓ | 192 | Ⓐ Ⓑ Ⓒ Ⓓ |
| 103 | Ⓐ Ⓑ Ⓒ Ⓓ | 113 | Ⓐ Ⓑ Ⓒ Ⓓ | 123 | Ⓐ Ⓑ Ⓒ Ⓓ | 133 | Ⓐ Ⓑ Ⓒ Ⓓ | 143 | Ⓐ Ⓑ Ⓒ Ⓓ | 153 | Ⓐ Ⓑ Ⓒ Ⓓ | 163 | Ⓐ Ⓑ Ⓒ Ⓓ | 173 | Ⓐ Ⓑ Ⓒ Ⓓ | 183 | Ⓐ Ⓑ Ⓒ Ⓓ | 193 | Ⓐ Ⓑ Ⓒ Ⓓ |
| 104 | Ⓐ Ⓑ Ⓒ Ⓓ | 114 | Ⓐ Ⓑ Ⓒ Ⓓ | 124 | Ⓐ Ⓑ Ⓒ Ⓓ | 134 | Ⓐ Ⓑ Ⓒ Ⓓ | 144 | Ⓐ Ⓑ Ⓒ Ⓓ | 154 | Ⓐ Ⓑ Ⓒ Ⓓ | 164 | Ⓐ Ⓑ Ⓒ Ⓓ | 174 | Ⓐ Ⓑ Ⓒ Ⓓ | 184 | Ⓐ Ⓑ Ⓒ Ⓓ | 194 | Ⓐ Ⓑ Ⓒ Ⓓ |
| 105 | Ⓐ Ⓑ Ⓒ Ⓓ | 115 | Ⓐ Ⓑ Ⓒ Ⓓ | 125 | Ⓐ Ⓑ Ⓒ Ⓓ | 135 | Ⓐ Ⓑ Ⓒ Ⓓ | 145 | Ⓐ Ⓑ Ⓒ Ⓓ | 155 | Ⓐ Ⓑ Ⓒ Ⓓ | 165 | Ⓐ Ⓑ Ⓒ Ⓓ | 175 | Ⓐ Ⓑ Ⓒ Ⓓ | 185 | Ⓐ Ⓑ Ⓒ Ⓓ | 195 | Ⓐ Ⓑ Ⓒ Ⓓ |
| 106 | Ⓐ Ⓑ Ⓒ Ⓓ | 116 | Ⓐ Ⓑ Ⓒ Ⓓ | 126 | Ⓐ Ⓑ Ⓒ Ⓓ | 136 | Ⓐ Ⓑ Ⓒ Ⓓ | 146 | Ⓐ Ⓑ Ⓒ Ⓓ | 156 | Ⓐ Ⓑ Ⓒ Ⓓ | 166 | Ⓐ Ⓑ Ⓒ Ⓓ | 176 | Ⓐ Ⓑ Ⓒ Ⓓ | 186 | Ⓐ Ⓑ Ⓒ Ⓓ | 196 | Ⓐ Ⓑ Ⓒ Ⓓ |
| 107 | Ⓐ Ⓑ Ⓒ Ⓓ | 117 | Ⓐ Ⓑ Ⓒ Ⓓ | 127 | Ⓐ Ⓑ Ⓒ Ⓓ | 137 | Ⓐ Ⓑ Ⓒ Ⓓ | 147 | Ⓐ Ⓑ Ⓒ Ⓓ | 157 | Ⓐ Ⓑ Ⓒ Ⓓ | 167 | Ⓐ Ⓑ Ⓒ Ⓓ | 177 | Ⓐ Ⓑ Ⓒ Ⓓ | 187 | Ⓐ Ⓑ Ⓒ Ⓓ | 197 | Ⓐ Ⓑ Ⓒ Ⓓ |
| 108 | Ⓐ Ⓑ Ⓒ Ⓓ | 118 | Ⓐ Ⓑ Ⓒ Ⓓ | 128 | Ⓐ Ⓑ Ⓒ Ⓓ | 138 | Ⓐ Ⓑ Ⓒ Ⓓ | 148 | Ⓐ Ⓑ Ⓒ Ⓓ | 158 | Ⓐ Ⓑ Ⓒ Ⓓ | 168 | Ⓐ Ⓑ Ⓒ Ⓓ | 178 | Ⓐ Ⓑ Ⓒ Ⓓ | 188 | Ⓐ Ⓑ Ⓒ Ⓓ | 198 | Ⓐ Ⓑ Ⓒ Ⓓ |
| 109 | Ⓐ Ⓑ Ⓒ Ⓓ | 119 | Ⓐ Ⓑ Ⓒ Ⓓ | 129 | Ⓐ Ⓑ Ⓒ Ⓓ | 139 | Ⓐ Ⓑ Ⓒ Ⓓ | 149 | Ⓐ Ⓑ Ⓒ Ⓓ | 159 | Ⓐ Ⓑ Ⓒ Ⓓ | 169 | Ⓐ Ⓑ Ⓒ Ⓓ | 179 | Ⓐ Ⓑ Ⓒ Ⓓ | 189 | Ⓐ Ⓑ Ⓒ Ⓓ | 199 | Ⓐ Ⓑ Ⓒ Ⓓ |
| 110 | Ⓐ Ⓑ Ⓒ Ⓓ | 120 | Ⓐ Ⓑ Ⓒ Ⓓ | 130 | Ⓐ Ⓑ Ⓒ Ⓓ | 140 | Ⓐ Ⓑ Ⓒ Ⓓ | 150 | Ⓐ Ⓑ Ⓒ Ⓓ | 160 | Ⓐ Ⓑ Ⓒ Ⓓ | 170 | Ⓐ Ⓑ Ⓒ Ⓓ | 180 | Ⓐ Ⓑ Ⓒ Ⓓ | 190 | Ⓐ Ⓑ Ⓒ Ⓓ | 200 | Ⓐ Ⓑ Ⓒ Ⓓ |

# ANSWER SHEET: Practice Test Three

## Listening Comprehension

### Part I / Part II / Part III / Part IV

| | Answer | | Answer | | Answer | | Answer | | Answer | | Answer | | Answer | | Answer | | Answer | | Answer |
|---|---|---|---|---|---|---|---|---|---|---|---|---|---|---|---|---|---|---|---|
| | A B C D | | A B C D | | A B C | | A B C | | A B C | | A B C D | | A B C D | | A B C D | | A B C D | | A B C D |
| 1 | Ⓐ Ⓑ Ⓒ Ⓓ | 11 | Ⓐ Ⓑ Ⓒ Ⓓ | 21 | Ⓐ Ⓑ Ⓒ | 31 | Ⓐ Ⓑ Ⓒ | 41 | Ⓐ Ⓑ Ⓒ | 51 | Ⓐ Ⓑ Ⓒ Ⓓ | 61 | Ⓐ Ⓑ Ⓒ Ⓓ | 71 | Ⓐ Ⓑ Ⓒ Ⓓ | 81 | Ⓐ Ⓑ Ⓒ Ⓓ | 91 | Ⓐ Ⓑ Ⓒ Ⓓ |
| 2 | Ⓐ Ⓑ Ⓒ Ⓓ | 12 | Ⓐ Ⓑ Ⓒ Ⓓ | 22 | Ⓐ Ⓑ Ⓒ | 32 | Ⓐ Ⓑ Ⓒ | 42 | Ⓐ Ⓑ Ⓒ | 52 | Ⓐ Ⓑ Ⓒ Ⓓ | 62 | Ⓐ Ⓑ Ⓒ Ⓓ | 72 | Ⓐ Ⓑ Ⓒ Ⓓ | 82 | Ⓐ Ⓑ Ⓒ Ⓓ | 92 | Ⓐ Ⓑ Ⓒ Ⓓ |
| 3 | Ⓐ Ⓑ Ⓒ Ⓓ | 13 | Ⓐ Ⓑ Ⓒ Ⓓ | 23 | Ⓐ Ⓑ Ⓒ | 33 | Ⓐ Ⓑ Ⓒ | 43 | Ⓐ Ⓑ Ⓒ | 53 | Ⓐ Ⓑ Ⓒ Ⓓ | 63 | Ⓐ Ⓑ Ⓒ Ⓓ | 73 | Ⓐ Ⓑ Ⓒ Ⓓ | 83 | Ⓐ Ⓑ Ⓒ Ⓓ | 93 | Ⓐ Ⓑ Ⓒ Ⓓ |
| 4 | Ⓐ Ⓑ Ⓒ Ⓓ | 14 | Ⓐ Ⓑ Ⓒ Ⓓ | 24 | Ⓐ Ⓑ Ⓒ | 34 | Ⓐ Ⓑ Ⓒ | 44 | Ⓐ Ⓑ Ⓒ | 54 | Ⓐ Ⓑ Ⓒ Ⓓ | 64 | Ⓐ Ⓑ Ⓒ Ⓓ | 74 | Ⓐ Ⓑ Ⓒ Ⓓ | 84 | Ⓐ Ⓑ Ⓒ Ⓓ | 94 | Ⓐ Ⓑ Ⓒ Ⓓ |
| 5 | Ⓐ Ⓑ Ⓒ Ⓓ | 15 | Ⓐ Ⓑ Ⓒ Ⓓ | 25 | Ⓐ Ⓑ Ⓒ | 35 | Ⓐ Ⓑ Ⓒ | 45 | Ⓐ Ⓑ Ⓒ | 55 | Ⓐ Ⓑ Ⓒ Ⓓ | 65 | Ⓐ Ⓑ Ⓒ Ⓓ | 75 | Ⓐ Ⓑ Ⓒ Ⓓ | 85 | Ⓐ Ⓑ Ⓒ Ⓓ | 95 | Ⓐ Ⓑ Ⓒ Ⓓ |
| 6 | Ⓐ Ⓑ Ⓒ Ⓓ | 16 | Ⓐ Ⓑ Ⓒ Ⓓ | 26 | Ⓐ Ⓑ Ⓒ | 36 | Ⓐ Ⓑ Ⓒ | 46 | Ⓐ Ⓑ Ⓒ | 56 | Ⓐ Ⓑ Ⓒ Ⓓ | 66 | Ⓐ Ⓑ Ⓒ Ⓓ | 76 | Ⓐ Ⓑ Ⓒ Ⓓ | 86 | Ⓐ Ⓑ Ⓒ Ⓓ | 96 | Ⓐ Ⓑ Ⓒ Ⓓ |
| 7 | Ⓐ Ⓑ Ⓒ Ⓓ | 17 | Ⓐ Ⓑ Ⓒ Ⓓ | 27 | Ⓐ Ⓑ Ⓒ | 37 | Ⓐ Ⓑ Ⓒ | 47 | Ⓐ Ⓑ Ⓒ | 57 | Ⓐ Ⓑ Ⓒ Ⓓ | 67 | Ⓐ Ⓑ Ⓒ Ⓓ | 77 | Ⓐ Ⓑ Ⓒ Ⓓ | 87 | Ⓐ Ⓑ Ⓒ Ⓓ | 97 | Ⓐ Ⓑ Ⓒ Ⓓ |
| 8 | Ⓐ Ⓑ Ⓒ Ⓓ | 18 | Ⓐ Ⓑ Ⓒ Ⓓ | 28 | Ⓐ Ⓑ Ⓒ | 38 | Ⓐ Ⓑ Ⓒ | 48 | Ⓐ Ⓑ Ⓒ | 58 | Ⓐ Ⓑ Ⓒ Ⓓ | 68 | Ⓐ Ⓑ Ⓒ Ⓓ | 78 | Ⓐ Ⓑ Ⓒ Ⓓ | 88 | Ⓐ Ⓑ Ⓒ Ⓓ | 98 | Ⓐ Ⓑ Ⓒ Ⓓ |
| 9 | Ⓐ Ⓑ Ⓒ Ⓓ | 19 | Ⓐ Ⓑ Ⓒ Ⓓ | 29 | Ⓐ Ⓑ Ⓒ | 39 | Ⓐ Ⓑ Ⓒ | 49 | Ⓐ Ⓑ Ⓒ | 59 | Ⓐ Ⓑ Ⓒ Ⓓ | 69 | Ⓐ Ⓑ Ⓒ Ⓓ | 79 | Ⓐ Ⓑ Ⓒ Ⓓ | 89 | Ⓐ Ⓑ Ⓒ Ⓓ | 99 | Ⓐ Ⓑ Ⓒ Ⓓ |
| 10 | Ⓐ Ⓑ Ⓒ Ⓓ | 20 | Ⓐ Ⓑ Ⓒ Ⓓ | 30 | Ⓐ Ⓑ Ⓒ | 40 | Ⓐ Ⓑ Ⓒ | 50 | Ⓐ Ⓑ Ⓒ | 60 | Ⓐ Ⓑ Ⓒ Ⓓ | 70 | Ⓐ Ⓑ Ⓒ Ⓓ | 80 | Ⓐ Ⓑ Ⓒ Ⓓ | 90 | Ⓐ Ⓑ Ⓒ Ⓓ | 100 | Ⓐ Ⓑ Ⓒ Ⓓ |

## Reading

### Part V / Part VI / Part VII

| | Answer | | Answer | | Answer | | Answer | | Answer | | Answer | | Answer | | Answer | | Answer | | Answer |
|---|---|---|---|---|---|---|---|---|---|---|---|---|---|---|---|---|---|---|---|
| | A B C D | | A B C D | | A B C D | | A B C D | | A B C D | | A B C D | | A B C D | | A B C D | | A B C D | | A B C D |
| 101 | Ⓐ Ⓑ Ⓒ Ⓓ | 111 | Ⓐ Ⓑ Ⓒ Ⓓ | 121 | Ⓐ Ⓑ Ⓒ Ⓓ | 131 | Ⓐ Ⓑ Ⓒ Ⓓ | 141 | Ⓐ Ⓑ Ⓒ Ⓓ | 151 | Ⓐ Ⓑ Ⓒ Ⓓ | 161 | Ⓐ Ⓑ Ⓒ Ⓓ | 171 | Ⓐ Ⓑ Ⓒ Ⓓ | 181 | Ⓐ Ⓑ Ⓒ Ⓓ | 191 | Ⓐ Ⓑ Ⓒ Ⓓ |
| 102 | Ⓐ Ⓑ Ⓒ Ⓓ | 112 | Ⓐ Ⓑ Ⓒ Ⓓ | 122 | Ⓐ Ⓑ Ⓒ Ⓓ | 132 | Ⓐ Ⓑ Ⓒ Ⓓ | 142 | Ⓐ Ⓑ Ⓒ Ⓓ | 152 | Ⓐ Ⓑ Ⓒ Ⓓ | 162 | Ⓐ Ⓑ Ⓒ Ⓓ | 172 | Ⓐ Ⓑ Ⓒ Ⓓ | 182 | Ⓐ Ⓑ Ⓒ Ⓓ | 192 | Ⓐ Ⓑ Ⓒ Ⓓ |
| 103 | Ⓐ Ⓑ Ⓒ Ⓓ | 113 | Ⓐ Ⓑ Ⓒ Ⓓ | 123 | Ⓐ Ⓑ Ⓒ Ⓓ | 133 | Ⓐ Ⓑ Ⓒ Ⓓ | 143 | Ⓐ Ⓑ Ⓒ Ⓓ | 153 | Ⓐ Ⓑ Ⓒ Ⓓ | 163 | Ⓐ Ⓑ Ⓒ Ⓓ | 173 | Ⓐ Ⓑ Ⓒ Ⓓ | 183 | Ⓐ Ⓑ Ⓒ Ⓓ | 193 | Ⓐ Ⓑ Ⓒ Ⓓ |
| 104 | Ⓐ Ⓑ Ⓒ Ⓓ | 114 | Ⓐ Ⓑ Ⓒ Ⓓ | 124 | Ⓐ Ⓑ Ⓒ Ⓓ | 134 | Ⓐ Ⓑ Ⓒ Ⓓ | 144 | Ⓐ Ⓑ Ⓒ Ⓓ | 154 | Ⓐ Ⓑ Ⓒ Ⓓ | 164 | Ⓐ Ⓑ Ⓒ Ⓓ | 174 | Ⓐ Ⓑ Ⓒ Ⓓ | 184 | Ⓐ Ⓑ Ⓒ Ⓓ | 194 | Ⓐ Ⓑ Ⓒ Ⓓ |
| 105 | Ⓐ Ⓑ Ⓒ Ⓓ | 115 | Ⓐ Ⓑ Ⓒ Ⓓ | 125 | Ⓐ Ⓑ Ⓒ Ⓓ | 135 | Ⓐ Ⓑ Ⓒ Ⓓ | 145 | Ⓐ Ⓑ Ⓒ Ⓓ | 155 | Ⓐ Ⓑ Ⓒ Ⓓ | 165 | Ⓐ Ⓑ Ⓒ Ⓓ | 175 | Ⓐ Ⓑ Ⓒ Ⓓ | 185 | Ⓐ Ⓑ Ⓒ Ⓓ | 195 | Ⓐ Ⓑ Ⓒ Ⓓ |
| 106 | Ⓐ Ⓑ Ⓒ Ⓓ | 116 | Ⓐ Ⓑ Ⓒ Ⓓ | 126 | Ⓐ Ⓑ Ⓒ Ⓓ | 136 | Ⓐ Ⓑ Ⓒ Ⓓ | 146 | Ⓐ Ⓑ Ⓒ Ⓓ | 156 | Ⓐ Ⓑ Ⓒ Ⓓ | 166 | Ⓐ Ⓑ Ⓒ Ⓓ | 176 | Ⓐ Ⓑ Ⓒ Ⓓ | 186 | Ⓐ Ⓑ Ⓒ Ⓓ | 196 | Ⓐ Ⓑ Ⓒ Ⓓ |
| 107 | Ⓐ Ⓑ Ⓒ Ⓓ | 117 | Ⓐ Ⓑ Ⓒ Ⓓ | 127 | Ⓐ Ⓑ Ⓒ Ⓓ | 137 | Ⓐ Ⓑ Ⓒ Ⓓ | 147 | Ⓐ Ⓑ Ⓒ Ⓓ | 157 | Ⓐ Ⓑ Ⓒ Ⓓ | 167 | Ⓐ Ⓑ Ⓒ Ⓓ | 177 | Ⓐ Ⓑ Ⓒ Ⓓ | 187 | Ⓐ Ⓑ Ⓒ Ⓓ | 197 | Ⓐ Ⓑ Ⓒ Ⓓ |
| 108 | Ⓐ Ⓑ Ⓒ Ⓓ | 118 | Ⓐ Ⓑ Ⓒ Ⓓ | 128 | Ⓐ Ⓑ Ⓒ Ⓓ | 138 | Ⓐ Ⓑ Ⓒ Ⓓ | 148 | Ⓐ Ⓑ Ⓒ Ⓓ | 158 | Ⓐ Ⓑ Ⓒ Ⓓ | 168 | Ⓐ Ⓑ Ⓒ Ⓓ | 178 | Ⓐ Ⓑ Ⓒ Ⓓ | 188 | Ⓐ Ⓑ Ⓒ Ⓓ | 198 | Ⓐ Ⓑ Ⓒ Ⓓ |
| 109 | Ⓐ Ⓑ Ⓒ Ⓓ | 119 | Ⓐ Ⓑ Ⓒ Ⓓ | 129 | Ⓐ Ⓑ Ⓒ Ⓓ | 139 | Ⓐ Ⓑ Ⓒ Ⓓ | 149 | Ⓐ Ⓑ Ⓒ Ⓓ | 159 | Ⓐ Ⓑ Ⓒ Ⓓ | 169 | Ⓐ Ⓑ Ⓒ Ⓓ | 179 | Ⓐ Ⓑ Ⓒ Ⓓ | 189 | Ⓐ Ⓑ Ⓒ Ⓓ | 199 | Ⓐ Ⓑ Ⓒ Ⓓ |
| 110 | Ⓐ Ⓑ Ⓒ Ⓓ | 120 | Ⓐ Ⓑ Ⓒ Ⓓ | 130 | Ⓐ Ⓑ Ⓒ Ⓓ | 140 | Ⓐ Ⓑ Ⓒ Ⓓ | 150 | Ⓐ Ⓑ Ⓒ Ⓓ | 160 | Ⓐ Ⓑ Ⓒ Ⓓ | 170 | Ⓐ Ⓑ Ⓒ Ⓓ | 180 | Ⓐ Ⓑ Ⓒ Ⓓ | 190 | Ⓐ Ⓑ Ⓒ Ⓓ | 200 | Ⓐ Ⓑ Ⓒ Ⓓ |

# ANSWER SHEET: Practice Test Four

## Listening Comprehension

Part I · Part II · Part III · Part IV

| | Answer | | Answer | | Answer | | Answer | | Answer | | Answer | | Answer | | Answer | | Answer | | Answer |
|---|---|---|---|---|---|---|---|---|---|---|---|---|---|---|---|---|---|---|---|
| | A B C D | | A B C D | | A B C | | A B C | | A B C | | A B C D | | A B C D | | A B C D | | A B C D | | A B C D |
| 1 | Ⓐ Ⓑ Ⓒ Ⓓ | 11 | Ⓐ Ⓑ Ⓒ Ⓓ | 21 | Ⓐ Ⓑ Ⓒ | 31 | Ⓐ Ⓑ Ⓒ | 41 | Ⓐ Ⓑ Ⓒ | 51 | Ⓐ Ⓑ Ⓒ Ⓓ | 61 | Ⓐ Ⓑ Ⓒ Ⓓ | 71 | Ⓐ Ⓑ Ⓒ Ⓓ | 81 | Ⓐ Ⓑ Ⓒ Ⓓ | 91 | Ⓐ Ⓑ Ⓒ Ⓓ |
| 2 | Ⓐ Ⓑ Ⓒ Ⓓ | 12 | Ⓐ Ⓑ Ⓒ Ⓓ | 22 | Ⓐ Ⓑ Ⓒ | 32 | Ⓐ Ⓑ Ⓒ | 42 | Ⓐ Ⓑ Ⓒ | 52 | Ⓐ Ⓑ Ⓒ Ⓓ | 62 | Ⓐ Ⓑ Ⓒ Ⓓ | 72 | Ⓐ Ⓑ Ⓒ Ⓓ | 82 | Ⓐ Ⓑ Ⓒ Ⓓ | 92 | Ⓐ Ⓑ Ⓒ Ⓓ |
| 3 | Ⓐ Ⓑ Ⓒ Ⓓ | 13 | Ⓐ Ⓑ Ⓒ Ⓓ | 23 | Ⓐ Ⓑ Ⓒ | 33 | Ⓐ Ⓑ Ⓒ | 43 | Ⓐ Ⓑ Ⓒ | 53 | Ⓐ Ⓑ Ⓒ Ⓓ | 63 | Ⓐ Ⓑ Ⓒ Ⓓ | 73 | Ⓐ Ⓑ Ⓒ Ⓓ | 83 | Ⓐ Ⓑ Ⓒ Ⓓ | 93 | Ⓐ Ⓑ Ⓒ Ⓓ |
| 4 | Ⓐ Ⓑ Ⓒ Ⓓ | 14 | Ⓐ Ⓑ Ⓒ Ⓓ | 24 | Ⓐ Ⓑ Ⓒ | 34 | Ⓐ Ⓑ Ⓒ | 44 | Ⓐ Ⓑ Ⓒ | 54 | Ⓐ Ⓑ Ⓒ Ⓓ | 64 | Ⓐ Ⓑ Ⓒ Ⓓ | 74 | Ⓐ Ⓑ Ⓒ Ⓓ | 84 | Ⓐ Ⓑ Ⓒ Ⓓ | 94 | Ⓐ Ⓑ Ⓒ Ⓓ |
| 5 | Ⓐ Ⓑ Ⓒ Ⓓ | 15 | Ⓐ Ⓑ Ⓒ Ⓓ | 25 | Ⓐ Ⓑ Ⓒ | 35 | Ⓐ Ⓑ Ⓒ | 45 | Ⓐ Ⓑ Ⓒ | 55 | Ⓐ Ⓑ Ⓒ Ⓓ | 65 | Ⓐ Ⓑ Ⓒ Ⓓ | 75 | Ⓐ Ⓑ Ⓒ Ⓓ | 85 | Ⓐ Ⓑ Ⓒ Ⓓ | 95 | Ⓐ Ⓑ Ⓒ Ⓓ |
| 6 | Ⓐ Ⓑ Ⓒ Ⓓ | 16 | Ⓐ Ⓑ Ⓒ Ⓓ | 26 | Ⓐ Ⓑ Ⓒ | 36 | Ⓐ Ⓑ Ⓒ | 46 | Ⓐ Ⓑ Ⓒ | 56 | Ⓐ Ⓑ Ⓒ Ⓓ | 66 | Ⓐ Ⓑ Ⓒ Ⓓ | 76 | Ⓐ Ⓑ Ⓒ Ⓓ | 86 | Ⓐ Ⓑ Ⓒ Ⓓ | 96 | Ⓐ Ⓑ Ⓒ Ⓓ |
| 7 | Ⓐ Ⓑ Ⓒ Ⓓ | 17 | Ⓐ Ⓑ Ⓒ Ⓓ | 27 | Ⓐ Ⓑ Ⓒ | 37 | Ⓐ Ⓑ Ⓒ | 47 | Ⓐ Ⓑ Ⓒ | 57 | Ⓐ Ⓑ Ⓒ Ⓓ | 67 | Ⓐ Ⓑ Ⓒ Ⓓ | 77 | Ⓐ Ⓑ Ⓒ Ⓓ | 87 | Ⓐ Ⓑ Ⓒ Ⓓ | 97 | Ⓐ Ⓑ Ⓒ Ⓓ |
| 8 | Ⓐ Ⓑ Ⓒ Ⓓ | 18 | Ⓐ Ⓑ Ⓒ Ⓓ | 28 | Ⓐ Ⓑ Ⓒ | 38 | Ⓐ Ⓑ Ⓒ | 48 | Ⓐ Ⓑ Ⓒ | 58 | Ⓐ Ⓑ Ⓒ Ⓓ | 68 | Ⓐ Ⓑ Ⓒ Ⓓ | 78 | Ⓐ Ⓑ Ⓒ Ⓓ | 88 | Ⓐ Ⓑ Ⓒ Ⓓ | 98 | Ⓐ Ⓑ Ⓒ Ⓓ |
| 9 | Ⓐ Ⓑ Ⓒ Ⓓ | 19 | Ⓐ Ⓑ Ⓒ Ⓓ | 29 | Ⓐ Ⓑ Ⓒ | 39 | Ⓐ Ⓑ Ⓒ | 49 | Ⓐ Ⓑ Ⓒ | 59 | Ⓐ Ⓑ Ⓒ Ⓓ | 69 | Ⓐ Ⓑ Ⓒ Ⓓ | 79 | Ⓐ Ⓑ Ⓒ Ⓓ | 89 | Ⓐ Ⓑ Ⓒ Ⓓ | 99 | Ⓐ Ⓑ Ⓒ Ⓓ |
| 10 | Ⓐ Ⓑ Ⓒ Ⓓ | 20 | Ⓐ Ⓑ Ⓒ Ⓓ | 30 | Ⓐ Ⓑ Ⓒ | 40 | Ⓐ Ⓑ Ⓒ | 50 | Ⓐ Ⓑ Ⓒ | 60 | Ⓐ Ⓑ Ⓒ Ⓓ | 70 | Ⓐ Ⓑ Ⓒ Ⓓ | 80 | Ⓐ Ⓑ Ⓒ Ⓓ | 90 | Ⓐ Ⓑ Ⓒ Ⓓ | 100 | Ⓐ Ⓑ Ⓒ Ⓓ |

## Reading

Part V · Part VI · Part VII

| | Answer | | Answer | | Answer | | Answer | | Answer | | Answer | | Answer | | Answer | | Answer | | Answer |
|---|---|---|---|---|---|---|---|---|---|---|---|---|---|---|---|---|---|---|---|
| | A B C D | | A B C D | | A B C D | | A B C D | | A B C D | | A B C D | | A B C D | | A B C D | | A B C D | | A B C D |
| 101 | Ⓐ Ⓑ Ⓒ Ⓓ | 111 | Ⓐ Ⓑ Ⓒ Ⓓ | 121 | Ⓐ Ⓑ Ⓒ Ⓓ | 131 | Ⓐ Ⓑ Ⓒ Ⓓ | 141 | Ⓐ Ⓑ Ⓒ Ⓓ | 151 | Ⓐ Ⓑ Ⓒ Ⓓ | 161 | Ⓐ Ⓑ Ⓒ Ⓓ | 171 | Ⓐ Ⓑ Ⓒ Ⓓ | 181 | Ⓐ Ⓑ Ⓒ Ⓓ | 191 | Ⓐ Ⓑ Ⓒ Ⓓ |
| 102 | Ⓐ Ⓑ Ⓒ Ⓓ | 112 | Ⓐ Ⓑ Ⓒ Ⓓ | 122 | Ⓐ Ⓑ Ⓒ Ⓓ | 132 | Ⓐ Ⓑ Ⓒ Ⓓ | 142 | Ⓐ Ⓑ Ⓒ Ⓓ | 152 | Ⓐ Ⓑ Ⓒ Ⓓ | 162 | Ⓐ Ⓑ Ⓒ Ⓓ | 172 | Ⓐ Ⓑ Ⓒ Ⓓ | 182 | Ⓐ Ⓑ Ⓒ Ⓓ | 192 | Ⓐ Ⓑ Ⓒ Ⓓ |
| 103 | Ⓐ Ⓑ Ⓒ Ⓓ | 113 | Ⓐ Ⓑ Ⓒ Ⓓ | 123 | Ⓐ Ⓑ Ⓒ Ⓓ | 133 | Ⓐ Ⓑ Ⓒ Ⓓ | 143 | Ⓐ Ⓑ Ⓒ Ⓓ | 153 | Ⓐ Ⓑ Ⓒ Ⓓ | 163 | Ⓐ Ⓑ Ⓒ Ⓓ | 173 | Ⓐ Ⓑ Ⓒ Ⓓ | 183 | Ⓐ Ⓑ Ⓒ Ⓓ | 193 | Ⓐ Ⓑ Ⓒ Ⓓ |
| 104 | Ⓐ Ⓑ Ⓒ Ⓓ | 114 | Ⓐ Ⓑ Ⓒ Ⓓ | 124 | Ⓐ Ⓑ Ⓒ Ⓓ | 134 | Ⓐ Ⓑ Ⓒ Ⓓ | 144 | Ⓐ Ⓑ Ⓒ Ⓓ | 154 | Ⓐ Ⓑ Ⓒ Ⓓ | 164 | Ⓐ Ⓑ Ⓒ Ⓓ | 174 | Ⓐ Ⓑ Ⓒ Ⓓ | 184 | Ⓐ Ⓑ Ⓒ Ⓓ | 194 | Ⓐ Ⓑ Ⓒ Ⓓ |
| 105 | Ⓐ Ⓑ Ⓒ Ⓓ | 115 | Ⓐ Ⓑ Ⓒ Ⓓ | 125 | Ⓐ Ⓑ Ⓒ Ⓓ | 135 | Ⓐ Ⓑ Ⓒ Ⓓ | 145 | Ⓐ Ⓑ Ⓒ Ⓓ | 155 | Ⓐ Ⓑ Ⓒ Ⓓ | 165 | Ⓐ Ⓑ Ⓒ Ⓓ | 175 | Ⓐ Ⓑ Ⓒ Ⓓ | 185 | Ⓐ Ⓑ Ⓒ Ⓓ | 195 | Ⓐ Ⓑ Ⓒ Ⓓ |
| 106 | Ⓐ Ⓑ Ⓒ Ⓓ | 116 | Ⓐ Ⓑ Ⓒ Ⓓ | 126 | Ⓐ Ⓑ Ⓒ Ⓓ | 136 | Ⓐ Ⓑ Ⓒ Ⓓ | 146 | Ⓐ Ⓑ Ⓒ Ⓓ | 156 | Ⓐ Ⓑ Ⓒ Ⓓ | 166 | Ⓐ Ⓑ Ⓒ Ⓓ | 176 | Ⓐ Ⓑ Ⓒ Ⓓ | 186 | Ⓐ Ⓑ Ⓒ Ⓓ | 196 | Ⓐ Ⓑ Ⓒ Ⓓ |
| 107 | Ⓐ Ⓑ Ⓒ Ⓓ | 117 | Ⓐ Ⓑ Ⓒ Ⓓ | 127 | Ⓐ Ⓑ Ⓒ Ⓓ | 137 | Ⓐ Ⓑ Ⓒ Ⓓ | 147 | Ⓐ Ⓑ Ⓒ Ⓓ | 157 | Ⓐ Ⓑ Ⓒ Ⓓ | 167 | Ⓐ Ⓑ Ⓒ Ⓓ | 177 | Ⓐ Ⓑ Ⓒ Ⓓ | 187 | Ⓐ Ⓑ Ⓒ Ⓓ | 197 | Ⓐ Ⓑ Ⓒ Ⓓ |
| 108 | Ⓐ Ⓑ Ⓒ Ⓓ | 118 | Ⓐ Ⓑ Ⓒ Ⓓ | 128 | Ⓐ Ⓑ Ⓒ Ⓓ | 138 | Ⓐ Ⓑ Ⓒ Ⓓ | 148 | Ⓐ Ⓑ Ⓒ Ⓓ | 158 | Ⓐ Ⓑ Ⓒ Ⓓ | 168 | Ⓐ Ⓑ Ⓒ Ⓓ | 178 | Ⓐ Ⓑ Ⓒ Ⓓ | 188 | Ⓐ Ⓑ Ⓒ Ⓓ | 198 | Ⓐ Ⓑ Ⓒ Ⓓ |
| 109 | Ⓐ Ⓑ Ⓒ Ⓓ | 119 | Ⓐ Ⓑ Ⓒ Ⓓ | 129 | Ⓐ Ⓑ Ⓒ Ⓓ | 139 | Ⓐ Ⓑ Ⓒ Ⓓ | 149 | Ⓐ Ⓑ Ⓒ Ⓓ | 159 | Ⓐ Ⓑ Ⓒ Ⓓ | 169 | Ⓐ Ⓑ Ⓒ Ⓓ | 179 | Ⓐ Ⓑ Ⓒ Ⓓ | 189 | Ⓐ Ⓑ Ⓒ Ⓓ | 199 | Ⓐ Ⓑ Ⓒ Ⓓ |
| 110 | Ⓐ Ⓑ Ⓒ Ⓓ | 120 | Ⓐ Ⓑ Ⓒ Ⓓ | 130 | Ⓐ Ⓑ Ⓒ Ⓓ | 140 | Ⓐ Ⓑ Ⓒ Ⓓ | 150 | Ⓐ Ⓑ Ⓒ Ⓓ | 160 | Ⓐ Ⓑ Ⓒ Ⓓ | 170 | Ⓐ Ⓑ Ⓒ Ⓓ | 180 | Ⓐ Ⓑ Ⓒ Ⓓ | 190 | Ⓐ Ⓑ Ⓒ Ⓓ | 200 | Ⓐ Ⓑ Ⓒ Ⓓ |